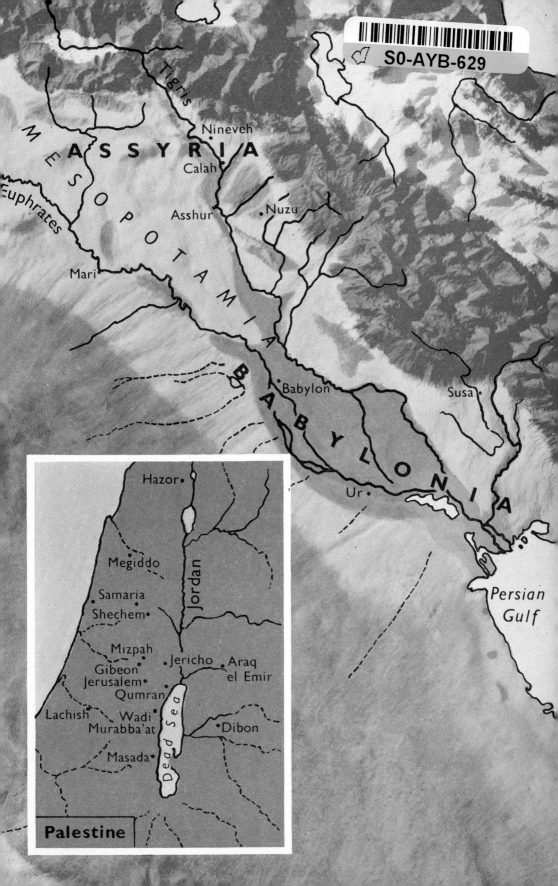

SO-AYB-629

MESOPOTAMIA

ASSYRIA

Tigris

Euphrates

Nineveh

Calah

Asshur

Nuzu

Mari

BABYLONIA

Babylon

Susa

Ur

Persian
Gulf

Palestine

Hazor

Megiddo

Jordan

Samaria

Shechem

Mizpah

Gibeon

Jerusalem

Qumran

Jericho

Araq
el Emir

Lachish

Wadi
Murabba'at

Dead Sea

Dibon

Masada

ARCHAEOLOGY IN
BIBLICAL RESEARCH

ARCHAEOLOGY IN BIBLICAL RESEARCH

WALTER G. WILLIAMS

LUTTERWORTH PRESS
LONDON

First published in Great Britain, 1966

Printed in Great Britain
by Billing & Sons Limited
Guildford and London

TO
MARY ESTHER

PREFACE

A preface frequently resembles a postscript. Permit me instead to use this as a salutation.

This is salutation to many teachers in and out of the classroom, to whom I am forever indebted. The footnotes and the bibliographies recognize some of the teachers whose work has added to my own knowledge. Many of these instructors I have never seen, but their influence is nonetheless important and appreciated. Some are fellow members of professional societies and would, perhaps, consider themselves to be colleagues in a common task, but their presentations in the societies, in journals, and in books have made me debtor as their student. But, like all good students I have not always agreed with my teachers. Agreement or disagreement, their teachings have stimulated my own thinking. This is another way of saying that most of the material in this volume did not originate with me, but I bear full responsibility for the form in which the information and ideas are expressed.

This is salutation to my own students and to the many students in distant lands who have offered me the courtesy of a hearing. Students' questions have frequently alerted me to the fact that an idea of mine was not clearly stated or that the concept was built upon false premises or insufficient evidence. In such situations students turn teacher, and I gratefully acknowledge my indebtedness to them.

This is salutation to my colleagues at The Iliff School of Theology, who have been a source of encouragement and who sometimes have been patient listeners to portions of this document. In the informal gathering we dignify by the title Faculty Colloquium they have listened attentively, and then in good faculty fashion have inquired, "But have you considered these facts?" Their many suggestions have smoothed out rough places and have called my attention to pertinent material I might otherwise have missed. I am particularly indebted to Martin Rist, friend of many years, co-laborer in the biblical field, and resourceful director of our library program. Our conversations and discussions have been a fruitful source of information and inspiration to me. He and his co-workers in the library have given unstintingly of their time in order that journals and books, the tools of the teacher, would be available as I needed them. I owe a special word of thanks also to William R. Griffiths, my student and colleague, whose patience has not been exhausted by the

7

demands I have put upon him. He has read critically much of the material prepared for this volume, and many of his suggestions have been accepted with appreciation. My student assistants, Miss Lila Jean Phillips and the Reverend C. Leslie Reiter, have been a great help in preparing the materials for the indexes, and I take this opportunity to thank them.

I bear full responsibility for all drawings and maps, but their clarity is due to the skill and penmanship of my colleague William R. Griffiths and my son Edwin Ross. My thanks to each of them.

This is salutation to those who have worked hard and long in the mechanics of the preparation of material for the printing press. To Sue Brown, who has prepared all the typescript in its various editions, I say a special word of thanks. Her own plans and those of her family have been upset and interrupted many times because of her sense of dedication to this project. She has worked faithfully and well.

This is far more than salutation to the one to whom this volume is dedicated, my companion of thirty-five years. Together we have roamed the world, excavated in strange places, agonized over readability of copy, and shared the sorrows and joys of parsonage and classroom. Without her understanding and love, her guardianship of my time and health, and her gift for saying just the right word at just the right time, this study could not have been brought to completion.

> The heart of her husband trusts in her.
> . . . .
> Her children rise up and call her blessed.

WALTER G. WILLIAMS

CONTENTS

Part I
Essence of Biblical Archaeology

1. Aims and Ideals of Biblical Archaeology 15
2. Archaeology Becomes a Science 23
3. Controls, Aids, and Sources of Information 37

Part II
Aspects of Archaeology

4. Surface Survey 49
5. Excavation 60
6. Accidental Discoveries, Established Tradition,
   and Objective Evaluation 72
7. Field Preservation, Museum Display, and Publication 85

Part III
The World in Which the Bible Was Written

8. Interpretation of Evidence 99
9. The Location of Bible Sites 103
10. Expanded Knowledge of Hebrew History 115
11. Recovered Nations 128
12. Cultural Diffusion 140
13. Parallels to Biblical Customs 154
14. New Knowledge of Ancient Languages 168
15. Biblical and Extra-Biblical Manuscripts 182

Conclusion and a Beginning 196

Bibliography 209

Indexes 215

9

LIST OF ABBREVIATIONS

AASOR	*Annual of the American Schools of Oriental Research*
AJSL	*American Journal of Semitic Languages*
ANET	James Bennett Pritchard, editor, *Ancient Near Eastern Texts* (rev. ed.; Princeton, N.J.: Princeton University Press, 1955)
AOT	Hugo Gressman, *Altorientalische Texte zum alten Testament* (Berlin, 1926)
ASOR	American Schools of Oriental Research
BA	*Biblical Archaeologist*
BASOR	*Bulletin of American Schools of Oriental Research*
IB	*Interpreter's Bible* (12 vols.; Nashville: Abingdon Press)
IDB	*Interpreter's Dictionary of the Bible* (4 vols.; Nashville: Abingdon Press, 1962)
JBL	*Journal of Biblical Literature*
JBR	*Journal of the Bible and Religion*
JNES	*Journal of Near Eastern Studies*
JPOS	*Journal of the Palestine Orient Society*
LXX	The Septuagint—Greek translation of the Old Testament
MT	Masoretic Text—Hebrew Old Testament
NEB	*New English Bible*
OIP	*Oriental Institute Publications*, University of Chicago
PEF	Palestine Exploration Fund
Sam.	Samaritan Pentateuch
SAOC	*Studies in Ancient Oriental Civilizations*, University of Chicago
ZAW	*Zeitschrift für die Alttestamentliche Wissenschaft*

ILLUSTRATIONS

PLATES

Between pages 112-113

1. Sennacherib's prism
2. The surrender of Lachish from a relief from Sennacherib's palace at Nineveh
3. Olive stones found during excavations at Lachish
4. An ostracon recording gold shipments from Ophir
5. The Babylonian account of the Flood
6. The Hammurabi Code
7. Brick tower at Susa where the Hammurabi Code was found
8. The Rosetta stone
9. An Assyrian dictionary
10. The Rock of Behistun
11. Al Muqayyer, "the mound of bitumen"
12. The harp from the Royal Cemetery at Ur
13-14. Stages in the excavation of the harp
15. Excavations at Jericho
16. A plastered skull found at Jericho
17. A Middle Bronze Age tomb from Jericho
18. Cave IV in Wadi Qumran
19. A portion of a Dead Sea Scroll of Isaiah
20. Aerial view of the Essene settlement at Qumran
21. Evidence of an earthquake in a cistern at Qumran
22. "The Treasury", Petra
23. The Palace Tomb, Petra
24. The Temple of the Snake, Petra
25. Procession of gods at Boghazköi
26. The tell at Dhiban
27. The Mesha stele
28. A limestone figure of a king found at Amman

11

DRAWINGS AND OUTLINE MAPS

Pages 201-208

1. Plan of excavated buildings, Dhiban (1950-51)
2. City gate, Tell en-Nasbeh
3. Developments from pictographic writing
   Early Sumerian picture writing
   Development of cuneiform signs after Arno Poebel
   Inscriptions from Mount Sinai mines
   Egyptian "alphabet"
4. Forms of alphabetic writing—West Semitic
   1. Ugaritic cuneiform
   2. Early Phoenician
   3. Moabite (Mesha Stone)
   4. Hebrew (square characters)
   5. Samaritan
5. The ancient Near East
6. Palestine
7. Samaria and Judaea
8. (Left) Araq el-Emir. (Right) Qumran Area

ACKNOWLEDGEMENTS

The Publishers would like to thank the following for permission to reproduce the photographs of which they hold the copyright: British Museum: 1, 2, 3, 5, 8, 9, 12, 13, 14; Department of Antiquities, Jordan: 26, 28; Israel Department of Antiquities: 4; Dr. Kathleen Kenyon: 15, 16, 17; Keystone Press Agency: 19; Palestine Archaeological Museum: 18, 20, 21, 22, 23, 24, 27; Paul Popper: 6, 7, 10, 11, 25.

PART I

Essence of Biblical Archaeology

1.

AIMS AND IDEALS
OF BIBLICAL ARCHAEOLOGY

The purpose of the archaeologist is to recover and study the remains of ancient civilizations so that historians may reconstruct the story of ancient people. He must always be aware that he can recover artifacts, or man-made objects, but of necessity he can only recover a very small part of the evidence. Perishable materials, except under unusual conditions, have long since disappeared. Yet evidence of perishable material can sometimes be recovered indirectly if the archaeologist possesses the necessary skills.

Scientific techniques in archaeology were introduced first in the last part of the nineteenth century and have been developed largely during the twentieth century. Many of the excavation techniques are the same the world over, with special adaptation to the climatic and topographical conditions of the country being investigated. Technologically there may be little difference between the archaeologists in Jordan and Israel and those in northern Europe, but their interests are centered in different cultures and records of different nations. It is, therefore, quite permissible to speak of biblical archaeology. Such designation indicates that the archaeologist is confining his efforts to those geographical areas generally associated with the writing of the Bible.

The biblical archaeologist is primarily concerned with recovering the story of the people associated with the Bible so that we may obtain insight concerning the message of the Bible. He must always remember that he can deal only with evidence which reveals history, its setting, and the history of culture, including religion. Whether or not his discoveries will support or deny the dogmas of any religious group is beyond his responsibility. He can only spell out the record as he sees it. He may even be able to recover enough information to document a political and social history of ancient periods. He may discover cult objects and relics and religious records which tell something of the beliefs and practices of an ancient people, and that this people believed that their god led them to victory over a neighboring people. Whether or not modern man shall accept or reject this religious position is not the responsibility of the archaeologist or historian.

There are many ways, nevertheless, in which the archaeologist is helpful to the reader of the Bible. Jews and Christians alike believe that God has revealed himself to man in history. It is important, therefore, for us to know something about history. Of particular importance is the need to recognize that Bible characters have their roots in history. For too many people such individuals as Noah, Abraham, Isaiah, and Jeremiah are unreal people who live only in the pages of a book or perhaps are portrayed in the windows of

15

their churches. Through the work of the archaeologist many Bible figures may stand firmly on the solid ground of historical fact.

Similarly, until the work of the archaeologist provides source material it is not always possible to write credible histories of Bible times. Two things are involved. First, there is paucity of chronological material throughout the Old Testament with which to provide the skeleton of history. Second, precise dates, except in terms of reigns of kings or natural catastrophes such as earthquakes, are lacking. There had not yet been one great turning point in history upon which all dates could be based, as we now compute dates in terms of before or after the birth of Jesus. We now have much fuller knowledge of the people who were contemporaries of the Hebrews. By studying their histories and making cross checks with biblical records the history of the Hebrews can be constructed. It is now possible to equate such histories with our own calendars and to construct chronologies which have meaning today.

Neighboring nations and tribes are mentioned frequently in the Bible, but the Bible gives little or no identification of such people. It was, in fact, a practice in some circles in the last century to dismiss such people as myths or at least legends. Many ancient tribes and nations have now been recovered by the archaeologist and their histories have been written. The poorly known Babylonians, Assyrians, Persians, Phoenicians, Syrians, and Egyptians now stand clothed in glorious cultures, and we are aware also of their influence upon the culture of the Hebrews themselves. Other nations which were completely unknown have now been recovered from oblivion. We read in the Bible (KJV) of the "Sons of Heth," but the Hittites (RSV) are now known to us as an important nation during most of the second millennium B.C. Nowhere in the Bible nor in classical literature is there any reference to the Sumerians. There is reference in Genesis to Shinar, a term used in early Bible times to designate Babylonia. This area actually covered the countries of Akkad and Sumer, but such differentiation of territory was unknown to the Bible writer. We still do not know the ethnic background of the Sumerians, but we know much about their residence in Mesopotamia. We also have discovered that this is the people which taught ancient Mesopotamia to write and that the Sumerians are the people who formulated the earliest law codes yet discovered.

The "Horites" are also mentioned in the Old Testament. Older commentaries identified the Horites as cave dwellers, based upon the Hebrew word for cave. Through the careful work of archaeologists and linguists the west Horites now stand revealed as the Hurrians, a people of high culture who were active in the middle of the third and to the end of the second millennium B.C.[1]

[1] E. A. Speiser, "Horite," *IDB*, p. 645.

We find additional help for the translation and interpretation of the Bible as we understand the languages, literature, and customs of the people who lived next door to ancient Palestine. Hebrew is a language which has many linguistic relations. Many of these related languages and dialects have been recovered and studied. Insights are thereby provided concerning meanings of hitherto obscure Hebrew words. Like all people, as the Hebrews came into contact with people who used other languages they borrowed words and expressions from them, frequently with changed meanings. Only by studying those related languages can we fully understand the Hebrew usage of borrowed expressions.

We have known for many years that the Hebrews not only borrowed individual expressions, but sometimes borrowed whole stories, poems, and even traditions. They adapted them to their own culture and used them as vehicles to convey great truths discovered by the Hebrews themselves. Even before archaeology became a science and was concerned chiefly with collecting antiques, we learned that there was a large body of Babylonian literature which bore striking resemblances to Hebrew stories. One of the early expeditions, commissioned by the British newspaper *Daily Telegraph*, sent George Smith to Nineveh to find the remaining portion of the Babylonian story of the flood, the first part of which had been translated by Smith. The amazing thing is that Smith was successful in his quest. Other parallels have been found. We, in fact, have been so intrigued with parallels that we have sometimes ignored the significant differences, and thereby, overlooked the particular religious genius of the Hebrew people which they conveyed through adopted but adapted literature. As we have come to understand the ancient literature of the entire Near and Middle East we have grown in our appreciation for the depth of Hebrew religious culture.

Many customs recorded in Scripture puzzle us, or at least are not fully understood because the customs are unknown in modern cultures. Sometimes a Bible writer knew that an explanation was necessary because customs had already changed in his own day. For example, Ruth 4:7 explains the significance of drawing off the sandal to indicate renunciation of one's rights. But even if the author had not given us an explanation we would now know the significance of the custom because of the work of the archaeologist. Tablets have been recovered from near Kirkuk (ancient Nuzu), Iraq, which explain this particular practice. Other unexplained customs can now be understood. Gen. 31:30 ff. records Laban's anguish because his teraphim or household gods had been stolen. Unknown to her husband Jacob, Rachel had taken these images. The incident seems to have little significance except for the increased tension between Jacob and Laban. Through the Nuzu tablets we now know why the tension was increased and, more important, why Rachel risked possible injury or death in taking the images. Ancient law among the tribes provided that whoever owned the family gods inherited the family estate, or in other cases, became the recognized head of the clan.[2] Rachel was seeking to protect her own and Jacob's just inheritance. New commentaries contain many such insights which come as a direct result of the work of the archaeologist.

"Treasure-hunting," said the noted archaeologist Leonard Woolley, "is almost as old as man, scientific archaeology is a modern development, but in its short life of about seventy years it has done marvels." [3] We shall discuss in the next chapter the steps which led from plundering to scientific techniques. In the meantime a quick glance at a few artifacts will serve to emphasize the purposes and skills of the modern archaeologist.

Several objects in my study have elicited many questions—a piece of carved stone, some beads, a few fragments of an old jug, a handful of grain, some coins, and a small clay tablet. People get excited about them because they are obviously very old and reputedly come from Bible times and places. The beauty of the beads can even conjure up an aesthetic thrill and make an emotional appeal. These objects can serve us well to illustrate what archaeology is and how it is a major area of research in the biblical field.

The piece of stone was given to me by a guide in Egypt. He claimed that it had been cut from the tomb of one of the pharaohs. It does bear the image of an enthroned figure together with the cartouche, an oval symbol enclosing the name of the pharaoh, Ramses II. Careful examination indicates that, while the stone is old, the carved symbols were probably placed there by modern craftsmen who capitalize on the gullibility of tourists. To go through the Bible lands and to be aware of associations is a deeply emotional experience. Unfortunately the emotions of travelers are sometimes played upon by skillful natives, with the result that the travelers are persuaded to purchase "guaranteed antiques." Tragically, there are many such objects in museums across the world. It is lucrative business. The archaeologist must be able to distinguish between the genuine and the false.

The beads were purchased from a reputable and licensed antiquities dealer. The governments of the various countries associated with the Bible story are doing much to rid their respective countries of illicit trading in antiquities and of the sales of fake antiques to unsuspecting customers. In making my purchase I was given a certificate guaranteeing the approximate date of the necklace. The merchant also indicated the probable queen's tomb from which the necklace came, but would not go beyond probabilities. Since the beads are beautiful, they did serve the purpose of a gift to my wife. The necklace is an antiquity, guaranteed, but of no significant value to the archaeologist or historian because the object is completely out of its historical context.

[2] Moshe Greenberg, "Another Look at Rachel's Theft of the Teraphim," *JBL* (September, 1962), pp. 239-48; C. H. Gordon, *Geschichtliche Grundlagen des A. T.* (Zurich, 1961), p. 123. Cf. Chap. 13, p. 15.
[3] *Digging Up the Past* (New York: Charles Scribners Sons, 1931), p. 20.

In its essence Field Archaeology is the application of scientific method to the excavation of ancient objects, and it is based on the theory that the historical value of an object depends not so much on the nature of the object itself as on its associations, which only scientific excavation can detect. The casual digger and the plunderer aim at getting something of artistic or commercial value, and there their interest stops.[4]

The fragments of the old jug usually elicit the comment, "Of what use are those things?" Frequently in excavation such "things" are the only immediately available evidence for determining the stage of history which is being uncovered. Clay, by its very nature, is not easily destroyed. If it has been baked into a jug or written document it can be smashed, but its pieces can be reassembled and it will still tell a story. Because clay is readily obtainable it has been used for a variety of purposes.[5] Clay is cheap, and therefore, objects made from it were easily abandoned and replacements were quickly made. When ancient houses were destroyed by storms or enemy attack the cheap clay vessels were left in the ruins. These are found in great quantities today. It was the great English archaeologist Sir W. Flinders Petrie who discovered and stressed the scientific importance of dating occupation levels by studying the pottery types. Each age and culture had its own characteristic shapes of vessels, forms and colors of decoration, and composition of clay. The jug fragments in my study do not need to be glued back together to be useful. The characteristic markings show clearly that this vessel was made in the early Byzantine period. From such pieces, and there were literally thousands of them, there is abundant evidence that the building at Araq el Emir, erected in the early part of the second century B.C., was reoccupied from the fourth through the sixth centuries of the Christian Era. Clay vessels contain for the archaeologist much more than food or beverage which the vessel originally held.

The handful of grain is part of the supply of wheat uncovered at Dhiban during the spring campaign, 1952.[6] Samples of this grain were tested by physicists and given the carbon 14 test. From the pottery found with the grain archaeologists had already determined that the grain must have been placed there about the middle of the ninth century B.C. The carbon 14 tests confirmed this and gave the date 851 B.C. (plus or minus a hundred years) as the time when the grain was harvested. This method of dating is relatively new and is but one of the many techniques used in modern archaeology to date ancient material.[7] The process served the purpose of confirmation or cross

[4] *Ibid.*, p. 16.
[5] See below, Chap. 4, pp. 58-59.
[6] Tests made by Jason R. Swallen, Head Curator, Department of Botany, Smithsonian Institution, identified the grain as "probably a wheat relative." See *BASOR* (April, 1957), pp. 6-10.
[7] E. H. Willis, "Radiocarbon Dating," Don Brothwell and Eric Higgs, editors, *Science in Archaeology* (New York: Basic Books, Inc., 1963), pp. 35-46.

checking. Such cross checking is always advisable where it is at all possible.

The discovery of the grain gave us evidence of farming activity in that area in the ninth century B.C. and also of the food habits of the people. History often deals only with those facts which men have thought worthy of recording. Archaeology uncovers details of common life which gives us fuller aspects of history. Historians and archaeologists have become aware that history is the record of what happened to people, not merely the annals of emperors and accounts of battles.

Coins are interesting for their own sake, as any coin collector will tell you. A coin, unless badly worn, is usually identifiable as to date, location, and mintage. Finding a number of coins in an ancient building provides one means of dating the occupation of that room, but not necessarily the date of its building. On the other hand, if a coin has been accidentally dropped by a workman during construction and is embedded in the wall, it is a fair assumption that the date of the coin is immediately prior to the building of that wall. In any case the date of the wall is later than the date of the coin. Robbers may, on occasion, be forced to hide their loot of coins in an abandoned building perhaps many years after the date of its construction. The number and location of the discovered coins is all-important for dating occupation and construction.

On the other hand, coins also give us much information concerning the period in which they were minted. By the titles monarchs used on coins they tell us much about themselves. Symbolism of the period sometimes reflects religious beliefs. We have on a coin information concerning the language in use at that particular location and evidence concerning the form of the writing used, but we must always be alert to the problems presented by archaizing.[8] Coins help significantly in etching in details of history not always to be found in historical documents.

The clay tablet in my study bears an inscription written in cuneiform, or wedged-shaped characters, and dated in the first half of the second millennium B.C. It tells about a common commercial transaction, the sale of sheep. Such a tablet can be read without difficulty because of the work of early archaeologists and linguists. Languages and forms of writing completely unknown to us a few years ago have been deciphered by scholars. Ancient kings, priests, scribes, and businessmen wrote documents of various kinds. Some are records of business transactions; others are letters dealing with affairs of state, written instructions to generals of armies, records of military engagements written by victors and vanquished, lists of donors to sanctuary building and current expense funds, personal letters, et cetera. The variety is as wide as the cross section of the activities of the community. From such documents histories have been written of ancient nations, most of whom were not well known and

---

[8] "Archaizing" is a term used, particularly by students of writing, to designate attempts by ancient writers to make their documents look older than they really are by using forms of letters typical of an earlier period than the age in which they are writing.

some of whom were completely buried under the sands of time. No document can be ignored. One scholar made a detailed study of the prices at which a variety of commodities were sold. He discovered that it was true in ancient days, as it is today, that when there is war or other national emergency there is a marked change in prices. But when he constructed his price charts he found that peak prices occurred at times for which there was no record of war or other emergency. He carefully checked other records and discovered that his price charts were correct. There had been other wars of which there was little information. More complete histories of those countries have now been written.[9]

It is often assumed that the historian is concerned with the story of mankind in the periods after man has learned to write and make records, and that the archaeologist must be concerned with preliterary periods, or "prehistory." The fact is that the histories of the nations in the Near and Middle East could not be written until the archaeologist had uncovered and deciphered the written documents and materials from which the historian could compile his histories. A major function of the archaeologist is to uncover the past, and to uncover it so skillfully that it can be reconstructed in minute detail. Frequently, before the reconstruction can take place, the archaeologist must decipher languages and scripts and so make intelligible information available to the historian.

This suggests that in addition to field archaeologists who uncover artifacts there are also scholars who devote themselves to the preparation of material for intelligible display, and there are still others whose task it is to discover the secrets of ancient writings. Such scholars are included in the company of those who consider themselves archaeologists. Increasingly the term "field archaeologist" is being used. Such a term seeks to distinguish between a major task of archaeology, that of searching for evidence in the field through excavation, exploration, et cetera, and the work of research and interpretation of the products of the field archaeologist. In later chapters we shall give attention to these various aspects of archaeology.

One other aspect of archaeology needs our attention at this particular point in our study. While we believe that modern archaeology is solidly committed to scientific procedures and can be, and ought to be, as objective with its evidence as any physical science, the fact remains that there is a major difference between archaeology and most other sciences. The procedures of field archaeology are essentially destructive. As the archaeologist excavates he must of necessity destroy one layer of history before he can study the next. He cannot say to fellow scientists, "Follow these procedures in this precise situation and you will confirm my conclusions." The experiment cannot be done over again. There can be similar procedures in parallel situations, but not in the same situation. Walls are gone; pottery has been removed from the place in

[9] W. H. Dubberstein, "Prices and Interest Rates in Babylonia (625-400 B.C.)" (Doctoral dissertation, University of Chicago, 1934).

which it has lain for centuries; and even the charcoal from the fireplace has been swept up and may now repose in a cellophane bag instead of between fire place stones. It is, therefore, basic to modern work in the field that detailed and accurate records be kept of every procedure and every scrap of evidence. From the archaeologist's records of the day it should be possible to put everything back into place. His notes should tell anyone as much about the structure of an ancient building as an architect's drawings tell the builder about a building under construction. This is the less glamorous side of the archaeologist's task. After a long, hard day's work, when the native workers have gone to their tents, the archaeologist must write detailed records from notes made during excavation. He must make drawings and take photographs. He must spend time with his co-workers and his director examining all artifacts which have been recovered that day, selecting all items which have real significance in telling the story of that particular place in man's history. These are the aspects of archaeology which were too often completely omitted in the days of "pot-hunting" and prescientific archaeology.

2.

ARCHAEOLOGY
BECOMES A SCIENCE

Man's insatiable curiosity about himself and his origins has caused him to examine with interest any object which he believes has been made by his predecessors. Modern excavators uncovered ancient Assyrian libraries in Mesopotamia only to discover that the Assyrians in turn were indebted to collectors from Babylonian times. The Babylonian collectors had gathered Sumerian as well as Babylonian tablets, many of them quite ancient, into a library.

The Royal Library of Nineveh, for example, has had a long history. Part of the collection dates back to the time of Tiglath-pileser III (744-727). Sargon II (722-705) added many astrological works. Sennacherib (705-680), known popularly as a ruthless and cruel oppressor, ordered his scribes to add Assyrian documents, short stories, and miscellaneous inscriptions. He caused the entire collection to be moved from Calah to Nineveh. There Esarhaddon (680-668) added many historical and mythological works. It was, however, Ashurbanipal (668-626) who made it into the magnificent collection which was recovered in the middle nineteenth century.[1]

Professor A. T. Olmstead notes that Ashurbanipal had been schooled in both Akkadian and Sumerian.[2] On some of Ashurbanipal's bookmarks he says: "In agreement with the original tablets and documents I caused copies of the Assyrian, Sumerian, and Akkadian to be written, compiled and revised in the chancellery of the experts, and as precious possessions of my royalty."[3] In the J. Pierpoint Morgan Library there is a copy of the Gilgamesh Epic which was found at Nineveh. It is a copy of a much older version. The scribe has signed the copy and even indicated with the word "broken" where the original was defective.[4]

As man sought for additions to his collection he became aware of the beautiful works of art produced by bygone generations. These discoveries stimulated his acquisitive activities even more. It has been said that man has something of the nature of the pack rat, and certainly the earliest collections of which we have knowledge indicate that pride of possession was the chief motivation. Jacquetta Hawkes called attention to a Thracian princess of the

[1] Carl Holliday, The Dawn of Literature (New York: The Thomas Y. Crowell Company, 1931) p. 53.
[2] History of Assyria (New York: Charles Scribners Sons, 1927) p. 489.
[3] Ibid., p. 491.
[4] James Baikie, "The Cradle of Civilization," National Geographic Magazine (February, 1916), p. 168, 170.

fifth century B.C. who made a collection of stone axes from prehistoric sites.[5] Yet even in Sennacherib's day there seems to have been an investigative spirit which led man to inquire whether or not writers in the past had anything to teach men of a later generation.

The stories of rivalry and piracy between explorers in the first half of the nineteenth century, particularly the British and French, reveal more nationalistic pride than scientific zeal. There was a constant race between the competing teams to see which could make the first and biggest acquisitions. Much material was destroyed in the process, partly because the workers had no comprehension of the nature of the material with which they were working, but mostly because they had not yet learned techniques of preservation for the highly friable objects they handled. Haste made much waste. We are, nevertheless, deeply indebted to the early workers in the field.

Any observant traveler in the Near and Middle East immediately becomes aware that even with rigid supervision from departments of antiquities many ancient objects are thoughtlessly destroyed. For centuries such monuments as the great pyramids of Egypt were used as quarries from which to extract building stone. After the first season of work at Dhiban the excavation was left in charge of the local police whose duty it was to protect the site until work could be resumed in the second season. Upon his return to the site the director discovered to his horror that the chief of police had helped himself to enough stone to build a new police station. In the process he had destroyed important base lines in the excavation necessitating the reestablishment of key measuring points before the work could be resumed.

It is not unusual to go into a simple native home and discover that the threshold stone was once an important inscription in a nearby temple or palace. And the man who purloins the stone is not always thoughtful enough to place the stone with the inscription down so that it will not be erased by the tramp of many feet.

Fine statues have been smashed beyond recognition because the devout Muslim believes that carving such statues is a violation of the commandment prohibiting the making of images. Inaccessibility is the only thing which preserved such carvings as may be seen at the top of the great columns at Baalbek. In other cases depth of soil and sand has protected monuments against zealous iconoclasts. In addition, natives discovered many generations ago that ancient mounds provide a ready supply of stone from which lime can be slaked. Many a crude cottage has been adorned with lovely whitewash at the expense of destroyed palace walls.

A further factor has resulted in attempts to garner the beautiful and ignore the more important but less attractive objects. There is great expense in archaeological research. A typical way to raise funds for an expedition is to promise the donor that recovered objects will be publicly displayed with proper

[5] Jacquetta Hawkes, editor, *The World of the Past* (New York: Alfred A. Knopf, Inc., 1963), I, 27.

notation concerning the generosity of the person who made the expedition possible. It is understandable that such a donor is more likely to be flattered if the objects displayed have great intrinsic value and beauty of form. A golden crown or a richly carved alabaster vase seem to be much more important than rough clay jugs, which are probably cracked to boot. One teacher sought financial backing from his school only to have the trustees ask, "What do we get out of it?" They were finally persuaded by the administrator that there would be important advertising value for the school. Investment in knowledge is hard to sell. One school did rally support with the unusual slogan, "Shekels for Shechem!"

Henry Layard, inspired by the Frenchman Paul Émile Botta, made England aware of the rich treasures to be found in Mesopotamia, but when the British Museum finally was persuaded to make 2,000 pounds available for excavation it was with the strict provision that Layard was "to obtain the largest possible number of well-preserved objects of art at the least possible outlay of time and money." [6]

Archaeology is popularly associated only with excavation. If, however, archaeology is the study of antiquities, then it must be occupied with much more than excavation. Excavation, in fact, is only one of the techniques by which antiquities are made available for study. We shall need to stress this fact throughout our studies.

In Mesopotamia and Palestine most antiquities are recovered painstakingly through excavation, but in Egypt much material is already above ground and is readily available for study. Such objects as the pyramids and temple walls were so well known that when Napoleon went to Egypt on a military campaign he took scientists with him to study these famous monuments. A major project of the Oriental Institute of the University of Chicago was the recording of every known hieroglyphic inscription at Thebes in Egypt. Many of these had long been above ground, and others had to be uncovered by excavation. The major part of the project was photographic, and much time was spent checking the photographs against the original inscriptions.

In the early centuries of Christianity interest turned to the land where Christianity originated, and many travelers made their way to Palestine. Much of the travel was little more than idle curiosity or emotional response to scenes hallowed by the memories of Jesus and the apostles. Occasionally an explorer stopped to investigate ruins and to make inquiry concerning local traditions. Such inquiry helped to identify locations of ancient villages and cities.

According to Western tradition Saint Helena, mother of Constantine, was an early pilgrim to Palestine. Her name is associated with the identification of the place of the Crucifixion and with the building of the Church of the Holy Sepulchre and the Church of the Holy Nativity, but there is no confirmation of such activity in the writings of Eusebius of Caesarea (260-340),

[6] Leonard Woolley, *History Unearthed* (London: Ernest Benn, Ltd., 1958), p. 19.

Bishop Cyril of Jerusalem (315-386), or the Pilgrim of Bordeaux (ca. 333).

Eusebius left a record of his search for holy places in his book *Onomasticon*. This in turn was translated by Jerome from Greek into Latin. The revised edition contained over a thousand place-names, and about one third of them were given definite location.

The Crusaders in the eleventh to the thirteenth centuries sought out holy places and made many identifications, many of them quite erroneous. The Crusades, nevertheless, stimulated new interest in Palestine, but because of the failure of the Crusades to free the Holy Land from the Muslims travel still remained difficult.

In the fifteenth century an Italian merchant (born in Ancona in 1391), Cyriac de Pizzicolli, interested himself in ancient coins, and works of art and in copying inscriptions. He traveled in Egypt and Greece. Because of the care he gave to systematic records and orderly investigation he is one of the men known as "father of archaeology." He died about 1449, and his collections have been scattered.

Also in the fifteenth century extensive travel in Palestine was undertaken by courageous individuals. Felix Schmidt (Fabri) made his first journey about 1480 but gathered little information. He made a second journey in 1483 and this time was more successful. He was able to make critical checks on locations, to verify historical claims, and to record some notes on the manners and customs of the people. He explored the country from Jerusalem to Mount Sinai.

In the following century (1575) Leonhard Rauchwolff (Rauwolf) made notes on natural history and botany, and eleven years later (1586) Johann Zuallart made a special study of architecture and other antiquities. It was also in the sixteenth century that Johann van Kootwyck (Cotovicus) brought back accurate descriptions of the country.

In the seventeenth and eighteenth centuries much additional information was gathered by Quaresimus (1639), Pietro della Valle (1650), Michael Nau (1679), Henry Maundrell (1703), Bishop Pococke (1738), and Adrian Reland (1709) whose book on ancient monuments was published in 1714. This book, entitled *Palaestina ex Monumentis Veteribus Illustrata*, was hailed as a most significant publication.

Investigation and travel were sharply increased at the close of the eighteenth and the beginning of the nineteenth centuries. In 1798 Napoleon Bonaparte took a party of 175 scholars, artists, and scientists with his army to Egypt. This group made careful search in both Upper and Lower Egypt. In addition to making drawings of monumental buildings, they collected many moveable artifacts. With the defeat of the French by the British, these artifacts became the property of the British in 1802. The French, however, were able to retain rights of publication of their discoveries, and seven volumes appeared between 1809 and 1822. The artifacts were removed to the British Museum where they form part of the display in the Egyptian section. Napoleon's plans included a four-month campaign into Palestine and Syria to protect his troops from attack by the Turks. Among his company was a corps of geographers. The chief geographer, M. Testevuide, was assassinated in Cairo. His nephew Pierre Jacotin replaced him. In spite of the difficulty of making maps under the hazardous conditions of a fast military campaign, Jacotin surveyed more than four hundred places. These were located on five maps and published later in Paris.[7]

It was at this time that serious work was first carried on in Mesopotamia. C. J. Rich was resident in Baghdad from 1808 to 1821 and during his residency was able to excavate small mounds near Baghdad. Later he extended his investigations as far as Kirkuk and Mosul. The artifacts recovered were the first antiquities brought to England from Mesopotamia. The French consul in Mosul, P. E. Botta, worked across the River Tigris in 1842, and still later at Khorsabad, where he uncovered the palaces of Sargon II.

Work for the British was carried on by Austen Henry Layard at Nimrud (ancient Calah), twenty miles south of Mosul. The palaces of Ashurnasirpal (884-858), Shalmaneser III (858-823), and Esarhaddon were identified. He also dug at Kuyunjik (part of ancient Nineveh) and found two more palaces— those of Sennacherib and Ashurbanipal. Botta's materials were sent to Paris and Layard's to the British Museum. There was great rivalry between the two countries and their agents. In the race for quantities of material untrained workers were left in charge of sites uncovered while the leaders went in search of new fields for plunder.

Much valuable material was recovered, but fantastic amounts of important writing were forever destroyed. Much of the excavation was done by tunneling into mounds. Poor light and complete lack of experience by which important and unimportant material could be differentiated were major causes of destruction. Only the most solid objects such as stone walls and statues appeared to be worth salvaging. No attention was given to sherds, but whole pieces of pottery were thought worthy of preservation.

Clay tablets were assumed to be important largely because they had been collected in an ancient day and stored as a library. The excavators had no way of preserving tablets which were in poor condition, however. Many were badly damaged in excavation and shipment.

Botta's work was followed by that of Victor Place at Khorsabad and by that of Fulgence Fresnel and Jules Oppert. Layard trained Hormuzd Rassam who continued work at Kuyunjik, and Henry C. Rawlinson became an adviser and promoter for the English.

From 1854 to 1873 there was little excavation in Iraq, but in 1873 George Smith found a 30,000 tablet library at Nineveh. Smith was an employee of the British Museum, and during his work there had learned to read cuneiform writing. During his work as a translator he had found part of the Babylonian

[7] C. M. Watson, "Bonaparte's Expedition to Palestine in 1799," *Quarterly Statement of the Palestine Exploration Fund* (1917), pp. 17-35.

story of a great flood. As we have already noted, he was then commissioned by a London newspaper to go to Mesopotamia to recover the other half of the tablet. Such was the innocent comprehension of the task of the archaeologist held by most people at that time. Amazingly enough, Smith did find the rest of the story of the Babylonian flood, as we have already noted.[8]

In Palestine work moved steadily in the direction of scholarly and scientific investigation. From 1805 to 1807 Ulrich Jasper Seetzen explored Transjordania, with special attention being given to Caesarea Philippi, Amman, and Jerash. Johann Ludwig Burckhardt worked from 1801 to 1812, making three major contributions: The discovery of Petra, a city of major importance in the history of the Nabateans; the careful recording of Arabic place-names; and the copying of inscriptions, which Burckhardt identified as "Muslim."

A few years later (1817-18) C. L. Irby and James Mangles traveled in Palestine and Transjordan making drawings of many sites and recording evidences of ancient occupation. They gave us the first important information concerning Araq el-Emir, traditionally associated with Tobias in the second century B.C. This site was architecturally surveyed by Howard Crosby Butler of Princeton University in 1904 and more recently was excavated by The American Schools of Oriental Research. The first real plans for the city of Jerash were made by James Silk Buckingham in 1821.

It is generally recognized that a most important step forward was taken by Edward Robinson and Eli Smith in 1838. These men were a perfect team. Robinson was well schooled in the ancient languages, and during his residency at Andover Theological Seminary he had made a translation of Gesenius' *Hebrew Lexicon* and had written *A Greek and English Lexicon of the New Testament*. He had just been appointed professor of biblical literature at Union Theological Seminary but had accepted that position on condition that he be allowed to continue with his plans to explore Palestine. His companion, the Reverend Eli Smith, was a former student and a missionary to Lebanon. Smith spoke fluent Arabic and was well acquainted with conditions in Palestine and with the problems of travel. A three-volume work resulted from their travels and was published under the title *Biblical Researches in Palestine, Mount Sinai, and Arabia Petrea* (1841).

In 1867 Titus Tobler of Germany published the results of topological research he had made in four trips to Palestine. His first trip in 1835 was largely for pleasure, but it was on that trip that he accepted the challenge to become a scientific explorer. In 1845-46 his attention was directed to the city of Jerusalem. In 1857 he studied Judea, and his work in 1865 was an exploration of Nazareth.

The most comprehensive topographical survey of west Palestine was that conducted by C. R. Conder and H. H. Kitchener from 1872 to 1878, a project under the sponsorship of the Palestine Exploration Fund. About 6,000 square miles were surveyed, and approximately 9,000 names were plotted

[8] See above, Chap. 1, p. 17.

on 26 sheets, to a scale of 1 inch to 1 mile.[9] The Hauran and North Trans-jordania were explored by G. Schumacher in 1884 and following. In 1933 Nelson Glueck began explorations in Transjordan from the Aqabah to Syria, and in 1952 he began similar explorations in the Negeb of the new State of Israel.

Excavation techniques were placed on a scientific basis both in Egypt and in Palestine by W. Flinders Petrie, a British archaeologist who afterwards was knighted by his government in recognition of his contributions to the field of archaeology. Petrie was the first to work out techniques by which succeed-ing levels of occupation could be differentiated from one another. Heinrich Schliemann, excavating at Hissarlik in 1871 and Mycenae in 1876, had recog-nized that cities had been built upon the ruins and remains of preceding cities. Petrie recognized that pottery and other artifacts could be used to dis-tinguish various periods of man's occupation of a site. Pottery had distinctive shapes in different periods of history and in different nations. The shape or decoration of the vessel, as well as the quality of the clay used, was peculiar to each period. Using this as a key, Petrie developed new Egyptian and Palestinian archaeological techniques.

In 1890, under the auspices of the Palestine Exploration Fund, Petrie ex-cavated at Tell el-Hesi, a mound some 120 feet in height. He spaced his diggers a few feet apart down the side of the mound and had each worker dig into the hillside at that point. The result was a long trench, cut step fashion from top to bottom of the tell.[10] Petrie's workers kept all artifacts separated according to the step in the trench from which they had been re-covered. Petrie was then able to demonstrate that different levels had dis-tinctively different types of pottery. These were later correlated with specific dates in the city's history. As a result of his work and that done later by Frederick J. Bliss eight different strata of occupation were identified.

The question immediately arises, how were these different strata formed. Two statements from the teachings of Jesus serve well to illustrate the con-ditions which produced the layers of a tell. Jesus said, "A town that stands on a hill cannot be hidden" (Matt. 5:14 N.E.B.). Most towns and villages in the Middle East stood on hills either natural or artificial. They were so placed as to give military advantage and perhaps protection from flood waters.

Second, Jesus told the parable of two men who built houses (Matt. 7:24-27). One dug a foundation and built upon the rock. Presumably he had not only solid foundation but sturdy building materials for the superstructure. The other man built upon the sand. Such an individual merely scratches the

[9] *Map of Western Palestine in 26 Sheets from Surveys Conducted for the Committee of the Palestine Exploration Fund by Lieutenants C. R. Conder and H. H. Kitchener, R. E., During the Years 1872-1877,* (London, 1880).

[10] "Tell" is the Arabic word for "hill." The plural form is "Tulul." British publications tend to use the spelling "tall." The map *Holy Land Today,* published by the National Geographic Society (December, 1963), uses "tall" or "tell" for locations in the Hashemite Kingdom of Jordan, and "tel" within the boundaries of the State of Israel.

ground level and builds his house of mud brick. The life span of that kind of house is relatively short. When a mud brick house falls into decay, the ground is again leveled off and a new house built on top of the leveled debris.

Even the sturdy houses were destroyed in time. Sometimes their end was hastened by earthquake, fire, or enemy action. Sometimes the stubs of stone walls were used as foundations for new buildings, but such reuse can usually be detected without too much difficulty. Differences in available building material, techniques of laying the courses, and sometimes the establishment of a new floor level will reveal reuse of walls.[11]

Sometimes the reoccupation is immediate, resulting in a new level in the particular building but no new level or break in history in the town or village. In the fall, 1961, campaign at Araq el-Emir[12] there was clear evidence that during the Byzantine period a succession of floor levels in one building was due to the fact that the roof had caught fire and fallen onto the floor. The occupants apparently quickly covered the ashes with stones and dirt and laid down a new floor of limestone chips. There was no change in pottery type above and below the line of fire.

It is essential to distinguish between the occupation levels of individual buildings and the occupation levels of a city. Carefully kept records and drawings will help the archaeologist to coordinate the complete record.

The great depths at which ancient cities are found is difficult for some Westerners to comprehend because it is our practice in much of the West to remove all debris of previous buildings from a site before we build anew. In addition, it is the practice in many cities of the United States to establish the ground level of a building in accordance with a building code and at a point indicated by a surveyor's level. Visitors to the Holy Land talk easily about "walking the streets which Jesus or the prophets walked." As one climbs over the brow of the Mount of Olives this may be possible because the trail is nothing but bare rock, but it is not possible in any settled community such as Jerusalem, Bethlehem, et cetera. The streets of ancient days are many feet underground and only occasionally are they uncovered. A few illustrations will suffice.

When the ancient city of Ugarit (Ras Shamra) on the north Syrian coast was excavated it was necessary to dig down between sixty and seventy feet to get below the level of the most ancient occupation of that site. The latest city was destroyed by an invading enemy about 1200 B.C. and there has been nothing but farmers' fields there for many centuries. This town lies directly below the surface, but the original city was at the equivalent of the height of an eight-story building beneath the surface.

In 1951 I journeyed to Damascus, Syria. Repairs were being made to a city sewer. As the workers dug into the ground, about three feet down, the top of

---

[11] See plate I, Mosque at Luxor.
[12] See BASOR (October, 1963), pp. 8-39.

an arch was discovered. Archaeologists were called in. When I returned to Damascus in 1954 I visited this same street. The ancient arch had been removed from the ground and rebuilt above the surface. The top of that arch now stands some eighteen feet above ground instead of three feet below. Some experts have dated the arch as having been standing in the days of Paul. Here is evidence that approximately one foot of debris each century has been laid down on the city of Damascus.

The archaeologist is aware that the mound he proposes to excavate is a history book. He must turn its pages with care. He is also aware of two important facts as he excavates.

First, he begins with the last chapter written and proceeds step by step to the first chapter. The most recent occupations are, with few exceptions, on top. Yet his task is not quite as simple as turning the pages of a book, with everything neatly in order, nor is it as orderly as taking off the levels of a layer cake. Many things prevent geometrically perfect levels. Level is not geometric, but cultural. If correct records are kept of artifacts, floor levels, et cetera, careful separation between occupation levels is not difficult to determine. And in turn the levels can be grouped into strata of history. Normally the term "level" is used in connection with building occupation, and stratum is used in connection with recognized breaks in or levels of history, such as Middle Bronze, Early Iron, et cetera.

Second, an excavator, by the very nature of his work, destroys the book of history as he reads it. In order to read early chapters he must destroy later chapters. If, for example, he uncovers a house which dates from Roman times, and there is evidence that it is built on top of something else, then the Roman house must be demolished before any investigation can be made of the building below. Therefore, it is imperative that exact records be kept of everything which is uncovered. If possible, photographs should be taken of every aspect of the uncovered building and notation made of everything found in and around the building. Occasionally archaeologists do misinterpret the evidence, but this is not an extremely serious matter if proper records have been kept. Another investigator can read the record and correctly interpret the evidence and no permanent damage is done, except perhaps to the reputation of the first investigator.

Many refinements have been added to the method established by Petrie, but stratigraphical excavation is accepted as basic in modern archaeological expeditions. In addition, much has been added to our knowledge of ancient pottery and its various forms. Further consideration will be given to this aspect of archaeology in another chapter.[13]

The basic principle of scientific excavation is to dig by levels in pits or by the use of the trench. In a sounding (test examination) or a dig of limited personnel and funds it is sometimes the practice to excavate a pit five to ten

[13] See below, Chap. 4, pp. 57-59 ff.

meters square. Work then proceeds by levels as we have noted. In other cases a trench is dug across a mound, instead of from top to bottom, as was done by Petrie. This is done so that work can begin at the highest level, or latest period of occupation, and proceed to the earliest level of occupation. In addition, such a trench will give a cross section of the town's history, and for the whole length of the trench all digging proceeds to virgin soil. It is a better sampling of the evidence of occupation.

Another variation is to dig a series of pits either at random or in an established pattern. One method is to dig a series of pits in such a way as to give cross sections on two axes of the mound, east and west, north and south![14] In a few cases attempts have been made to excavate the entire mound layer by layer as at Megiddo (Tell el Mutesellim). This is expensive, and few organizations can afford excavation on a grandiose scale. In addition, it is the considered judgment of many excavators that even if money is available no one expedition should excavate the entire city. Enough should be left so that later scientists, as techniques are more sharply refined, will be able to make further checks on that particular site.[15]

As we have already stated,[16] the work of the archaeologist covers preliterary as well as literary periods in the story of man. Man became literate toward the close of the fourth millennium B.C. The archaeological record stretches back into time many millennia prior to the days when man could write and read. It has therefore been necessary for the archaeologist to discover means other than literary to date the various periods of man's history. A time schedule, therefore, has been worked out in terms of man's cultural development. The terminology has been borrowed, at least in part, from the related study, anthropology.

The oldest evidence we have of man comes from the crude stone tools he used. There may have been a period prior to this when he used wood, such as the branches of trees, to help him, but such evidence has completely disappeared. Stone tools have remained. His first stone tools were crudely shaped. This period is known as the Old Stone, or Paleolithic Age. It may have begun as early as 200,000 years ago. About 10,000 years ago man entered a new stage in his development and became a food raiser instead of a food gatherer. His tools were still made from stone. This period, lasting from 8000 to 6800 B.C., is designated the Mesolithic, or Middle Stone Age. The Neolithic, or New Stone Age (6800-4000 B.C.), was characterized by highly polished and shaped stone tools and by the development of man's farming skills and his first use of clay vessels.[16a] Approximately another 2,000 years elapsed in this period. A period known as the Chalcolithic period, lasting about 700 years, or 4,000-

[14] See drawing 1 showing excavation squares at Dhiban.
[15] See below, Chap. 5, pp. 60-71 for further discussion of excavation techniques.
[16] See pp. 21 and 23 above.
[16a] The work of Miss Kenyon at Jericho necessitates the dating of pre-pottery Neolithic as early as the eighth or seventh millennium B.C.

3300 B.C., saw the change from stone to metal tools. Man discovered that copper could be shaped into useful tools. At first man could only hammer out the malleable metal, but later he discovered that heat made the metal more readily useful.

About 3300 or 3000 B.C. the true metal age arrived in Palestine. Sometimes the term Copper Age is used, but the practice has developed of referring to this period as the Bronze Age. It lasted until man had discovered how to process iron, or until about 1200 B.C. Careful examination of changing types and patterns of pottery has enabled the archaeologist to subdivide the Bronze Age into several divisions. At first the division was made into Early, Middle, and Late. In turn each of these has been subdivided: Early and Middle are divided into four subdivisions, and Late Bronze into three.

Early Iron, or Iron I, lasted for about 300 years from 1200-900 B.C. Iron II, sometimes called Middle Iron, lasted another 300 years. Late Iron, or Iron III, runs well into historical times and is usually referred to as the Persian Period. It, too, covers approximately 300 years.

The other periods are designated by historical terms: Hellenistic, 300-63 B.C.; Roman 63 B.C.-A.D. 323; Byzantine A.D. 323-636; and Islamic from A.D. 636 to the present. With written documents and many coins it is often possible to date exactly to a given year, but in the case of artifacts, especially pottery and statuary, dating to a period is the only possible procedure.[17]

Special attention needs to be called to the technique necessary for the clearing of a tomb. The word "clearing" is more appropriate than excavation in most cases. Tombs cut into rock are sealed against the kind of intrusion and debris to which a house is subject.[18] A tomb also may be used over a much longer period of time than a house. It may be owned by a family and used generation after generation. So long as space remained in the tomb nothing was disturbed and nothing comparable to "levels of occupation" occurred. Then when the tomb was full the practice was to push all bones and objects aside and begin over again. Tombs, however, have a distinct advantage over houses for the archaeologist in the quality of artifacts to be found. Most of the pottery found in houses is broken, but very fine specimens can often be found buried with the deceased. Coins are sometimes found. Beads and clothing are also more frequently found in the tomb than in the town. In addition, the objects buried with the deceased and the position of the body may give us information concerning religious beliefs, particularly belief in immortality.

Extreme care is necessary for the clearance of a tomb. The objects are frequently so tightly put together that there is little room for any individual to stand so as to be able to make proper investigation. In addition, ancient skeletal material, clothing, and objects of wood are in such friable condition

---

[17] A convenient table is available in "Archaeology," *IDB*, pp. 206-7. See comparative chart at the end of this chapter, p. 36.

[18] Sometimes rains and rivulets will wash debris into the tomb.

that the possibility of complete destruction is ever present. The chemist and the physicist have aided the archaeologist in working out techniques of preservation which have contributed much to our information. An excellent example of care in clearing, skill in preservation, and imagination in reconstruction may be seen at the Jordan Archaeological Museum in Amman, Jordan. One of the important displays is the reconstruction of a tomb from ancient Jericho. Every piece of bone, now permanently preserved; every piece of pottery; all articles of clothing; may be seen by any visitor to the museum. Alongside the reconstructed tomb is a photograph taken at the time of the discovery of the tomb. Careful comparison shows that the reconstruction is faithful to the last detail. Such a reconstruction would have been impossible a century ago; indeed, it would have been thought unimportant. Most of the evidence from the tomb would have been completely ignored.[19]

In the last few paragraphs we have noted the importance of techniques of preservation. This is true not only for tomb clearing, but in all aspects of archaeological research. Care of observation coupled with skill in preservation sometimes give us information which is extremely valuable. A few examples will suffice to show the importance of observation. When Sir Leonard Woolley was excavating at Ur two small holes in the ground were observed. Obviously the holes could not have been made by rodents or reptiles. Wax was poured into the ground and allowed to congeal. The ground was then carefully removed, and to their astonishment the excavators found that the wax had taken the form of a harp frame. In addition, pieces of lapis lazuli and other decorative material were imbedded in the wax. The holes had resulted from the disintegration of the wood, and the decoration which once adorned the wood was now imprisoned in the wax. From the wax form, a new frame was constructed. It is now possible to see the actual form of a harp from the time of Abraham. Care preserved the evidence which otherwise would have been lost.

Henry Field of the Chicago Museum of Natural History related the story of the discovery of an ancient chariot and its steed. As excavation proceeded sand suddenly fell away, leaving a wall surface in which a clear outline of a chariot appeared. Nothing remained but decayed wood. Thick coats of varnish were applied to the decayed wood. Layer on layer was applied. Finally, it was possible to remove the thick layers of varnish from the soil and with them the evidences of the chariot. A reconstructed chariot was afterward placed on display at the Museum in Chicago.

Most metals deteriorate with age. Silver is notoriously unstable. The famed Chalice of Antioch would long since have fallen to dust had not a thin coating of gold been put over the silver many centuries ago. Even so, the present owner of the chalice lived in constant fear while it was on display at the Chicago World's Fair. He was not afraid of attempted theft because the chalice was guarded day and night with extreme care. His fear was that some

[19] See Woolley, *Digging Up the Past*, pp. 81 ff.

sudden movement would shake it to dust and no restoration would be possible. Techniques are now available to give stability to metals which have been changed by time to salts. The copper scroll recovered from Cave III at Qumran is an excellent example of this.[20]

These paragraphs are by no means the complete story of the transition from plundering to scientific investigation of antiquities. Enough has been said, however, to indicate the major steps and to prepare the reader for the record which follows. We now turn to a consideration of the sources of information available to an archaeologist and to the variety of conditions under which he must work in different parts of the Near and Middle East.

[20] See John Marco Allegro, *The Treasure of the Copper Scroll* (Garden City, N. Y.: Doubleday & Company, Inc., 1960); J. T. Milik, "Le Rouleau de Cuivre de Qumran (3Q 15)," *Revue Biblique*, LXVI (1959), 321-57; G. Vermes, *The Dead Sea Scrolls in English* (Pelican Books, 1962), pp. 248 ff.

COMPARATIVE DATES OF ARCHAEOLOGICAL PERIODS

	DATE ACCORDING TO: Wright*	Harding**	Van Beek***
Paleolithic	100,000-8000	200,000-8000	omits
Mesolithic	8000-5500	omits	"Natufian" 8000-6000
Neolithic	5500-4000	8000-4500	"Pre-Pottery" 6000-5000 "Pottery" 5000-4000
Chalcolithic	4000-3300	4500-3000	4000-3200 "Esdraelon" 3200-3000
Early Bronze	3300-2000	3000-2100	I 3000-2800 II 2800-2600 III 2600-2300 IIIB or IV 2300-2100
Middle Bronze	2000-1500	2100-1500	I 2100-1900 IIa 1900-1700 IIb 1700-1600 IIc 1600-1550
Late Bronze	1500-1200	1500-1200	I 1550-1400 IIa 1400-1300 IIb 1300-1200
Early Iron or Iron I	1200-1000	"Iron Age" 1200-330	Ia 1200-1150 Ib 1150-1025 Ic 1025- 950 Id 950- 900
Iron II	1000-600	see above	IIa 900-800 IIb 800-700 IIc 700-600
Iron III	600-330	see above	"Iron III, Late Iron, or Persian" 600-300
Hellenistic	333-63	331-63	300-63
Roman	63 B.C.-A.D. 325	"Rome and Byzantium" 63 B.C.-A.D. 636	63 B.C.-A.D. 323
Byzantine	omits		A.D. 323-636
Islamic	omits	A.D. 636	A.D. 636 to present

* See George Ernest Wright and Floyd V. Filson, editors, *The Westminster Historical Atlas to the Bible* (rev. ed.; Philadelphia: The Westminster Press, 1956) pp. 15-16; and Wright, *Biblical Archaeology* (Philadelphia: The Westminster Press, 1957), pp. 30-39.

** G. Lankester Harding, *The Antiquities of Jordan* (London: Lutterworth Press, 1959) pp. 26 ff. See Chronological Table, pp. 210-11.

*** G. W. Van Beek, "Archaeology," *IDB*, pp. 206-7.

3.

CONTROLS, AIDS,
AND SOURCES OF INFORMATION

"I have gazed on the face of Agamemnon." In a telegram to the King of Greece Heinrich Schliemann announced in these words his great discovery at Mycenae. He has since been proved wrong.

In spite of his mistakes in identification at Troy and Mycenae, Schliemann made significant contributions to archaeology. In the first place he demonstrated that ancient tradition may contain more than a grain of truth and should be thoroughly checked out. Second, particularly in his work at Troy, he showed that an ancient site is frequently a succession of cities, one being built on top of another. In the case of ancient Troy he identified seven cities; these were later subdivided by American excavators into forty-six building periods.[1]

Schliemann's methods, however, were not too far removed from the plundering stage. There is little point in condemning him for not using methods which were not yet in existence. He did get into serious difficulty, however, because he had smuggled out of Turkey everything of value he discovered at Troy. For this reason he was permitted by the Greeks to excavate at Mycenae only after he agreed (1) to have his work supervised by the Archaeological Society of Greece, and (2) to guarantee that anything discovered would be turned over to the Greeks. This was the beginning of control in Greece. Similar protections were taken in other lands.

We have already noted the contests between representatives of the British and French as they sought for antiquities in Mesopotamia. Yet it must be observed that much material was being destroyed by the natives in their own building operations. They were not interested in history but in ready access to building supplies.

When, as a result of the exhibits in London and Paris, the world showed interest in antiquities, the Turks in control of Mesopotamia sought to shut off all excavation. This was not because they believed that control of scientific method was desirable, or even that the country of origin should have prior claim to antiquities, but so that the pockets of the Turkish officials could be lined with gold from selling antiquities.

It was not until the latter part of World War I that any adequate controls were imposed in Iraq. At that time the British were given mandate over Mesopotamia. The British High Commissioner was responsible for the enactment of laws governing excavation. Miss Gertrude Bell, an experienced traveler and excavator, was appointed first director of antiquities in 1917. She was replaced by Sidney Smith who remained in charge until he returned to Lon-

[1] Hawkes, *The World of the Past*, I, 59.

don to replace H. R. Hall as director at the British Museum. With the termination of the mandate and the admission of Iraq to the League of Nations, Iraqis assumed leadership. Among them were Naji al Asil, Saty al-hasri, Taha Baqir, and Fuad Safar. Messrs. Baqir and Safar received their training at the Oriental Institute of the University of Chicago. Under their direction the Department of Antiquities of Iraq has been housed in beautiful new buildings which include a carefully planned museum.[2]

Controls did begin much earlier in Egypt, but in the beginning the control was in favor of the French and not the Egyptians. The scholars who accompanied Napoleon to Egypt in 1798 were assigned the task of recording and studying the ancient buildings, such as the pyramids and the sphinx, which had been known for many centuries. In addition, they searched for objects which had not yet received recognition. By the misfortunes of war, the movable objects which had come into their possession became the property of the British and ended up in the British Museum instead of the Louvre. The French, however, were permitted to publish the result of their investigations, and by 1822 several volumes had been printed.

The French have been amazingly fortunate in their archaeological endeavors, and many objects of historical and cultural significance have come into their purview, some of them accidental discoveries by natives. Of major importance was the discovery in 1799 of a section of inscribed stone, found by French soldiers as they dug among foundations of a fort near Rosetta. We shall further discuss this discovery later. We need only note here that this stone, now known as the Rosetta Stone, gave scholars the key to the reading of the ancient Egyptian language.

Giovanni Battista Belzoni, an Italian born at Padua in 1778, left Rome when it was occupied by the French and moved his residence to England in 1803. There he divided his time between acting and studying hydraulics. After nine years he journeyed, by way of Portugal, Spain, and Malta, to Egypt. He made his living as a dancer, but his real purpose in going to Egypt was to sell his services as a hydraulic engineer. On advice from Burckhardt[3] he became interested in archaeology. Belzoni was a showman, a physical giant 6 feet 7 inches in height and already known for his great strength. His reputation continued, and in his search for antiquities he often resorted to brute force. The battering ram was frequently used. He forced his way into the second of the pyramids at Gizeh, and later discovered the tomb of Seti I in the Valley of the Kings, 400 miles up the River Nile from Cairo. Many of the artifacts discovered by Belzoni were sent to the British Museum. He published his findings in 1820.

Belzoni's career indicated quite clearly the need for better control in Egyptian excavations. More adequate supervision came thirty-five years

[2] These men were students of mine at Chicago. During my study in Iraq they extended many courtesies to me. It is a pleasure to acknowledge their courtesies in this way.
[3] See above, Chap. 2, p. 28.

after the death of Belzoni in 1823 with the appointment of Auguste Édouard Mariette to the post of Conservator of the Monuments and Antiquities, with the title Bey. Later he was promoted to Pasha.

Mariette was born at Boulogne-sur-Mer in 1821 and was educated in France. In 1839 he went to England as a teacher of French and drawing. He returned a year later and renewed his education, turning his interest to archaeology. He obtained a position in the Egyptian Museum of the Louvre in 1848 and in 1850 was sent to Egypt to collect manuscripts in Coptic, Syriac, Arabic, and Ethiopic. While searching for the site of ancient Memphis Mariette uncovered the avenue of sphinxes. This lead in turn to the Serapeum, the burial places of the sacred bull-gods Apis. More than 2,000 sphinxes and 4,000 statues, inscriptions, bas-reliefs, and ancient structures were uncovered. It was Mariette who excavated around the base of the Great Sphinx at Gizeh. He discovered it to be cut from solid rock. He also uncovered the entrance to the structure.

In 1854 he returned to Paris and was made assistant conservator at the Louvre. In 1855 he studied Egyptian collections in the German museums. Three years later when he returned to Egypt he was appointed to take charge of Egyptian antiquities. He was given financial support annually for his research and for the establishment and maintenance of a museum at Bulak. The present Egyptian Museum of Antiquities in Cairo was an outgrowth of Mariette's work and was built in 1895 by the Khedive Abbas Pasha. Mariette made important discoveries at Tanis, Thebes, and Abydos, and his list of publications is a long one.

Of great significance was his insistence that all excavation should be controlled by the Egyptian authorities and that no work could be done without express permission from his office. He also recognized that antiquities belonged of right to the country in which they had originated. He set patterns, which with modification, have been accepted in other countries.

In Palestine, control of any significance was quite late. That unhappy land no longer exists as an entity but has been divided into two new countries; the State of Israel and the Hashemite Kingdom of Jordan.

At the close of World War I the old Ottoman Empire was replaced by mandates under the French in Lebanon and Syria, and under the British in Palestine and Transjordan. Rising Arab nationalism and political Zionism forced further changes in the map of the Near and Middle East.

With the withdrawal of the British from Palestine on May 15, 1948, the State of Israel came into being, and a small portion of the old Palestine west of the River Jordan was combined with the Emirate of Transjordan to create the new country now known as the Hashemite Kingdom of Jordan.

Under the British mandate of Palestine the government set up a modern department of antiquities in 1920. John Garstang of the University of Liverpool, himself an experienced archaeologist, gave direction to the program. A more liberal policy enabled excavators from various nations to carry on their work with less difficulty than formerly.

With the establishment of the Emirate of Transjordan G. Lankester Harding was made the chief curator of antiquities, and later the director of antiquities of the Hashemite Kingdom of Jordan. He remained in this position until he was dismissed with other British leadership in 1956. Later the work was taken over by Awni Dajani as Director, and Joseph Saad was named director of the Palestine Archaeological Museum in Jerusalem. A personal gift of $2,000,000 from John D. Rockefeller, Jr., made possible the museum in Jerusalem, one of the best-organized displays of archaeological material to be found anywhere. The Department of Antiquities has recently completed the Jordan Archaeological Museum on the Citadel in Amman.

Digging in Israel is carried out by the Department of Antiquities in the Ministry of Education and Culture, the Hebrew University, and the Israel Exploration Society. As new villages have been established and new foundations dug, many archaeological sites have been uncovered up and down the country. At the new site of Hebrew University in Jerusalem a special building known as "The Shrine of the Book" is being constructed, in which the earliest found of the Dead Sea Scrolls are to be displayed. Provisions will be made also for the display of other antiquities.

The establishment of departments of antiquities and adequate display facilities in various countries has made it possible for laws to be established and controls of field procedure to be enforced. Many scientific groups have been organized, and we shall discuss more of their importance in the next section of this chapter. We must, however, recognize immediately that full cooperation between departments of antiquities, the several governments, and the scientific societies resulted in the adoption of basic rules which govern archaeological expeditions.

Permission to excavate, in all cases, must be obtained from the department of antiquities of the country in which the work is to be carried on. Free-lance excavation is now forbidden in most civilized countries (with the exception of the United States).

Permission is granted under the following conditions:

1. The department must be satisfied that the excavators have professional competence and will maintain approved scientific procedures.

2. The department must be permitted to inspect the work and the records of the expedition periodically. At the close of the season an inspector from the department will make a final check before the excavators are permitted to leave the site.

3. Financial guarantees must be made (a) that the work at a particular site will be completed, if necessary in a series of seasons, and (b) that publication will be made of the results of the expedition. Usually in this last case a financial deposit must be left with the department.

4. The department has the right to keep any and all artifacts, but normally

there is an equable distribution between the excavator and the department. It is recognized that the department will keep objects of special historical and cultural significance.

5. Artifacts permitted to the excavator may be brought out of the country, but only on condition that such objects will be placed on permanent public display.

6. Each excavator must agree that his discoveries will be made available to other scientists.

7. The excavator is normally given prior rights to publication of any discovery.

The field of archaeology has become so extensive and so interrelated to other fields of study that no archaeologist can work alone. The most skilled workers in the field regularly consult other experts and seek authoritative information from scholars in those fields of learning in which they recognize that they have limited competence. Frequent consultation in the field is an increasing practice of competent workers. It was for mutual help and encouragement of scholarship that many of the national and international societies were founded.

In 1864 the Palestine Exploration Fund was founded and on June 22, 1865, it was incorporated as a society. From the beginning its purpose was to encourage the systematic exploration of Palestine "for biblical verification and illustration." Work began immediately to determine which sites should be investigated. From 1867 to 1870 work continued with attempts to verify holy places. A survey of western Palestine was conducted from 1872-77 and a survey of eastern Palestine in 1881. This work was headed by C. R. Conder and H. H. Kitchener.[4] Many major excavations have been conducted by the fund.

The fund has published a quarterly statement since 1869 and an annual since 1911. These publications are major sources of information concerning archaeological activity in the field.

An American Palestine Exploration Society was established in 1870. The Deutscher Palästina-Verein was formed in 1878. The Deutsche Orient-Gesellschaft was founded under the auspices of the German Emperor in 1898.

Special schools also came into existence with headquarters in Jerusalem. One of the oldest is the École Biblique et Archéologique Française, associated with St. Stephen's Church and the library of the convent. It stands on the traditional site of the Byzantine Basilica of St. Stephen erected by the Empress Eudoxia in A.D. 460. It has been destroyed, but its site was recovered in 1882 by the Dominican Fathers, who built on the old ruins. Since 1893 the Dominicans have published Revue Biblique, a basic source of information concerning archaeological work in Palestine.

Within a short walking distance are two other important headquarters of archaeological work. The American Schools of Oriental Research, founded

---

[4] See above, Chap. 2, pp. 28-29.

in 1900, is an association of now about 130 universities, colleges, and theological schools of the North American continent. In 1910 its present school building was erected on Saladin Road, just a short distance north of Herod's Gate. This organization also has headquarters, established in 1923, though no building, in Baghdad, Iraq. Its publications are many.[5] Member organizations are kept currently informed by means of a newsletter published several times a year.

The American Schools of Oriental Research is an outstanding example of cooperative endeavor.[6] As we have noted, its membership is comprised of educational institutions, plus some outstanding patron individuals. It is at once the representative of member institutions in archaeological research and the headquarters from which many of the expeditions of participating institutions work. Tools and equipment may be stored in its buildings. Archaeological equipment may be costly and the ASOR makes possible joint ownership of some types of equipment. Its library is specialized for field archaeology. Investigators looking for information in related areas have easy access to the magnificent libraries at l'école Biblique and the Palestine Archaeological Museum. The director of the ASOR is regularly named as one of the trustees of the museum, and this makes for close cooperation between institutions.

Flinders Petrie founded the British School of Archaeology in Egypt in 1895, and shortly afterwards a parallel organization was set up in Jerusalem. For many years it operated in close association with the American Schools, but in recent years it has operated from its own headquatrers three blocks north of the American School.

Hebrew University was situated on Mount Scopus just northeast of Jerusalem. With partition in 1948 the university moved to west Jerusalem. It is the center of much archaeological activity, the place of publication of many books and journals, and the headquarters of The Hebrew University Department of Antiquities.

These and many other organizations and their publications are great aids to archaeologists, both field workers and others who seek to keep abreast of field results.

Opportunities exist today for training and experience in archaeological research which were completely unknown but a few years ago. It is not the purpose of this book to be a primer to field archaeology, but to give the general reader enough background information so that reports from the field and the various books on archaeology may be read intelligently. For readers who may be interested in preparing themselves for an archaeological career, the Bibliography gives reference material. Especially good are: Kathleen Kenyon, *Beginning in Archaeology*, and Sir Mortimer Wheeler, *Archaeology from the Earth*.[7]

[5] See special reference list at the close of this chapter.
[6] Photo, Plate II.
[7] Kenyon (rev. ed.; London: Phoenix House, Ltd., 1960); Wheeler (London: Oxford University Press, 1954).

It is important to recognize, however, that opportunities do exist for excellent training both in the classroom and in the field. The new spirit of cooperation between individuals and institutions makes possible observation in the field and the sharing of newly developed techniques. Excellent collections of pottery from various centuries and cultures make it possible for neophytes and experts to improve skills in study of pottery. All the institutions referred to in the preceding paragraphs have such collections. It should be noted, also, that the Palestine Archaeological Museum in Jerusalem has, in addition to its regular public displays, special drawers of pottery types. The student may handle and learn the feel and sound of characteristic material. Similar collections may be found in Amman, at the Jordan Archaeological Museum; in Jerusalem, Israel, at the Hebrew University; in Baghdad, Iraq, at the Iraqi Museum; and at Chicago House, Luxor, Egypt; to name but the most outstanding.

The publication of material from excavations goes through various steps. As we have already noted, publication is required by the host countries, but quite apart from this, publication is basic to the world of scholarship. Even the more sordid motive of a scholar's reputation may urge him on to publication.

In general there are four accepted ways of reporting or publication. First, there is a report by the archaeologist to his sponsoring institution or organization. This may be a private matter to account for funds expended, or it may be a lecture or series of lectures to which other scholars or the general public is invited. Or it may take the form of the brief telegram such as was sent by Howard Carter to inform his sponsor Lord Carnarvon that he had found King Tutankhamen's tomb and urging Lord Carnarvon to join him immediately in Egypt.[8]

The second is the formal presentation of a paper to one of the learned or professional societies. In the United States there are many such societies, somewhat international in character, which are recognized as major sources of current information. If one is to know what is happening currently it is well to belong to and attend such societies. Books on the subject are usually delayed many years. Some final reports in fact have never been printed.

There are annual and sectional meetings of such organizations as the Society of Biblical Literature and the American Oriental Society. There is an annual meeting of the corporation of the American Schools of Oriental Research which meets jointly with the Society of Biblical Literature, usually in New York. This meeting is generally devoted to receiving reports on current activities from the field. Reports may be made to the Archaeological Institute of America, and occasionally a paper of archaeological significance is given at an annual or regional meeting of the American Academy of Religion, formerly known as the National Association of Biblical Instructors.

[8] The telegram read: "At last have made wonderful discovery in valley; a magnificent tomb with seals intact; re-covered same for your arrival; congratulations."

In addition, there are regional organizations such as the Chicago Society of Biblical Research.

A paper presented at one of the organization meetings may then go on to the third method of reporting, that of publication in the journal of the society or in a departmental journal of a university. The outstanding journals for the publication of this type of material are listed below.

It is through such journals that information concerning archaeological discoveries is first made available. In the secular press information is frequently published in the *Illustrated London News*, the *New York Times*, *Life*, *Time*, and *Newsweek*, et cetera.

Eventually publication is made in book form. The more formal of these is often the publication through one of the university presses. Such publication is very expensive and can normally be done only by an underwriting of the cost of publication. Universities engaged in Archaeological work sometimes provide a means of publication in a special series. For example, the Oriental Institute of the University of Chicago has published a series of monographs under the title *Oriental Institute Communications;* another is titled *Oriental Institute Publications*. Other universities have similar means of communication. The current series of official publications concerning the Dead Sea Scrolls (discovered in Jordan) is being published by the Oxford University Press.

Publications are divided between those which deal exclusively with one excavation or closely related excavations and those which draw upon and seek to interpret the significance of archaeology. It can normally be expected that the first are written by the scholars involved in the excavation. It is the exception where this is not true.

The second group is produced by a variety of writers, some of whom have little knowledge of the methods of archaeology and are interested only in the results. Sometimes they are unable to distinguish between poor and excellent reports from the field. Or they may be written by men who are misusing archaeology to support a particular point of view, such as the verbal inspiration and literal accuracy of the Bible. For example, a recent publication ignored or dismissed all evidence of man's existence on the earth prior to 4000 B.C., because the writer belongs to a group which accepts Archbishop Henry Ussher's date of 4004 B.C. as the actual date of creation. Fortunately this type of publication is now on the decrease. An examination of the preface to a book will usually indicate the writer's purpose in writing and will often reveal any particular bias, if there is one.

In general the reader should remember that publications later than World War II are to be preferred to those prior, particularly those published from the turn of the century to the time of World War I. Most recent findings will appear in the journals, and only later will more definitive reports be available in book form.[9]

[9] See Bibliography, pp. 94-95; 209-14.

The following are generally recognized to be the more important journals:

Journal	Publisher

American Journal of Archaeology—Archaelogical Institute of America
Anatolian Studies—British Institute of Archaeology at Ankara
Annual of the American Schools of Oriental Research
Annual of the Department of Antiquities of Jordan (Amman)
Antiquaries Journal—Society of Antiquaries of London
Archaeologia—Society of Antiquaries of London
Archaeological Journal—Royal Archaeological Institute of Great Britain and
    Northern Ireland
Archaeology—Archaeological Institute of America
'Atiqot—Journal of the Israel Department of Antiquities, Jerusalem, Israel
Biblical Archaeologist—American Schools of Oriental Research
Bulletin of the American Schools of Oriental Research
Bulletin of Antiquities of the State of Israel
Bulletin of the British School of Archaeology in Jerusalem—Jordan (not
    currently being published)
Bulletin of John Rylands Library—Manchester University Press
Expedition—Bulletin of the University Museum of the University of
    Pennsylvania
Illustrated London News—Illustrated London News and Sketch, Ltd.
Iraq—British School of Archaeology in Iraq (Baghdad)
Israel Exploration Journal—Israel Exploration Society (Jerusalem)
Journal of the American Oriental Society
Journal of Bible and Religion—American Academy of Religion (Chambers-
    burg, Pa.)
Journal of Biblical Literature—Society of Biblical Literature (Philadelphia)
Journal of Cuneiform Studies—American Schools of Oriental Research
Journal of Egyptian Archaeology—Egypt Exploration Society
Journal of Near Eastern Studies—University of Chicago (continuing The
    American Journal of Semitic Languages)
Journal of the Palestine Oriental Society
Palestine Department of Antiquities Quarterly (ceased publication in 1948)
Palestine Exploration Quarterly—Palestine Exploration Fund (London)
Revue Biblique—Librairie Lecoffre (Paris)
Revue de l'Histoire des Religions—Presses Universitaires de France (Paris)
Revue de Qumran—(Paris)
Syria—(Paris)
Vetus Testamentum—International Organization of Old Testament Scholars
    (Leiden)
Yediot—Israel Exploration Society (continuing the Bulletin of the Israel
    Exploration Society)
Zeitschrift für die Alttestamentliche Wissenschaft—Berlin
Zeitschrift des Deutscher Palästina-Vereins—Leipzig

PART II

Aspects of Archaeology

4.

SURFACE SURVEY

Archaeology is popularly associated with excavation, but there is far more to archaeology than digging up artifacts.[1] To be sure, as we have already noted, much of the work of the archaeologist is literally that of uncovering the past. There is, however, evidence already available on the surface. It is such surface evidence with which we are to be concerned in this chapter.

It is quite obvious that before an excavator begins to dig he must have reasonable evidence that the site at which he proposes to dig will be worth the time, energy, and money expended. He does not dig at some site randomly chosen. The site is carefully selected after examination of surface evidence. Building materials and stubs of ruined walls protruding from the ground are obvious indications of former habitation of that place. Such open evidence may not be present, however. The trained archaeologist recognizes other signs which are equally informative.

The shape of a hill or mound is generally indicative of whether it has been formed or modified by human occupation or is merely the end result of geological processes. The Arabic word for any hill is "tell" (plural tulul), but in practice the archaeologist uses this word to indicate specifically a hill or mound which covers the ruins of an ancient community. A tell is easily recognized by its fairly flat top and characteristically sloping sides.[2] Archaeological survey maps of Palestine generally indicate the more obvious tells.[3]

An archaeologist does at times excavate a mound simply because it shows evidence of former human occupation. He would, however, prefer to know, if possible, the traditional identification of that particular site so that he may judge its probable historical importance. Funds for archaeological work are scarce and difficult to obtain, as any excavator knows, and he must justify the use of his funds to his sponsoring group or individual. Second, an archaeologist may have a period of history in which he is primarily interested. If he is a specialist in early Hebrew history he will not want to spend his time excavating a mound which was occupied only during Roman times, or what to him is less historically interesting, a late Arabic period. Here again surface examination can give him much information.

As we noted earlier,[4] characteristic pieces of pottery can be found in each level of occupation. Similar pieces of pottery may be found on paths leading to the mound and particularly at the edges of the mound, where they have worked to the surface or have been exposed by weather. By examining the

[1] Artifacts are man-made or man-modified articles.
[2] See Plate III (Dothan).
[3] See work of Conder and Kitchener, Map of Western Palestine.
[4] See above, Chap. 2, p. 29; see also the special appendix to this chapter, pp. 57-59 ff.

D

sherds [5] a general history of the mound's occupation may be discovered. If the sherds are early Roman or later the excavator who is primarily interested in earlier historical periods will not be encouraged to excavate at that particular site.

It should be noted, however, that there is division of opinion among excavators concerning the completeness of occupational history recovered in this way. One excavator, an expert in pottery, places great trust in surface evidence. In field trips on surface survey he completely ruled out the possibility of early occupation of certain sites because he found no evidence of early pottery. Yet he himself was engaged in excavating a site at which the surface pottery was all Arabic and Byzantine. The building remnants above the surface, as well as local tradition, indicated occupation during late Hellenistic times, in which he has special interest. As excavation proceeded it was discovered that the building rested on Middle Bronze Age foundations. In this one case at least surface evidence was incomplete. In any case surface evidence must be checked with other sources of information to get as complete a picture as possible.

Great quantities of sherds in one location can normally be taken as evidence of settled occupation. Wandering people, such as the modern Bedouin,[6] prefer utensils of more lasting quality than the fragile clay vessels used in sedentary communities. They use goatskin containers and other less breakable materials.

A third and highly important method of detecting ancient sites is careful observation of the terrain from an elevation at a distance and in varying lights. Photographs taken from an airplane or even a hilltop will often reveal the location of an ancient site which cannot be detected from the surface. The reasons are simple: There is greater perspective, and light and shadows are more clearly discernible; where ground has been disturbed by occupation vegetation grows more readily and usually to a greater height. Sir Leonard Woolley tells of seeing "the entire plan of a Roman villa spread out before me where no spade had ever dug." [7] In another situation a slight variation in the color of the stone chips became apparent only at a short period immediately before sunset. Woolley and his companion McIver marked the darker spots. When excavation was made the next day the Arab workers discovered at each marked spot a square rock-cut shaft to an Egyptian tomb.[8] Ability to detect and interpret such evidence often distinguishes the master craftsman from the rest.

Surface survey is often related to and associated with geographic exploration. One of the most important and useful studies was that done by Nelson

[5] A sherd is a fragment of something brittle, usually pottery. See Plate IV.

[6] Wandering Arabs. Arabs who have settled on the land are known as Fellahin (singular, fellah).

[7] *Digging Up the Past* (New York: Charles Scribners Sons, 1931), p. 28.

[8] *Ibid.,* p. 29.

Glueck, president of Hebrew Union College, Cincinnati, Ohio, in which he surveyed the terrain east of the Dead Sea and the Jordan River.[9] Glueck traced the bed of every river, stream, and wadi [10] to its source. On the assumption that man has tended to reside near rivers, springs, and wells, he believed that by tracing old watercourses he could find evidences of human occupation in places where there is now little or no memory of that occupation. His belief was justified, and he has been able to map not only the watercourses, but many sites of man's residence two or three millennia ago. Pottery and sherds played an important part in that investigation.

Two discoveries during Dr. Glueck's Transjordanian investigations have particular importance for readers of the Old Testament. The first sheds some light on the vexed problem of the Exodus from Egypt and the date of the arrival of the Hebrew people in the land of Palestine. The second gives insight concerning the activities of King Solomon and the economy of his kingdom.

The date traditionally associated with the conquest of Palestine by the Hebrew tribes is 1400 B.C. It has long been recognized by historians and biblical scholars that this date can no longer be claimed with the assurance that it once was. On the basis of archaeological discoveries in Palestine, new knowledge of the history of Egypt, and better understanding of some biblical passages, an alternate date of 1250 to 1200 B.C. has been proposed. The question is far from being settled, but it is now recognized by many biblical historians that the campaign of the conquest of Palestine was a far more complicated series of events than the simple story of a quick onslaught and victory, as it is usually told.[11]

In Num. 20:14-21 there is part of the record of the journey from Sinai and the attempt of Moses and his followers to pass through the land of Edom. Permission was requested for that passage, but the king of Edom refused to give it. The tribesmen were forced to detour around that little country. A similar request was made of Sihon, king of the Amorites. Permission was refused, and Sihon moved in battle against Israel. The Israelites were victorious. They also overran the territory of the Ammonites and the Moabites, countries east of the Dead Sea and the River Jordan.

Glueck informs us that no sedentary kingdoms, according to evidence from surface survey, existed east of the Dead Sea and the Jordan River between the Early Bronze Age and the thirteenth century B.C. He says, therefore, that if the Hebrew tribes had come that way prior to that time "The Israelites

---

[9] See Glueck, *The Other Side of the Jordan* (New Haven, Conn.: American Schools of Oriental Research, 1940); *Rivers in the Desert* (New York: Farrar, Strauss & Cudahy, Inc., 1959); and *The River Jordan* (Philadelphia: The Westminster Press, 1946).

[10] A wadi is the bed of a watercourse, dry except in the rainy season.

[11] See H. H. Rowley, *From Joseph to Joshua* (London: Oxford University Press, 1950); cf. also H. J. Franken and C. A. Franken-Battershill, *A Primer of Old Testament Archaeology* (Leiden: E. J. Brill, Publisher, 1963), p. 15.

would have found neither Edomite nor Moabite kingdoms"[12] Moses would have had to seek permission from no one. The way would have been free for any group, large or small, to pass with no hindrance, except perhaps from small groups of brigands. Glueck's position was supported by evidence from the Dhiban Expedition of 1965 in which we found little evidence of sedentary occupation of that site between the Early Bronze and Iron ages.

The Old Testament glories on the one hand in the grandeur of Solomon's reign, but on the other hand warns later kings against the tyrannous financial burden such as was imposed by Solomon upon his people.[13] Solomon, aware of the financial burden entailed by his building program and his large household, sought to relieve the situation by adopting three means of obtaining money and labor. The first was the adoption of the system of forced labor, the corvée (I Kings 9:20-21). Second, he traded horses and chariots between the Egyptians, Hittites, and Aramaeans (I Kings 10:26-29). Finally, he entered into the copper smelting business on the shore of the Red Sea at Ezion Geber. Scripture does not describe his copper enterprise, but does name the place of operation as the harbor from which his ships plied the seas (I Kings 9:26-28), a possible fourth means of income. The details of his copper mining and processing have been given to us by Glueck.

While doing surface survey in the area of Ezion-geber Glueck discovered some heaps of slag, clearly the remains of metal processing. Further investigation was clearly called for, and Glueck proceeded to excavate in the area. Among other things he uncovered the actual furnaces used in the process of smelting. Chemical analysis of the slag revealed that the metal refined had been copper, and that the processing had been so carefully done that it would pay no modern industry to reprocess the slag. Further insight came again from surface observation. It was discovered that the doors of the furnaces were oriented to the north in every case. Then the archaeologists noted that the prevailing wind was from the north and at high pressures. Anyone acquainted with the terrain of Palestine is aware of the great geological fault which begins between the Lebanons and the Anti-Lebanons and continues south to create the Jordan Valley, the Dead Sea, and the Arabah. Geologists have indicated that this same fault continues into the continent of Africa. Winds pour down this great declevity in the earth's surface as if through a wind tunnel and create enormous pressures. Solomon's engineers took advantage of this natural phenomenon and combined it with skillfully constructed furnaces. The result was that enough heat was created from simple fuel to smelt copper at 2000° Fahrenheit.[14]

[12] See Glueck, The Other Side of the Jordan, pp. 146-47.
[13] See Deut. 17:16-18.
[14] See Glueck, The Other Side of the Jordan, p. 50-88. The story is partially reprinted in Glueck's own words in Leo Deuel, editor, The Treasures of Time (Cleveland, Ohio: World Publishing Company, 1961), pp. 193-206, under the title "King Solomon's Pittsburgh."

Related to the plotting of ancient waterways is the tracing of irrigation systems. Such irrigation systems tell us of agricultural activities as well as urban planning. New Testament Jericho lies in the Jericho Plain some 1½ miles to the southwest of Old Testament Jericho. Old Testament Jericho, as does the modern village of Jericho, depended upon water from the spring associated with Elisha (II Kings 2:19-22). This spring is still called "Elisha's Fountain." The Roman road from Jerusalem to Jericho came down through the canyon known at its lower end as the Wadi Qelt. The road clung tenaciously to the south side of the canyon and entered the Plain of Jericho immediately at the Wadi Qelt; Herod's palace dominated the scene on the south bank. Human habitation was possible only because of the supply of water from the Wadi Qelt. On both sides of the Wadi the old irrigation trenches can readily be traced.

There is little rainfall in the Plain of Jericho or the Dead Sea region. It is estimated at two to three inches per year. Water in the Dead Sea is useless for human consumption. The region has, therefore, until the recent drilling of deep wells, been completely dependent upon the spring whose water had to be carefully conserved. One wonders why such a city as Jericho more than 830 feet below sea level has been maintained across the centuries in spite of the heat and the limited supply of water. There are several important reasons, as a visit to the city quickly demonstrates. First, the site is of strategic military importance. No one can cross the Jordan or approach the pass which leads to Jerusalem without being seen by guards at Jericho. Second, the weather at Jericho during the winter is a welcome relief from cold Jerusalem. It will be remembered that Herod went to Jericho during the winter months. Just on the outskirts of modern Jericho is a hotel which is known as "Winter Palace." Third, and of increasing importance in Jordan's economy, proper irrigation produces lucious subtropical fruit. We bought all the "makings" for typical American Thanksgiving and Christmas dinners from a Jericho farm, including vegetables, fruit, and turkey.

The caves in which the now famous Dead Sea Scrolls were discovered lie in the high bluffs several miles southwest of Jericho at Wadi Qumran. We shall have occasion to discuss later the significance of the scrolls. We need to consider at this point the irrigation system at Khirbet Qumran.[15] The high bluffs west of Khirbet Qumran are marked with heavy water stains from the torrents of water which have come from the heights beyond during the rainy season. The channels through which the water was brought into the Qumran community are readily traceable. In the community many storage cisterns were cut. The storage capacity was great, as it needed to be to sustain the community throughout the year both with water for human consumption and for various manufacturing processes. Steps leading to the bottom of the cisterns made the water available at whatever level it reached. Much of the discussion concerning whether or not the cisterns were used for baptism by immersion

---

[15] "Khirbet" is the Arabic word for a ruin.

could have been shortened or omitted if a sound knowledge of water usage had been considered. On the other hand, the position of Del Medico, that it never rains in the Dead Sea region, is clearly incorrect. We were discussing his theory one day as we drove through the mud and the wet sand on the way to Khirbet Qumran.

In recent years much archaeological work has been done by various organizations in the Negeb[16] with full cooperation from the State of Israel. Glueck has again given leadership in many aspects of archaeology, but especially in various forms of surface survey. He has recovered many places in which there is evidence of a special kind of irrigation system particularly suited to transportation of water in marginal lands where evaporation by the sun rapidly dries up most water courses. Water was channeled underground. This was effected by digging pits and connecting the pits by channels dug underground. This is the method still used in Mesopotamia, Persia and Arabia. Water is brought to the surface where needed just as water is drawn from a well. By this method water can be carried long distances with very little loss. Glueck points out that the use of such a system provided water for a far larger population in the Negeb than has been known for centuries. It is the recovery of this knowledge which gives hope to the new State of Israel that the Negeb can support a sizeable population.[18]

Water is a scarce commodity in most of Palestine, and it must be conserved by heroic means wherever possible. Even today water storage is a part of every building program. In the modern sections of Jerusalem in both Jordan and Israel large cisterns are incorporated into the buildings. Under the wing sections of the American School of Oriental Research in Jerusalem (Jordan) there are the equivalents of full-sized basements. Their function is solely that of storing rain from the roofs for use in case of failure of the city water supply. An understanding of the importance of water conservation is essential to interpretation of many ancient monuments.

At the juncture of Nablus Road and Saladin Road on the northern outskirts of Jerusalem, Jordan, there is a large monument called "The Tombs of the Kings." It was excavated by DeSaulcy in about 1850 and still belongs to the French authorities.[19] The date of its construction was not prior to the first century A.D. The tombs were closed with a rolling stone such as is described for the tomb of Jesus, and this is one of the few places where a "rolling stone" can be seen. The whole monument, with its series of tombs, was cut from an enormous outcropping of solid rock. A gigantic stairway

---

[16] The Negeb is the biblical term for south Palestine, south of Beer-sheba. The term has been revived in the State of Israel. Note: Glueck refers to the Negeb in his earlier reports, but to Negev in the later ones. In the Hebrew language some consonants have softened pronunciation following a vowel, and "B" becomes "BH" or "V."

[18] See Glueck, BASOR (December, 1958), p. 19.

[19] Cf. R.A.S. Macalister, A Century of Excavation in Palestine (London: Religious Tract Society, 1925), pp. 26-38.

leads down to the tomb area. The stairway and much of the leveled rock have been carefully channeled to drain off rainwater into cisterns. This also served the purpose of keeping torrents of water from the tombs themselves.

The city of Petra lies on the east side of the Arabah, some forty-five miles south of the Dead Sea. It is completely ringed about with high mountains, and the only entrance to it is through a very narrow cleft in the mountains (called the Siq) varying from a half dozen to about twenty yards in width and continuing for slightly more than a mile. The rock walls of the Siq tower up on either side to great heights, and it is obvious that a handful of men stationed here could stop a whole army. One and a half miles from the entrance to the valley in which the city lies is the heart of the ancient city. It has been described as "The Rose Red City, half as old as time." [20] Actually most of the sandstone is dark red ochre and is shot through with bandings of yellow, green, grey, and almost pure white. The edifices, many of them ceremonial tombs, have not been built but have been carved out of the living rock. They have to be seen to be believed.

The city had been lost to modern knowledge until its discovery in 1812 by the Anglo-Swiss explorer Johann Burckhardt. Since then hostile tribesmen have learned to tolerate the scholar and, now, to welcome the tourist. Modern travel agencies have made travel from either Jerusalem or Amman relatively easy.

Petra is quite ancient; Miss Diana Kirkbride has found traces of Paleolithic man, hand axes from about 10,000 B.C. Surface evidence of early occupation has been found in at least three different sections of the area. The larger part of the tombs, however, were built by the Nabataeans between the second century B.C. and the third century A.D. The Nabataeans are mentioned as early as the seventh century B.C. in the Assyrian records.[21] One of the buildings, The Urn Tomb, was converted into a Christian church in the fifth century A.D., and Petra became the seat of a bishop.[22]

As one goes through the Siq he can trace the long water conduit which has been cut into the rock. Water was channeled from Ain Musa (The Spring of Moses) right to the heart of the city. The conduits were cut on both sides of the Siq and were capable of carrying large amounts of water. This seems not to have been the only supply of water at Petra, however. On the tops of the surrounding mountains a number of altars have been discovered. The largest is known as "The High Place of Sacrifice." The top of the mountain, solid stone, has been leveled off. Around the altar is a large flat area or basin cut so that a natural wall completely surrounds the space except for drain channels. It has been suggested that the blood of the sacrificed animal was removed in this way. But the size of the "basin"

[20] Cf. Robinson, Petra: Sarcophagus of an Ancient Civilization (New York: The Macmillan Company, 1930); see also Plate VI.
[21] ANET, p. 298.
[22] Cf. G. Lankester Harding, The Antiquities of Jordan (London: Lutterworth Press, 1959), pp. 114-35.

is out of proportion for such a purpose. Down the sides of the mountain channels are cut. There are also at least two cisterns. It would seem to be probable that the basin was cut to catch storm waters which were then channeled to the community in the valley. It may well be that the altar was erected to the storm god who answered with rain. In any case, there is evidence that all storm waters were captured on the tops of the mountains and brought by conduits into the residential area.

Confirmation of this proposal may be found in the patterns of water engineering of the Nabataeans recently observed by Glueck in the Negeb. A series of explorations have been carried on by the Hebrew Union College—Jewish Institute of Religion. In a three-hour aerial reconnaissance, March 13, 1959, Glueck observed boxed sections of terraced wadi-beds.[23] By means of carefully placed lateral walls, heaps of stones, et cetera, water was channeled onto terraced fields and into cisterns. Sometimes the hills were stone banked. In the campaign of 1957 flat-topped, walled hill sites were photographed. Glueck reported, "The walled hilltop was used as a necropolis, but this was only a secondary function. Its primary purpose, at first developed by the Nabataeans through an amazing feat of water engineering, was to serve as a catchment basin."[24] This is precisely the method noted at Petra, but there the cutting was of necessity done in rock.

From his explorations in the Negeb Glueck has been able to make other important contributions to our knowledge of ancient history and culture. First, he reported that by the close of the season of 1959 "450 ancient historical sites have been discovered in the Negev, dated primarily by fragments of pottery found on the surface. . . ."[25] He went on to say, "The general historical conclusions thus arrived at from the archaeological exploration of the whole region were tested and confirmed by the archaeological excavations at Dhiban (Biblical Dibon)."[26]

At the end of the seventh season in the preceding year, Glueck and his co-workers had assembled enough evidence to assert:

The archaeological exploration of the Negeb has shown that it was never an uninhabited desert in historical times, that the climate has not changed in the past ten thousand years or so, and that parts of this southern half of the modern State of Israel were occupied intermittently by advanced agricultural civilizations from the fourth millennium B.C. on. It was dotted with hundreds of settlements and criss-crossed with important roads that joined Egypt, Arabia, and Canaan from the earliest times on.[27]

[23] Glueck, "An Aerial Reconnaissance of the Negev," BASOR (October, 1959), pp. 2-13.
[24] "The Sixth Season of Archaeological Exploration in The Negeb," BASOR (February, 1958) p. 11.
[25] "Archaeological Exploration in the Negev in 1959," BASOR (October, 1960), p. 26.
[26] Ibid., p. 3; see also Winnett, BASOR (February, 1952), p. 20; Tushingham, BASOR (February, 1954), p. 26.
[27] "The Seventh Season of Archaeological Exploration in the Negeb," BASOR (December, 1958) pp. 18-19.

Through his reconstruction of the history of the Negeb, Glueck has also been able to shed some light on the patriarchal period. It has long been recognized that the older datings for the time of Abraham as early as the twenty-second or twenty-first centuries B.C. were probably too high. Some historians have reduced the date to as late as the eighteenth century B.C. Glueck adduces evidence to prove that the Age of Abraham cannot be later than the nineteenth century B.C. He says:

After that there was a break in the history of the agricultural settlement in the Negeb, which lasted till the establishment of the Judaean kingdom in the tenth century B.C. The only archaeological framework in which the person and period of Abraham in the Negeb can be placed is Middle Bronze I. In the eighteenth or seventeenth centuries B.C. Abraham would have found neither settlements nor safety in the Negeb.[28]

He goes on to point out that Abraham and his large retinue would have been good prey for the Bedouin who tented in the Negeb between the eighteenth and eleventh centuries B.C.

Surface survey, often designated as archaeological exploration, is intimately related to excavation, as we have noted in several instances. It supplies the context for individual excavations and supplies information in addition to that which is obtained in an individual location. On the other hand, its methodology is often the same. Both have great dependence upon knowledge of pottery types for dating. A major difference between surface survey and excavation is that the former has no sealed off levels of occupation. The surface will contain material from many periods of occupation, while normally pottery types at each level of occupation in an excavation site are discrete. In either case, ability to recognize pottery types and dates is basic. The reader of archaeological reports, whether they report on surface survey or excavation, will need to understand the archaeologist's dependence upon his study of pottery. The following discussion on clay and pottery is given, therefore, as a special appendix to this chapter, not as a handbook on ceramics, but to underline the particular importance of pottery in archaeological studies.

APPENDIX: THE IMPORTANCE OF CLAY AND POTTERY

Clay is one of the most easily obtained, the cheapest, and the least destructible of the natural resources available to man. Ancient man made many products from it for household use. Man early learned to bake clay and give it greater stability and so produce pottery. He learned to use clay before he had discovered how to shape it into pottery. Man was already using clay when the lowest levels of Jericho were built. He used clay to seal and round out the corners between floor and wall so that floors could

[28] *Ibid.*, p. 20.

more easily be washed down. A thin coating of plaster clay was continuous over walls and floor. Pre-pottery Neolithic culture also used clay for making brick. These bricks were shaped by hand, unbaked, but sun dried. The shape was characteristic, somewhat in the form of French bread, flat bottomed, rounded at the ends, and with indentations from fingers or thumbs on top. These indentations received the mud mortar for the next layer.[29]

Shortly after about 5000 B.C. pottery came into use at Jericho, in the level of occupation designated Neolithic A. This is the earliest known pottery in Palestine so far discovered, and perhaps in the Near and Middle East. The use of clay vessels was only partially curtailed by the discovery of copper. Poor people could never afford the costlier material, and metal containers were useless for cooling water and wine.

The manufacture and use of pottery remained integral parts of the human story throughout history. Much of the pottery for daily household and business use was cheap and could be broken or abandoned without great loss. When storms and time destroyed the mud-brick houses and the roofs fell in, no attempt was made to rescue dishware. In most cases the dishes were broken and useless. The result has been that pieces of pottery have been sealed into the ruins of buildings and have become the labels by which archaeologists can distinguish levels of occupation and their probable dates.[30]

The work of the potter is referred to many times in the Bible: I Chr. 4:23; Ps. 2:9; Isa. 29:16; 30:14; 41:25; 45:9; Jer. 18:1-5; 19:1-13; Lam. 4:2; Dan. 2:41; Matt. 27:7-10; Rom. 9:20-24; and Rev. 2:27. The utility, cheapness, and destructibility of the potsherd is referred in Job 2:8; Ps. 22:15; Prov. 26:23; and Isa. 45:9. In spite of the common usage of the potter's wheel, it is never referred to in the New Testament, and only once in the Old Testament, Jer. 18:3.

We easily associate household items commonly made of clay. The list includes bowls; cups; plates; cookpots; bottles; jugs; juglets; cruets; juglets with perforated bottoms for sprinkling; pitchers; cruses for wine, oil, and water storage; perfume bottles; and large jars for grain storage. But the list must be expanded greatly. Pottery took care of man's needs from the cradle to the grave. As a child his feeding bottle, his rattle, and many of his toys were made from clay. And at the end, in a few cases at least, his coffin was shaped from clay.

Religion was served by clay. Clay idols were of two types, free hand and pressed in a mold. Bulls, doves, stylized trees, snakes, and other symbols of religion were reproduced. Astarte figurines are found in great quantities, and usually these have been pressed from molds. Altars of baked clay were quite elaborate, many of them several storied.

[29] Kathleen Kenyon, Digging Up Jericho (New York: Frederick A. Praeger, Publisher, 1957), pp. 54-55.
[30] An excellent article, "Pottery," written by an outstanding authority, J. L. Kelso, is available in IDB, pp. 846-53. See also Plate VII.

Tools for daily use included loom weights and spindle whorls, lamps, buttons, braziers, canteens for pilgrims and soldiers, sling stones, and ink pots. Emperors and kings immortalized themselves with clay in many ways; three of these are worth noting. Clay tablets contained written records of their reigns. These we shall study more closely later. Buildings had their foundation deposits, much the same as our cornerstones, and in Mesopotamia it was the custom to insert baked clay "nails" into the structure. These nails bore the name of the king under whose auspices the building was being erected. Roads were also marked, with special bricks inserted into the pavement at frequent intervals. Such bricks were stamped with a "printing block" made of baked clay; they bore the name of the king. This means of printing on clay bricks was used chiefly in Mesopotamia and is the earliest method yet discovered of duplicating messages or announcements. Seals bearing the king's name were already in use, but such usage was very infrequent in comparison with the marking of bricks with a clay stamp.

Pottery was also used for cheap jewelry, gaming pieces, molds, and even theater tickets. Broken pieces could be used to scoop grain or ashes and to carry live coals from one neighbor to another. Sherds were also used to write quick messages. Some important pieces which have been recovered give us communications between those in charge of soldiers in the field and those at the home base.

Even when pottery was ground to small fragments and dust, it could still be used. Man early discovered that ground-up pottery was important for tempering the clay to make new pottery. Later he learned how to use such pottery dust to make waterproof plaster to be used for lining cisterns.

Knowledge of the various patterns of usage help us to know the dates of human occupation, but in addition, great insights are ours concerning the customs of people. We learn much about practices in the homes of rich and poor as the story is revealed by the clay products they used. The record of a king's reign is now seen to be more than a list of battles, and religion is a far bigger story than the activity of priests in the precincts of the temple. To these aspects of the story of archaeology we shall return later.[31]

[31] More technical discussions of pottery can be found in J. L. Kelso and J. Palin Thorley, "Palestinian Pottery in the Bible Times," BA, (December, 1945), pp. 82-93; AASOR, XXI-XXII "Processing of Pottery in Ancient Times"; G. E. Wright, The Pottery of Palestine from the Earliest Times to the End of the Early Bronze Age (1937); W. F. Albright, "The Excavation of Tell Beit Mirsim—The Pottery of the First Three Campaigns," AASOR, XII (1930-31); "The Excavation of Tell Beit Mirsim IA: The Bronze Age Pottery of the Fourth Campaign" AASOR, XIII (1931-32), 55 ff.; "The Excavation of Tell Beit Mirsim," III; "The Iron Age" AASOR, XXI-XXII (1941-43); and Paul W. Lapp, Palestinian Ceramic Chronology (New Haven, Conn.: American Schools of Oriental Research, 1961).

5.
EXCAVATION

An American newspaper publisher and owner of a large newspaper syndicate once told his reporters, "People are interested in three things: money, sex and archaeology—in that order!" Without debating priorities or associations, it is well known that people do have keen interest in and avidly read popular reports of archaeological discoveries. There is some debate whether an accidental discovery, such as the finding of the Dead Sea Scrolls, or the results of excavation, such as the discovery of King Tutankhamen's tomb, excite most interest. The layman's interest is in the thing discovered, not the technique or accident of its discovery. Too often the story is glamorized and little is said about the weary years of toil or the heartbreaking disappointment of an expedition which produces meager results.

Excavation usually begins with the excavator's choice of site. In some cases, however, the place of excavation is assigned rather than chosen. Any accidental uncovering of evidence of ancient human occupation, whether it be by a farmer plowing his field, a plumber laying water pipe or sewers, or a builder digging for a foundation, must be reported, and all work must stop until a check can be made of the evidence. We visited a new public school on the south side of Old Jerusalem. The building had been completed except for a separate building for toilets and washrooms. Three times attempts had been made to dig foundations for this additional building, but each time ancient ruins had been encountered and, under the law, digging had to stop. A fourth attempt had safely gone down into the ground for six feet. The frustrated principal said, "That's not quite as deep as the contractor wants to go, but I'm afraid to go any further. We'll build here." In each of the earlier cases, the department of antiquities sent in teams of excavators and uncovered important aspects of the battlements and approaches to ancient Jerusalem.

In most cases the archaeologist is free to choose his site on the basis of his own interests or those of his sponsors. Howard Carter searched the Valley of the Kings for six years before he finally found the entrance to King Tutankhamen's tomb, but he had been convinced from evidence carefully collected that the tomb must be in that valley somewhere.[1] Some sites are selected because they lie at an important location or crossroads known from ancient days, others because they are known to be important cities, as in the case of the excavations at Nineveh.[2] Once the site has been chosen, permission to excavate has been obtained, and excavation has started, the archaeologist has no choice but to continue. Work must proceed at modern excavations until virgin soil has been reached even

[1] Howard Carter and A. C. Mace, *The Tomb of Tut-Ankh-Amen* (3 vols.; New York: Cooper Square Publishers, Inc., 1923).
[2] George Smith, *Assyrian Discoveries* (1875).

though it takes several seasons. This requirement was not made in early excavations, and much evidence still lies many feet below disturbed soil and abandoned digs.

Permission, as we outlined in Chapter 3, must be obtained from the appropriate department of antiquities. Permission must also be obtained from the landowner, and this is sometimes much more difficult to get and is usually much more expensive. Much coffee has been consumed and the health of many ancestors has been thoroughly discussed for uncounted hours in efforts to make agreements with landowners. If digging is to be done at a spot where the landowner normally raises a scant crop rent must be paid for the land, and in addition, an appropriate price must be paid for the otherwise anticipated crop. No crop was ever more valuable than that which has not been sown because the land has been rented to an archaeological expedition.

Ownership of land is also a complicated thing, ofttimes with many branches of the family involved. The archaeologist must make sure that his agreement is binding upon all who claim interest in the land involved, otherwise he may be caught up in family feuds.

When all necessary permits have been cleared he begins the task of excavation. The size of the operation will determine, in part at least, the size of the skilled staff as well as the number of native workers employed. Many skills are required, and one archaeologist may possess more than one skill. We shall therefore consider the skills to be represented rather than the number of personnel. A director must be responsible for the complete coordination of all activities. Sometimes this responsibility is shared between co-directors or a director and an assistant director, but complete coordination is essential. This will include hiring of native workers as laborers; assignment of responsibilities to skilled personnel; the procurement of equipment, tools, and supplies; obtaining and disbursement of funds; housing, transportation, and food; arrangements for recording, cataloging, storage, disposition, and interpretation of all artifacts recovered; recording of daily proceedings including photographic records; and provision for handling of possible major or minor accidents and illnesses.

The entire project is divided into "fields" or geographical areas of work. It is an increasing practice to place a field supervisor in charge of each field or area of work. This supervisor is directly responsible to the director and is completely responsible for all personnel and activity in his area. This practice means that in every area of excavation a trained archaeologist is always available to give direction and to provide special skills of recovery and conservation. In the past great reliance was of necessity placed upon native foremen, but highly trained natives are few and far between. In addition, training of native workers was usually confined to development of selected field procedures, largely mechanical skills.

The field supervisor keeps a field notebook and later writes up more formal

61

daily reports on all excavation in his section of the dig. If the field supervisor needs special help he sends a messenger to the director. Work is not left unsupervised. Long hours after the native workers have finished their day's work the field supervisor will be hard at work. There are photographs to be taken, drawings to be made of the day's discoveries, cross section drawings to be made of the excavation, and measurements to be made of every important physical feature of the excavation. Theoretically, it should be possible to put everything back into the excavation in its exact original location simply by following the archaeologist's notebook.

Often a native is hired as general foreman to serve as liaison between the director and the hired laborers. Complexities of language and native customs make such an arrangement highly desirable. In addition, there is advantage in having a native foreman or leader in each field.

The field is divided into squares with balks between. Into each square one or more pickmen are placed. The pickman is in effect the leader of his particular crew. His job is to loosen the ground a few inches in depth over the entire square to which he is assigned. As he does so he carefully watches the ground for changes in color, texture, or feel, and for any signs of "antikas." [3] He is also responsible to see that as the ground is loosened the hoemen fill the baskets and the dirt and debris are removed from the working area.

The system of pay for native workers is a combination of daily wages and special bonuses, commonly called "bakshish." Some excavators are opposed to the bakshish system, but it is generally recognized that special awards for finding and reporting "antikas" results, on the one hand, in more care of recovery, and on the other, in honest reporting of things discovered. Small but important objects can too easily be hidden in loose-fitting long-flowing native garments and later sold on the black market.

Priorities are well established. The pickman has the first opportunity to discover and report any item of significance. If he fails to see the item the hoeman has the next opportunity. Finally, the basket carrier has his chance, which is slim. Ofttimes a basketman will report something after he has returned from the dump and claim that the object was discovered by him as he emptied his basket. Such information is usually worthless because the provenance cannot be demonstrated. Occasionally an object may have some intrinsic value and should be accepted. The basic rule is that nothing must be moved from the ground until after the report has been made and the archaeologist in charge has had time to make proper records and take photographs of the objects "in situ."

Salting is a term which comes from the early mining activities in the western part of the United States. It is a term still used in archaeological circles to describe the attempt of untrustworthy natives who try to hide

[3] "Antika" is the native name for an ancient object.

objects purchased on the black market and then conveniently "find" them so that they can claim bakshish. Since few natives possess the critical historical perspective necessary for archaeological work, their attempts are usually doomed to failure. If, for example, when work is being done at a level of occupation which has been recognized as belonging to the second millennium B.C. a workman reports that he has found some coins there is obviously something wrong, for coins were not in use until the seventh century B.C. The worker responsible should immediately be discharged.

The moving of dirt can be a major problem. It takes more space by far upon which to dump dirt than the area from which it is taken. Adequate provision must be made for this. In all cases care must be taken that dirt is not dumped where it is anticipated that there will be future excavation. In some cases it is necessary to transport dirt for a long distance. In such a case, a light railway with dump wagons can be used.[4] The basket carriers empty their baskets into the wagon which in turn is taken to the dump by the railway attendent. One problem is frequently present with the use of a railroad. Boys, big and little, love to ride the train. A native worker should have charge of the dump to see that dirt is properly placed and that the dump is kept within the property acquired for this purpose, otherwise there can be bitter arguments with owners of adjacent fields.

Before any soil or debris is removed some basic work must be done. First, a complete survey of the area must be made by a competent surveyor. Contour lines should be clearly shown and all material protruding above ground indicated and described.

The second step is that of establishing two points to be connected by an imaginary base line from which all measurements, lateral and vertical, can be made. Obviously the points must be in positions which will not be disturbed by excavation; at the same time they must be conveniently located so that measurements with respect to them can readily be made. By triangulation from the base points any object found can be specifically located on the plans. In addition, the depth at which any object is found can be exactly determined with respect to the base line, which is often given the arbitrary number zero; all depths are then minus feet or meters below the base line.[5]

Third, the field is marked off into squares, usually five to ten meters in length and breadth. The exact size of the squares is determined by the terrain and the extent of the field, et cetera. The squares are frequently oriented to the points of the compass, but the lay of the land must be a basic consideration. In any case all charts and maps will show relationship to the north. The squares are designated by letters in one direction and numerals in the other. Each square is therefore designated by letter and numerals.

[4] See Plate VIII.
[5] See Albright, *The Archaeology of Palestine* (Baltimore, Md.: Penguin Books, Inc., 1949), p. 15, fig. 1; p. 16, fig. 2.

As work proceeds any object found is designated by its square on the grid and by the level from which it was taken. All pottery and sherds are normally placed in a native basket called a "gufa." Each basket is marked with a label which bears: (1) Name of excavation, usually in initials; (2) date; (3) field number; (4) square designation; (5) basket number; and (6) the initials of the field supervisor. Since the field supervisor's notebook contains the exact level at which each basket was put into use, all necessary information is available. Special objects, such as pieces of glass, coins, metal of any kind, or whole vessels, are given special consideration, envelops being provided for the smaller pieces, and cartons or boxes for the larger pieces. In any case the label must contain complete information concerning place and date of discovery. Later, the individual articles will be assigned numbers, part of which will be designation of the place of discovery. Should question ever arise concerning the provenance of the object, reference can immediately be made to the field supervisor's report and evidence confirmed.[6]

Squares are dug in such a way that there is a balk between each square or series of squares. The faces of the balk will be kept perpendicular and the surface as clean and straight as possible. Examination of the balk will clearly indicate the various levels of occupation and intrusions into those levels. In case the archaeologist has failed to recognize a floor level while digging, the omission can be corrected from the face of the balk.[7]

As objects are recovered from the ground, other skills will be needed. All articles of any significance will need to be photographed "in situ." A photographer is a most important member of the staff. He must know how to take pictures under many adverse circumstances and under a wide variety of conditions. This will involve flash equipment, a special lens for close-up work, and a wide-angle lens for working in close quarters. If possible more than one camera should be available. Record pictures for publication and reports can be taken in black and white, but there are many occasions when color film is useful. Colored pictures are much more interesting for classroom and public lectures, and it is much easier with color to illustrate certain aspects of pottery and levels of occupation. An examination of professional reports in such journals as the *Annual of The American Schools of Oriental Research* will demonstrate the importance of photography.

An architect is another important member of the staff whenever buildings or ruins of buildings are encountered. He will not only draw the necessary sketches, but he can be very useful in interpreting the fallen ruins and suggesting the form of the original buildings. From brick and stone he can determine whether the building had one or more stories, what its decorative features were, and the probable purpose of rooms in the building. He may

[6] W. F. Badè, *A Manual of Excavation in the Near East* (Berkeley, Cal.: University of California Press, 1934), p. 26, fig. 4.
[7] See Plate IX.

even be able to deduce from the style of building the probable date of construction.

A staff member with thorough knowledge of pottery types is most important. W. F. Albright[8] has written "A specialist in Palestinian pottery is much more necessary than an epigrapher." [9] Little inscriptional material has been found in Palestinian excavations. The importance of the epigrapher has been heightened with the finding of the Dead Sea Scrolls and the more recent discoveries of the Samaria Papyri in the Wadi Daliyeh, but these have in no way minimized the basic importance of ability to interpret evidence from pottery.

In order to facilitate the "reading" of pottery, it is necessary to have the pots and sherds as clean as possible. A boy is employed to wash the pieces— more than one if necessary. It is important that he be able to read, at least enough to distinguish numbers on the basket tags. Each basket of sherds is washed separately, dried, then either returned to the proper basket or placed on mats or shelves. In either case the provenance tag never leaves the sherds or pots. An initial sorting of the pottery can be started by a well-trained washer. If the more significant pieces, such as necks, bases, handles, are put at the top of the basket evaluation of the pottery finds can be more quickly made. It is the custom on some expeditions to give special reward to the pot washer who discovers seal impressions on jar handles, or other significant markings.

If pieces are too fragile to be trusted to a native pot washer then any special treatment is given by a member of the staff, ofttimes a member of the recorder crew. In some cases the pottery itself would survive the rigors of pot washing, but the decoration could not. It is therefore important that all pieces put into the basket which normally would be processed by the pot washer shall be examined by the field supervisor or the pottery expert. Sherds can usually be brushed clean enough to see whether or not special treatment is needed. When it has been determined which pieces shall be permanently saved each such piece is given a serial number. This serial number, together with the provenance insigna, are marked in india ink on the artifact. At the close of the day, the field supervisors will discuss with the pottery expert and the director of the expedition the discoveries of the day. In this way the best possible evaluation of the pottery finds can be made at every stage of excavation. In addition, there can be coordination between the several fields.

Recording is basic to a well-planned and coordinated expedition. In addition, it is required by law that records be kept of all objects recovered. This work is under the care of a recorder and staff. The work consists of (1) keeping a card file or other record of all objects found, (2) making drawings or taking photographs of the more significant objects, and (3)

[8] *The Archaeology of Palestine,* p. 12.
[9] An epigrapher is one skilled in reading inscriptions.

keeping a register in duplicate (sometimes triplicate) of all such objects. One copy of the register is made available to the department of antiquities and becomes the basis of the division between the department and the expedition. Inspectors for the department can make periodic checks to determine whether or not honest recording has been done. Each expedition has its favorite tools and devices by which the task of the recorder can be simplified. These tools usually aid in such matters as quickly determining the height of vessels, et cetera. With such devices it is generally possible to determine the original shape and size of a vessel even though only a portion of it remains.

Knowledge of simple medicine can be useful—at least the ability to render first aid. There will be cuts and bruises; there may even be a broken bone. With snakes and scorpions part of the natural scenery, a first aid kit for bites should be at hand. Team members may suffer from the occupational hazard of dysentery, and natives are subject to malaria. If the natives house their families nearby there will be requests for remedies for anything from headache to childbirth, and it is confusing for natives to hear any member of the staff referred to as "doctor." Such a person, they believe, must be able to help the sick. Good public relations can be established through the distribution by a competent team member of simple remedies. Mothers are particularly grateful when their children are helped, and soothing "drops in the eyes" have an effect on employer-employee relationships.

In Mesopotamia and Egypt the epigraphist is very important. Technically an epigraphist deals only with inscriptions; a paleographist is one who reads ancient forms of writing. However, the term epigraphist is commonly used to indicate one who has the ability to read one or more ancient languages whether the message is cut into stone, pressed into or scratched on clay, or inscribed upon papyrus, leather, or parchment.

A written document may have no immediate relationship to the task of dating the level of occupation at which it was found. It may be a document which has been handed down from preceding generations. Even this fact tells us something about the people who had saved the document. On the other hand, if a foundation deposit is uncovered, there will be information about the king who assumed responsibility for building the edifice. The more quickly this information is made available to the excavator the more intelligently he can work.

A most important member of the native staff is the water boy. Provision should be made for easy access to water by workers. If the water supply is at some distance from the workers too much time will be consumed in frequent trips from the place of work to the water tank. A small boy can quickly bring water to the workers. The cry "Moya" (water) will frequently be heard, especially on hot dusty days. Water can be drawn from a nearby stream if there is one. Otherwise it may be necessary to contract for a man and a donkey to supply the workers with water. The water should be clean, but no such water should be drunk by Americans or Europeans until it has been boiled for at least fifteen minutes. It is the practice in many camps today to carry special supplies of filtered water for use of the staff members and to supply the native workers with local water.

Cooks can add much to the comfort or misery of a camp. Fortunate is that director who has access to a good cook who knows the curious eating habits of Americans and Europeans and who will observe carefully the special rules for processing food for them. A good director will know the importance of the purchase of food from reputable sources and the necessity of adhering strictly to cooking rules. Yet we have enjoyed wedding feasts and other celebrations with natives without serious discomfort.

Excavations vary considerably in size and therefore in the number of seasons involved. Old Testament Jericho has been excavated by several groups and has one of the longest records of excavation. A small examination of the mound now known as Tell es-Sultan was made by the Palestine Exploration Fund in 1873, but the first major excavations were done by Ernst Sellin and Carl Watzinger between 1907 and 1909. Professor John Garstang, former director of antiquities, made further investigations between 1930 and 1936. Miss Kathleen Kenyon carried on excavations from 1952 to 1964. Jericho has now been demonstrated to be the oldest known city in the world so far discovered, with a history which goes back to at least 8000 B.C.[10] Other excavations are of shorter duration and cover a shorter period of human occupation and history.

Where an excavation will be continued from season to season, it is essential that every precaution be taken to protect the site from marauders and mischief while it is "closed for the season." A guard hired from the community in which the site is located will usually suffice. It is a matter of local pride that nothing is disturbed or stolen when such a person is hired. He can sleep through most of the night, and usually does, but his tribal honor is at stake, and this is more powerful than the best of firearms. The same results cannot be obtained if an outsider is hired.

In the next chapter we shall discuss the techniques and procedures to be used in connection with monuments and other structures already above ground, but it should be noted here that excavation must often be used in conjunction with such sites. The major portion of the great pyramids of Egypt is well above the surface and needs no excavation to make the monuments apparent. There is a substructure in each, however. In addition there are buildings which stand at the foot of each pyramid. These have been covered by the sands of time, and it is necessary to excavate. Two important discoveries through excavation at Gizeh will illustrate the importance of excavation at such well-known places.

[10] See Kenyon, *Digging Up Jericho; Archaeology in the Holy Land* (London: Ernest Benn, Ltd., 1960); and Harding, *The Antiquities of Jordan*, pp. 164 ff.

The Sphinx is as well known as the pyramids, but its structure is less well known. The major portion of it is carved from an outcropping of rock. The forepaws and the hindquarters were built into the monument, and this portion has only been known in relatively recent years. In addition, a small temple stands alongside the Sphinx.[11] The lower part of the Sphinx and the temple had been completely covered over by drifting sands. According to Egyptian records the complete Sphinx has been rescued from the covering sands on more than one occasion.

At the foot of the pyramid of Khufu, soundings were made. Two large channels had been cut into the rock about the time of the building of the pyramid. Into these channels, later covered over, boats had been placed. These were there for the purpose of transporting the pharaoh along the Egyptian equivalent of the River Styx. The recovery of one of these boats has given us much information concerning Egyptian shipping as well as their beliefs concerning immortality of the pharaoh and funeral procedures.

Excavation not only supplements information recovered from examination of monuments already in the open, but often leads to a much fuller knowledge of the environment of that building than is suspected from surface evidence. Excavations at the often reported but never previously excavated "palace" at Araq el-Emir not only confirmed that the traditional building was constructed in the second century B.C., but also revealed the long history of the building site. The earliest foundations had been laid down in the Middle Bronze Age. After a long lapse of time the building of Tobiah was erected on the old foundations. After partial destruction by earthquake, the building was remodeled and used extensively during the Byzantine period. The whole terrain, as well as the long lapses from occupation of the building, support the probability that there were periods of strong agricultural economy in the region. A new picture is emerging of the importance of the land of Gilead—its wealth and political power. New research into the importance of Transjordan in the biblical story is indicated. At the same time, careful examination of evidence already above ground would have prevented obvious mistakes from appearing in print. In spite of the fact that Josephus[12] speaks of the brilliant whiteness of the structure, De Saulcy refers to the black stone.[13] A simple scratch on the surface of the stone removed the "blackness" of centuries and revealed brilliant white limestone. Similarly, Millar Burrows said, "Whether the Jewish historian had ever seen the place is doubtful, for the stone which he calls white is red sandstone, nor are the carved animals of such prodigious size as he would have his readers believe." [14] Even surface evidence must sometimes be scratched.

[11] See Plate X.
[12] *Antiquities* XII. iv. 11.
[13] See De Saulcy, *Voyage en Terre Sainte* (1865), II, 211-35.
[14] *What Mean These Stones?* (New Haven, Conn.: American Schools of Oriental Research, 1941), p. 133. (Through what is apparently a misprint, Burrows locates Araq el Emir east of Amman instead of west).

A number of new techniques have been developed in recent years to aid the excavator or to explore unique situations. Since, in some cases, extravagant claims have been made for them, they need at least to be reviewed. In other cases the claims are valid, and the alert excavator will want to know their merits.

Perhaps the most advanced techniques of excavating and reporting results of digging by levels, or stratigraphical excavation, have been developed under the leadership of Kathleen Kenyon. Excellent drawings of the various sections of her excavations at Jericho are to be found in several publications and are worth careful examination.[15] A publication by H. J. Franken and C. A. Franken-Battershill discusses the details of Miss Kenyon's excavation techniques in great detail.[16] Unfortunately the authors make the book an occasion to discuss the relative merits of Miss Kenyon's methods and the apparently much inferior methods and results of American excavators. They may be right, but constant reiteration does not strengthen their arguments. The important contribution of the volume is the careful spelling out of the older and newer techniques of stratigraphical excavation.

Underwater excavation is a new technique which has been developed during the last few years; it was made possible by scuba diving and aqualung equipment. Startling claims have been made that the destroyed cities of Sodom and Gomorrah have been found by this method, but such claims have not yet been supported by conclusive evidence.

Underwater excavations at Caesarea have uncovered the ancient harbor, and much excellent pottery and some coins have been recovered. Some success has resulted from the same method in connection with recovery of material lost in the Sea of Galilee when ancient ships and their cargoes went to the bottom in storms or possibly from attack. In both cases the recoveries were remarkable in view of the difficulties of operation and the fact that new equipment had to be developed to remove large quantities of sand and silt and to sift carefully through all the displaced sea bottom. By the very nature of the operation, digging by levels is usually impossible. Any dating of objects recovered by this technique must be by typology, not by stratigraphy.

Ancient objects have also been recovered from the south coast of Turkey and the adjacent islands. Much material has been salvaged from sunken ships.[17]

This same technique has been used with somewhat inferior equipment in

[15] See Kenyon, *Digging Up Jericho*, fig. 4, facing p. 268.
[16] *A Primer of Old Testament Archaeology*.
[17] Peter Throckmorton, "Oldest Known Shipwreck Yields Bronze Age Cargo," *National Geographic Magazine* (May, 1962), pp. 697-711. Page 700 shows scarabs from Syria inscribed with hieroglyphs. See also Throckmorton, "Thirty-three Centuries Under the Sea," *National Geographic Magazine* (May, 1960), pp. 682-703. Cf. George F. Bass, "Underwater Archaeology: Key to History's Warehouse," *National Geographic Magazine* (July, 1963), pp. 138-56.

Yucatan under the auspices of the National Geographic Society. Big natural wells, or cenotes, were used by the natives as places in which to make sacrifices to their gods. Many objects, including human sacrifices, were thrown into the cenotes. Deep sea diving techniques are now making possible the recovery of objects anciently sacrificed. Dating, is of necessity, by typology. The method is limited to salvage, not scientific recovery of evidence.[18]

It should be noted in passing that the work in Yucatan has called our attention again to the importance of the analysis of metals and minerals. Such analysis indicates that ancient peoples imported metals from other countries and tells us of trade and cultural exchange.

Dendrochronology is a method of dating from tree rings which is used to a considerable extent in Indian archaeology in the southwestern section of the United States. It is based upon the knowledge that tree rings vary in thickness according to annual rainfall. Since the rainfall varies each year, tree rings have different thicknesses. Comparison of many trees can establish a sequence of hundreds of years. By fixing definite dates in a sequence the rest of the dates are determined. The last ring, where a live tree has been cut down, presumably marks the date when the tree was used for building purposes. Tree rings can be readily read in charred stumps, in charcoal from a fire, and in trunks of trees used for building purposes.

Tree-ring dating has been little used in the Near and Middle East for two major reasons. First, wood exposed to the elements above or under ground rots and disappears, and, second, with the exception of the famous cedars of Lebanon, there is little timber in the Middle East of building quality for large buildings. Small tree branches are too small for working out sequences of dates. Archaeologists will have to be content with dating specimens of wood by the carbon 14 process. This has proved to be valuable in several instances.[19]

A very recent technique of exploration has been developed to speed up the process of preliminary examination of promising sites. Currently the method of investigating the worthwhileness of any site is to make a sounding. This means digging a test trench or trenches. It is always difficult to know when a "sounding" becomes a full scale "excavation." Departments of antiquities are still struggling with this question as it relates to the issuing of permits. There are cases of record where an archaeological team accepted the responsibility of testing or "sounding" a site. The evidence was clear that full scale investigation should be made. In the reports the sounding is later referred to as "the first season" of excavation. Presumably if the examination

[18] Luis Marden, "Up From the Wells of Time" (Dzibilchaltun), *National Geographic Magazine* (January, 1959), pp. 110-29.
[19] Andrew Ellicott Douglass, "The Secret of the Southwest Solved by Talkative Tree Rings," *National Geographic Magazine* (December, 1929), pp. 737-70. Note particularly the charts, p. 769, and the photo, p. 760.

is negative, the sounding remains a sounding. Iraq has recently ruled that a sounding may not last longer than thirty days, and all artifacts from a sounding belong to the department of antiquities.

Faced with the problem of uncovering Etruscan tombs in the cemetery of Monterozzi (forty miles northwest of Rome), archaeologists teamed up with other scientists. Aerial photographs had revealed the presence of many tombs, and the problem was which of these would be best to open since it was obvious that not all of them could be examined. Engineers were called in, and through the use of modern geophysical techniques such as are used in locating ore, oil, or water, tombs were detected. In turn special equipment was used to probe the discovered tombs. First, an electric drill bored a three inch hole through the ground to the top of the tomb. Then special tubing containing a camera and lighting equipment was inserted through the bore into the tomb. The camera was so mounted that it could be turned on a complete circle of 360 degrees. Each picture taken covered thirty degrees, thus with twelve pictures the entire tomb could be photographed. When photographs indicated that a tomb of rich decoration and furnishings had been discovered, then arrangements were made to excavate. Claim is made that through the use of such photography time is saved, but more important, knowledge of the actual entrance to the tomb is revealed, making it possible for the archaeologist to enter the tomb with the least disturbance to the contents.[20]

It is obvious that such a technique is appropriate only in such specialized situations as obtained in the instance cited. With emphasis upon discovering the "most fruitful tombs" there is danger that the excavator will again become a tomb plunderer looking for show pieces instead of the "ingredients of history."

Excavation is slow painstaking work. Results are often disappointingly meager. But across the years archaeologists have been able to reconstruct through their search the amazing story of the people who lived centuries ago. Our libraries and homes are now enriched by hundreds of volumes which help us to understand our indebtedness to bygone days, a heritage that is at once both sacred and secular. The specific details of this heritage will be discussed, at least in part, in Part Three: "The World in Which the Bible Was Written."

[20] Carlo M. Lerici, "Periscope on the Etruscan Past," *National Geographic Magazine* (September, 1959), pp. 336-50.

6.

ACCIDENTAL DISCOVERIES, ESTABLISHED TRADITION, AND OBJECTIVE EVALUATION

Important and startling discoveries have been made by simple peasants, people who have had no archaeological training or any understanding of its purposes and methods. Their only knowledge, usually, was that archaeologists are peculiar people who pay bakshish for antikas. So long as archaeologists are willing to give financial rewards for information leading to antikas the natives are polite enough to furnish the information and to refrain from speaking derisively of the donor's sanity, except in their own circles.

The archaeologist prefers to make his own discoveries and to know from the very beginning the precise circumstances and conditions under which the discovery is made. This, in many cases, is impossible. He must depend upon help from people of the country in which he is working. There are so many ways in which an accidental discovery can be made, and the scientist can only hope that he will be notified as quickly as possible and that the facts of the discovery will be given to him as accurately as possible. A quick glance at some accidental discoveries will show that natives of many lands have rendered valuable service. They have been alert and have reported their observations to someone who could channel the information, not always it must be confessed through legal channels, to the proper persons or organization.

In 1947, goatherds of the Ta'amireh Bedouin, tribesmen from the Wilderness of Judea, made one of the most exciting discoveries in the history of biblical archaeology, at least in this century. The discovery was accidental, and reports vary concerning details. One of the goatherds found a cave in the rocky hills about one mile north of the Wadi Qumran, close to the northwest shore of the Dead Sea. Temporarily frightened he fled, but quickly returned with reinforcements. An entrance to the cave was enlarged so that the men could force their way in.

Inside was discovered a number of jars, some of which had been broken by falling rock. The jars contained ancient leather scrolls now popularly known as "the Dead Sea Scrolls." The tribesmen knew nothing of the value of their discovery. The objects in the cave had an evil smell, but the tribesmen knew from experience that they would probably be "antikas."

How many scrolls were originally found is not known. About forty jars have been reconstructed from the fragments later found in the cave; each of these jars was capable of holding several manuscripts. Eleven portions were finally reported by the tribesmen, but these portions were later discovered to be seven scrolls. Fragments from many other scrolls were afterwards found by archaeologists, but whether the scrolls were removed from the cave in ancient or modern times has not yet been determined.

The tribesmen took their discoveries to Bethlehem. Through agents, illegal in this case, the scrolls finally found their way into the possession of the Syrian Orthodox Church in Jerusalem and the Hebrew University on the Israeli side of the lines. This was the period of bitter struggle in Palestine, and communication between the separate parts of Jerusalem was impossible.

Professor Sukenik of Hebrew University recognized that the scrolls were very old and were written in Hebrew. In the meantime the scrolls from the Syrian Orthodox Church were taken to the American Schools of Oriental Research in Jerusalem. John Trever, a fellow at the school that year, had the privilege of examining the scrolls with the permission of the Archbishop Samuel. Later, in the privacy of his study, Trever carefully studied the copies he had made of a column from one of the scrolls. He recognized quickly that the material before him was a part of the book of Isaiah. This in itself was exciting, but his parallel discovery was even more exciting.

From a careful comparison of the script he came to the conclusion that the scroll was very old, probably written as early as the second century before Christ. If that conclusion was correct, then the scrolls were of inestimable value for scholarship. Dr. Trever immediately contacted his former professor, William F. Albright of Johns Hopkins University, one of the world's outstanding archaeologists and an authority in the field of ancient writing. Dr. Albright confirmed Trever's opinion.

This meant that ancient Bible manuscripts were now available in Hebrew; these are more than a thousand years older than anything previously known in that language and several hundred years older than most manuscripts known up to that time in other languages. The fact that these manuscripts had been found in Palestine was doubly significant, for it meant that we now had Bible manuscripts from the country which had produced the writings, and second, that for the first time we had written materials, at least of any extent, from Palestine itself. Written materials, except a few fragments of stone and clay, had not been found in Palestine.[1] The weather is not conducive to the preservation of parchment and papyrus, the ancient materials used for paper. These scrolls were preserved because of the peculiarly dry atmosphere in the Dead Sea region and because the scrolls had been stored in sealed jars which protected them.

The scrolls first found in what is now called Cave I have all been identified. The four scrolls in possession of the Syrian Orthodox Church were a complete copy of the book of Isaiah; a commentary on the first two chapters

---

[1] New discoveries have recently been made by members of the Ta'amireh tribe. The newly discovered writing is apparently Samaritan and is from the fourth century B.C. See BA (December, 1963), pp. 110-21.

73

of Habakkuk; a book of rules and regulations for a religious community popularly called The Manual of Discipline,[2] but probably known in ancient times as HAGU; and a fourth scroll which defied being unrolled for several years. It is now in possession of the Hebrew University and has been unrolled by its experts. It is a collection of midrashim[3] in Aramaic of the book of Genesis, popular stories and legends associated with the heroes of that book. One story of more than passing interest is of the birth of Noah. On the day of his birth he made a long speech. Lamech, his father, immediately was suspicious of the child and denied its paternity. Lamech accused his wife of relationships with one of the divine beings mentioned in Genesis 6. In the argument that ensues Mrs. Lamech tells of the conception of Noah, and Mr. Lamech is finally convinced that it is his child.

The scrolls originally sold to Hebrew University, though in six pieces, turned out to be three manuscripts. One is another copy of the book of Isaiah, but not as complete or in as good condition as the first copy mentioned. One interesting scroll has been named "The Wars of the Children of Light and the Children of Darkness." Some scholars have called this scroll an apocalypse showing the final conflict at the end of the present age. Serious question needs to be raised concerning this classification. Another scroll is a collection of psalm-like hymns and has been entitled "The Book of Thanksgiving." It was found in four pieces.

Since the finding of the first cave others have been discovered, and in some cases there were even larger collections of manuscripts than was reported from the first cave. From Cave IV alone there have already been reported portions of about 330 separate documents, with some material still to be identified. More than two hundred caves have been examined. About thirty show evidence of having been occupied during the period from two centuries before Christ until toward the close of the first century A.D. From a dozen caves written materials have been recovered. Several hundred documents are now represented in materials so far identified. Other caves may be brought to light, and much material already found awaits preparation, study, and identification.

Much of the material is biblical. Every book in the Old Testament, except Esther, is now represented in whole or in part. The books of Isaiah; the Pentateuch, particularly Deuteronomy; and the Psalms have the most copies, and this may indicate preference in the community for these books. Most of the biblical material is in Hebrew; some is in Greek, and a little in Aramaic.

Other material is noncanonical and nonbiblical. Some of the books of the Apocrypha are represented. Other manuscripts are copies of the books collected under the title of Pseudepigrapha, and still others are works which

---

[2] This scroll was found in two pieces and in the original count was considered as two scrolls.

[3] "Midrash" (plural "midrashim") is a Hebrew term denoting a story which illustrates or explains a scriptural passage.

have not hitherto been known. The extent of intertestamental literature has been considerably enlarged and with it our knowledge of literature and religion in the 220 years from about 150 B.C. to A.D. 70.

Insights gained from the Qumran literature are already almost overwhelming. As further studies are made and as, perhaps, new materials are discovered, these insights will be further enriched. Our indebtedness to consecrated scholarship is already great. In the days immediately ahead that debt will be increased considerably.

The original discovery was made by a poor goatherd. The significance of the discovery is due to the painstaking work of the scholar.

Special circumstances and incorrect or incomplete information resulted in failure to notify the department of antiquities about the discovery of the Dead Sea Scrolls. This was the period, as we have noted, when the country was torn with internal strife which was finally resolved by the partition of Palestine. It was scarcely possible for Sukenik to notify the department, and later developments made it impossible for any Israeli to recognize the authority of the Jordanian department. In the meantime the Syrian Orthodox Church had contacted the American Schools of Oriental Research in Jerusalem. The information given to John Trever, however, gave him the impression that he was examining material which had been in possession of the Church for some time. He naturally assumed, as did all connected with the School, that the department already knew about this material. In any case, it was unfortunate that the director of the department, G. Lankester Harding learned of this important discovery first through a published notice in the Bulletin of American Schools of Oriental Research.

We shall have occasion to examine special aspects of the Qumran literature in Chapter 15. The importance of the material can scarcely be overestimated. Hundreds of articles and scores of books about it have been written.[4] It will be many years before the full significance of the young Arab's discovery is recognized. Indebted as we are to the painstaking work of international teams of dedicated scholars, their work could not have been started except for the observant eyes of Muhammed Ed Dib of the Ta'amireh Tribe and his companions.

In 1928 a poor farmer in the state of Lattaquié on the North Syrian coast was plowing his field when suddenly the point of his plow became wedged between two stones. Quick examination revealed that these stones had been shaped by hand and probably belonged to an ancient building. Fortunately the farmer reported his discovery to the police, who in turn reported to French authorities who had mandate over Syria. The director of the Service des Antiquites en Syrie et au Liban, Charles Virolleaud, made an investigation. The stone belonged to a tomb, identified as Mycenean by

⁴ See bibliography published serially by William S. LaSor, *Bibliography of the Dead Sea Scrolls* (Fuller Library Bulletin, 1958), and continued in *Revue de Qumran* (1958-63), Vols. 1-4; and see article "Dead Sea Scrolls," *IDB*, pp. 790-802.

L. Albanese. In April, 1929, digging was begun under the direction of Claude F. A. Schaeffer. It was decided that the extent of the cemetery indicated the existence of a town of fair size. The only possible place in which the ruins of an ancient town could be hidden was the nearby tell, which stood to the east of the cemetery. Work on the tell was begun early in May, and on May 20, 1929, the first of many tablets were found where they had been stored as part of an ancient library.

Because of the great size of the mound, and the interruptions of war, excavation still continues. The mound is approximately 66 feet high, and its greatest diameter approximately 3,300 feet, or three fifths of a mile. Excavation has uncovered evidence of settled human occupation from Neolithic time prior to 4000 B.C. until the area was destroyed by the invasion of the Sea People at the close of the thirteenth or the beginning of the twelfth century B.C. The ancient name of the city was Ugarit. The mound is known to the natives today as Ras Shamra, apparently for the fennel which grows in abundance there.

The ancient city was located at the junction of the great highway which comes up from Palestine and Egypt in the south and the highway which went from the sea to the River Euphrates in Mesopotamia. It was an important center on the great trade routes. Whether material came by road or by sea from Egypt to the north Syrian coast it had to go by caravan route to northern Mesopotamia. There it could be sent by river into Assyria and Babylonia. From the records found in the libraries it is known that the people in ancient Ugarit were acquainted with at least eight languages. It was a cosmopolitan community in ancient times even though it is quite isolated today.

The discovery of this ancient community is highly important for general historical information, for the history of culture, but especially for background material on biblical studies. The prompt publication of reports, including photographs and transcriptions of clay tablets enabled the world of scholarship to proceed at once to a solution of the new type of cuneiform writing which appeared on so many of the tablets. The first were published in the French archaeological journal *Syria*.[5] The earliest published attempt to solve the cuneiform alphabet was made by Hans Bauer,[6] and this was quickly followed by publications of two French scholars, Edouard Dhorme and Virolleaud.[7]

The date of the alphabetical tablets had been established archaeologically in the fourteenth century B.C. This meant that these tablets constitute, if not the oldest alphabetic writing in the world, at least the first material of

[5] Charles Virolleaud, "Les Inscriptions Cuneiforme de Ras Shamra," *Syria*, X (1929), 304-10, and plates.

[6] *Entzifferung der Keilschrifttafeln von Ras Schamra* (Halle: M. Niemeyer, 1930).

[7] Dhormé, "Un Nouvel Alphabet semitique," *Revue Biblique* 39 (1930), pp. 571 ff.; Virolleaud, "Le Dechiffrement des tablettes de Ras Shamra," *JPOS*, XI (1931), 1-6.

any length to be written in alphabetic form.[8] A large body of material has now been translated and published.[9]

The texts written in various languages may be divided into several distinct groups: (a) Myth and ritual; (b) historical and political; (c) administrative; (d) legal; and (e) commercial. Most of the nonreligious texts were written in Akkadian, the current international language. The religious texts were usually written in the alphabetic cuneiform Ugaritic, a form of proto-Phoenician and closely related to Hebrew. One small cuneiform tablet was apparently the result of a student's exercise and contains the complete alphabet of thirty signs, and in the same order as known to us traditionally. It is now on exhibit in the National Museum of Damascus as part of a special display of Ras Shamra materials.

Examination of the tablets containing myth and ritual indicates strong parallelism with the somewhat later Hebrew writings. The form of poetry is markedly similar.[10] Names for deity—El, Elhm (Elohim?)—and gods—Baal, Astarte, Anath, Dagon, Asherah, et cetera—are well known to us through the Old Testament records. Much has been made of the appearance of the name Daniel (actually Danel), but second thoughts indicate that his son Aqhat is the important figure, not his father Danel.

For the first time in history rituals and myths are available to us which give us a fairly full picture of the practices and beliefs of the followers of the religion of Baal. It is now possible for us to appreciate the strong hold that this religion had upon the Hebrew people and the desperate battle waged against it by the prophets of Yahweh.[11] Significantly, the descriptions of the rituals leave no doubt that real drama existed in the temples at this early period. The struggles of nature formed the basis of the plot. There was protagonist and antagonist, with lines and action designated for each. At times the tale is picked up by a chorus, but priests and temple women enact the major roles of gods and their consorts. Actual union of the male and female players was believed to bring about, through mimetic magic, the union of the lord of nature and mother earth so that great harvests and herds would bless the community. The use of wine usually turned the proceedings into

[8] Ignace J. Gelb, in his book A Study of Writing (Chicago: University of Chicago Press, 1952), insists that the Ugaritic cuneiform is not pure alphabet, but a stage between syllabic and alphabetic which he still calls "syllabic."

[9] Cyrus H. Gordon, Ugaritic Literature (Rome: Pontificio Instituto Biblico, 1949); Theodor H. Gaster, Thespis (New York: Henry Schuman, Inc., Publishers, 1950); G. R. Driver, Canaanite Myths and Legends (Edinburgh: T & T Clark, 1956); and H. L. Ginsberg, translations of mythological materials in ANET, pp. 129-55.

[10] See John Hastings Patton, "Canaanite Parallels in the Book of Psalms" (Ph.D. dissertation, Johns Hopkins University, 1944).

[11] W. G. Williams, "The Ras Shamra Inscriptions and Israel's Cultural Heritage" (Ph.D. dissertation, University of Chicago, 1934); "The Significance of the Ras Shamra Inscriptions for the History of Hebrew Religion," AJSL L (1934), 132-44; and, John Gray, The Legacy of Canaan; The Ras Shamra Texts and Their Relevance to the Old Testament (Leiden: E. J. Brill, Publisher, 1957).

a bacchanalian festival in which members of the community were invited to participate. There is little wonder that the great prophets struggled almost in vain against the teachings and practices of Baalism.

The great similarity between the language and vocabulary of the Ras Shamra tablets and ancient Hebrew made it possible for scholars to make quick translations once the problem of the alphabetic cuneiform had been solved. On the other hand, new words appeared, and better translation of our Hebrew Bible was made possible. To this phase of the Ras Shamra inscriptions we shall turn later.[12]

Our knowledge of both Egyptian and Palestinian history has been greatly increased through the accidental discovery made by a poor Egyptian woman. About two hundred miles up river (south) from Cairo in the ruins of el-Amarna near the village of et-Till, a poor woman was digging in the ground to recover some special soil which was known for its fertilizing power. She uncovered a cache of about three hundred clay tablets which were covered with cuneiform writing. She assumed these pieces of clay to be worthless and sold them to a neighbor for ten piastres, about thirty cents.

Stories vary considerably as to what happened to the tablets from the time of original discovery until various groups of them were made parts of collections in Egypt, England, Germany, and France. Apparently there was considerable rivalry and chicanery as agents of antiquities dealers and agents of museums sought to obtain possession of the tablets at advantageous prices. Part of the story is told by Sir Wallis Budge in his book *By Nile and Tigris*.[13]

Sir Ernest Alfred Thompson Wallis Budge became the keeper of Egyptian and Assyrian antiquities in the British Museum. He himself conducted a number of campaigns and became so skilled in his negotiations with natives that he obtained material where his competitors failed. Dr. Seton Lloyd, in connection with the story of Budge's exploits in Mesopotamia, says "Budge excuses himself for this very blatant piece of sharp practice on the grounds of the Turkish government's inability to enforce its own laws and acquire the tablets for the Imperial Ottoman Museum." [14] Budge's own record reads like an adventure story, with Budge being pursued by the representatives of the Egyptian department of antiquities. Nevertheless, it was probably this man who first recognized the historical significance of the Amarna tablets. He cannot be held responsible for the fact that agents of other governments sought to label the tablets as imitations or forgeries in order to keep down the price, nor for the fact that when four of the tablets, purchased in Cairo for one hundred Egyptian pounds, were shown to an English professor, the

[12] See Chap. 14, pp. 174-76.
[13] *By Nile and Tigris* (London: John Murray, Publishers, Ltd., 1920). A reprint of a portion of this book is now available under the title "The Tell el-Amarna Tablets" in Deuel, *The Treasures of Time*, pp. 47-55.
[14] *Foundations in the Dust* (London: Oxford University Press, 1947), p. 205.

professor dated them nine hundred years too late, failed to understand their real significance, and published a newspaper account which added nothing to knowledge but boosted the already rapidly growing price of the tablets.

From the original group and some small groups found since, more than eighty went to the British Museum; more than two hundred are in the Berlin Museum; some are in Cairo; and a few are to be found in Oxford at the Ashmolean Museum.[15] A few have been obtained by private individuals, and there are two in the Metropolitan Museum, New York. The tablets vary in size from 2″x2½″ to 3½″x9″. Budge does report that one tablet, which a native tried unsuccessfully to hide in his clothing, measured "about 20 inches long and as broad in proportion," but since this tablet was "smashed to pieces" as the smuggler boarded the train, it is quite possible that no such sized tablet ever existed.[16]

The reason for the early confusion about the tablets was that they were written in Babylonian, not in Egyptian as one would expect. In addition, many of the messages were from Egyptians to Egyptian pharaohs. This suggested to many people that the tablets were obviously forgeries. It soon came to be recognized, however, that they were genuine, and the explanation was that Babylonian was the *lingua Franca*, the international language of diplomacy and government business. These tablets had been written in Palestine and Syria. Some of them were reports from military leaders who were facing difficulties because of invading hordes from across the Jordan. Careful reading of the documents revealed that the Babylonian used was that language as it was known and used among the Canaanites.

The very fact that these documents were sent from Palestine and Syria attested to the fact that the Egyptians were in possession of those countries. The tablets were reports made to the pharaohs Amenhotep III (1412-1375) and Amenhotep IV (1375-1366). It was Amenhotep IV who moved the Egyptian capital to Amarna from Thebes. The ancient name of Amarna was Akhetaton given to it by Amenhotep IV who changed his own name to Akhenaton. The changes of both names were adopted to recognize that the great god of Egypt was now Aton, the sun disk, the "life giver." Other gods, particularly Amon, were denied. This was the closest to a monotheistic reform that the world had known up to that time. Some, indeed, have labelled Akhenaton's ideas to be clearly monotheistic. The term "henotheistic" [17] is more technically correct. The great "Hymn to Aton," written by the authority of Akhenaton, is accepted by many scholars to be the source of Psalm 104. Others would see this reform as background to

[15] J. A. Knudtzon and O. Weber, *Die El-Amarna Tafeln* (1915); and S. A. B. Mercer, *The Tell el-Amarna Tablets* (Toronto: Macmillan and Company, 1939).

[16] Budge, *By Nile and Tigris*, as quoted in Deuel, *op. cit.*, p. 55.

[17] Henotheism is the acceptance of one god to which one gives complete loyalty without denying the existence of other gods. Some scholars would say "complete loyalty to one god at a time," as opposed to "monolatry" which is "complete loyalty to one god at all times."

Moses' own "monotheistic" teachings.[18] It should be noted, however, that influence of Akhenaton upon Moses is scarcely probable because of the fact that Akhenaton's reform was completely reversed by the Theban priests and Tut-ankh-amen. All evidences of the reform were carefully expunged from the monuments and records. The fact that such a reform was ever instigated in Egypt had been erased from memory and only the skill of the modern archaeologist has re-established the record.

Perhaps the greatest matter of interest in the Amarna tablets was the constant reference to the Habiru, the invading people. The close similarity between "Habiru" and "Hebrew" was immediately noticed. Studies since have supported the theory that there is etymological relationship between the two words. The words "Sagaz" and "Shasu" also appeared regularly and in contexts which suggested that these two words were roughly synonymous with HABIRU. These two words clearly had no ethnic or gentilic connotations. Neither apparently had the word "Habiru." All these words connoted the enemy, perhaps in uncomplimentary terms. It is therefore important to note that the word "Hebrew" in our Bibles was not at first used by the Hebrews of themselves. It was applied to them by others. The "Hebrews" preferred to be known as the "Sons of Israel," or by the particular tribe to which they belonged. It was not until well along in the period of the monarchy that the term "Hebrew" was well accepted by the people known by that name. They took what was apparently a term of reproach and clothed it with honor and dignity. It was also given popular interpretation and associated with the verb meaning "to cross over." [19]

Regardless of etymology, we are still faced with the important question of the identity of the Habiru and the related question of possible identification of the Habiru with the invasion of Palestine by the tribes under Joshua. It is now generally admitted that the question of the invasion of Palestine is an involved one. Increasingly scholars recognize that the conquest could not have been a short campaign of a few years such as is portrayed by the Deuteronomic writer. Many of the chapters in Joshua and Judges clearly indicate that the process was a long and involved one. In addition, there is increasing recognition of the proposal that there may have been one major invasion and much infiltration before and after the major campaigns. These various thrusts have been gathered together as part of the great saga of the conquest. If this be true, then it is altogether possible that the marauding Habiri are a part of the story.

Thirty cents' worth of tablets have become priceless, not because of the manipulations of traders and museum agents, but because of the untiring

---

[18] E.g., James E. Breasted, *Dawn of Conscience* (New York: Charles Scribners Sons, 1933), pp. 281 ff. An excellent comparison of Psalm 104 and "Hymn to Aton" can also be found in this volume. See below Chap. 12, p. 144.

[19] See Albright, "Abram the Hebrew," *BASOR* (October, 1960), pp. 36-54; and A. Haldar, "Habiru," *IBD*, p. 506.

work of the scholar. Even though he may begin his studies handicapped because the provenance of the artifact is not scientifically controlled, his skill is such that obstacles are overcome and significant information is obtained.

There are untold instances where accidental discoveries have led to important information concerning the ancient world. It was a chance discovery that led to the Moabite Stone or Mesha Inscription, and small boys crawling through the Siloam Tunnel discovered the now famous Siloam Inscription. The stories are many and are often "embroidered" in the re-telling, but the instances cited above will serve to indicate the importance of accidental discoveries. There are, in addition, many remnants from ancient civilizations in full view and awaiting our careful study. They have become familiar because they have been known for many centuries, yet their secrets have remained with them, at least until someone determined to make a full and complete investigation of their significance.

The pyramids of Egypt, at least the ones at Gizeh,[20] have been known almost as long as recorded history. Because of their great size they resisted complete conquest by the sands of time. The Great Pyramid of Khufu (Cheops) is 450 feet high, but originally it was 481.4 feet. Its base is approximately 756 feet square, and covers slightly more than thirteen acres. The pyramids were considered one of the "Seven Wonders of the World," and indeed only they and one other wonder, the Colossi of Memnon, remain extant. They have excited wonder and curiosity for 4,600 years. For many people, even today, the purpose of the pyramids is to record predictions of future events, and pyramidologists are active interpreting measurements of the pyramids as they relate to events in the twentieth century.

It was, in fact, interest in such matters that first took Flinders Petrie to Egypt in the latter part of the nineteenth century. His father had stimulated his interest and had also taught him the importance of basing his conclusions upon verified evidence. Since understanding of prediction was based upon the measurements of the pyramids, the so-called "pyramid inch," and since there was disagreement concerning those basic measurements, Petrie decided that the first step was to make those measurements for himself. As he carefully measured the Great Pyramid he came across another enthusiast who was busily engaged in chipping away some stone at the base of the pyramid. When Petrie made inquiry he was blithely told that the measurements of the base did not quite permit the predictions to come out as they were obviously intended to; therefore a "correction" was being made. Petrie abandoned pyramidology forthwith and went on to become an outstanding archaeologist, one of the first of the scientific investigators in the field.[21]

Since the early days of Petrie much careful attention has been given to

---

[20] In addition to the three major pyramids at Gizeh approximately 80 others have been identified. See I. E. S. Edwards, *The Pyramids of Egypt* (Baltimore: Penguin Books, Inc., 1947), p. 16.

[21] See above, Chap. 2, pp. 29 f.

the pyramids. For a while they were objects of plunder, as we noted earlier.[22] The pyramids were tombs for the pharaohs, and a study of the burial practices of the ancient Egyptians has given us much insight concerning Egyptian religion. The pharaohs were accorded great honors in death as in life. It was believed that the pharaoh became the new Osiris, god of the land of the dead. Therefore the deceased pharaoh was provided in his tomb with all those things it was believed he would need for his new reign in the afterlife. In addition, full records of his life upon earth were carefully inscribed and buried with him. From these various records, together with inscriptions carved during the lifetime of the pharaohs, Egyptian history has been reconstructed. Historians are now in possession of historical records which compare very favorably with histories of modern nations. This is not to say that no further work needs to be done. There are many gaps in the records and there is considerable difference of opinion among scholars concerning dates of reigns and the political significance of events. Breasted wrote A History of the Ancient Egyptians in 1908. It was a magnificent piece of work and is still considered a standard work for some periods of Egyptian history. Much more information is now available. Breasted's work is now augmented by such books as G. Steindorff and Keith C. Seele, When Egypt Ruled the East, and John A. Wilson, The Burden of Egypt.[23] The later books follow the newer view that history is people, not merely the recording of the dates of kings' reigns, battles, invasions, et cetera. This in turn enables us to compare the various cultures and to recognize where the thought and practices of one people impinge upon or contribute to the life and welfare of another nation.

Two observations concerning the writing of Egyptian history may be helpful to the reader. First, it will be apparent that there is a decided difference in the datings of events as noted by the earlier and later historians. The earlier historians tended to use dates, particularly for the early dynastic period, that were higher by several centuries. These are the so-called "higher datings." Dates have, by reason of evidence, been reduced, in some cases quite drastically. The reader, aware of the differences, can avoid the confusion which could arise if some dates are taken from one system and others from another.

The Egyptian language can be easily read by anyone who will take the trouble to learn the hieroglyphic symbols and the structure of the language. Strangely enough, the language cannot be pronounced with any confidence. This is because Egyptian was written with pictures and symbols which do not indicate vocalization. Any attempt to pronounce Egyptian words can be made only as "neutral" vowels are used. This is why there is considerable discrepancy between the spelling of Egyptian names. Is it Ikh-en-aton, or

[22] See above, Chap. 3, pp. 37-38.
[23] James H. Breasted, History of the Ancient Egyptians (New York: Charles Scribners Sons, 1908). Georg Steindorff and K. C. Seele, When Egypt Ruled the East (Chicago: University of Chicago Press, 1942); and John Albert Wilson, The Burden of Egypt (Chicago: University of Chicago Press, 1951).

Akh-en-aton? Nefr-tite, or Nofer-ti-te? Arbitrary vocalization has, of necessity been used, and so far there has been no international agreement upon standardized spelling of ancient names.

We have indicated earlier [24] that the term archaeology is broadened popularly and practically to include special disciplines which may stand in their own right and are not primarily concerned with excavation. This is particularly true of epigraphy, which has the task of deciphering and translating ancient inscriptions. The keys by which unknown languages from the past were unlocked were sometimes found in strange places. One of these keys had been in full view of man for nearly twenty-six centuries, but it had never been recognized as a key until a little more than a hundred years ago.

At the end of a long range of rocky hills in the Zagros Mountains, and to the east of the plain of Kermanshah in Iran, there is a great rock face upon which are carved figures of gods, kings, attendants, and many lines of writing. The place, called by Arab geographers the mountain of Behistun, has long been known. The name comes from "Bhagistan," meaning the "place of the gods."

The rock face stands more than 350 feet above the plain at an altitude of approximately 3,800 feet. The monument was called to the attention of Henry Rawlinson who had been in the army of the East India Company. He was transferred as a military adviser in 1835 to Persia, and it was there he learned of the "rock." He learned Persian and had interested himself in antiquities. Rawlinson's own account of his adventure in copying the writing from the rock indicates that he combined great daring and courage with careful scholarship. On the other hand, he was sometimes guilty of precipitous action that bordered on foolhardiness. He nearly lost his life because he failed to understand the crudity and weakness of the native ladder he was using in his efforts to copy the Behistun inscription.

He did, however, provide the world of scholarship with a nearly complete copy of the inscription. By 1847 he had made squeezes[25] of most of the columns. It was later discovered that the inscription was written in three languages—Persian, Babylonian, and Elamite. Rawlinson was able to decipher the Persian first, then moved on to the Babylonian. By 1851 he was able to publish his own translation of the Babylonian, and by 1857 the Royal Asiatic Society was convinced that the problem of reading and translating Babylonian had been solved. In more recent years the famous inscription has been photographed by N. C. Debevoise[26] and completely copied in 1948 by George G. Cameron, who used a special preparation of rubber which could be sprayed onto the inscriptions. Dr. Cameron also was able to obtain for the first time

[24] See above, Chap. 1, p. 21.
[25] A "squeeze" is a copy obtained by pressing wet papier mâché onto the surface much as a small boy obtains the impression of a coin by pressing "silver paper" onto it.
[26] "A Photograph of Darius' Sculptures at Behistun," JNES, II (1943), plate II.

a complete transcription of the Elamite section of the monument.[27] Cameron's interests are primarily in linguistics and history, but it was necessary for him to follow archaeological methods to obtain the source materials so necessary to his investigation. In addition, as he examined the work of his predecessors he became convinced that new examination of an ancient monument was needed, and that with new materials, new techniques, and increased understanding of languages, better information could be made available to the linguist and historian. His own writings have demonstrated that he was correct.

[27] *Ibid.*, pp. 115-16; and Cameron, *History of Early Iran* (Cambridge, England: Cambridge University Press, 1936).

7.

FIELD PRESERVATION, MUSEUM DISPLAY, AND PUBLICATION

How often an archaeologist hears it said, "I wish that I could watch you as you discover exciting things." It is not often, nor even desirable, that the work of excavation should be made available to spectators, at least during working hours. Visitors do go to the more accessible places, but it should be remembered that taking an archaeologist away from his work to conduct a tour of "the mound" is like asking a surgeon to leave the patient on the operating table to guide interested people around the hospital. Most archaeologists are very gracious people. Their business is investigation, the inquiring mind, and the student. Normally, therefore, arrangements can usually be made for visitors to inspect a site, but they should come at a time when the archaeologists are not head over heels in supervising field work. Some important sites, such as Jericho, have become tourist attractions, and a small admission fee makes it possible for the traveler to have the services of a specially trained native guide.

For very practical reasons it is simply not possible for most people who are interested in the results of archaeology to participate in field trips in the Near and Middle East. There are, however, many excellent resources available to them so that they may experience some of the excitement and see the results of field archaeology. It is just as possible to be an "armchair archaeologist" as it is to be an armchair traveler. Proper preservation of artifacts in the field, adequate and informative museum displays, and superbly illustrated publications make this possible.

As we have already noted, every object and piece of evidence found in excavation must be properly recorded, carefully removed from the ground, and adequately housed in order that more detailed study can be given to it. It is often true, however, that the object cannot be taken from its place of discovery until it has been given treatment to make its removal safe. The lower stone of a grinding mill was uncovered at Araq el-Emir. Pressure of many tons of soil and stone above it had cracked the mill at several points. Before it could be removed two steps had to be taken. First, the millstone was carefully tied together with strong cord and rope. Such binding kept all the pieces in place but was not strong enough to ensure that they would stay together while the millstone was being lifted from the excavation to the ground surface, about six meters above. Therefore, the ground under the millstone was carefully removed and a specially built platform was slipped under the stone. It was then possible for the workmen to lift the stone with safety for them and the stone. Larger pieces cannot be handled in this way. It often becomes necessary to remove gigantic monuments which have been broken piece by piece. In such case, after photographs and drawings have been made, each piece is carefully numbered, and notations are made of the numbers at the proper places in the drawings. When all pieces have been removed, reconstruction can be made above ground where this is desirable. Sometimes reconstruction does not take place until the object is being placed on permanent display as in the case of the Winged Bull at the Oriental Institute of the University of Chicago.

Pieces of pottery present no particular problem, except for the reconstruction of broken vessels where characteristic or unique examples are discovered. A sandtray for supporting the pieces while in the process of being glued, an effective glue which will not discolor the clay, and infinite patience can suffice to meet most situations. Clay tablets present a very different problem. Some of these were baked after they had been written, others were not. In any case, during the long period while they were buried in the ground moisture has soaked into the clay and with the moisture various salts from the ground have impregnated the tablets. It is important to remove both the moisture and the salts, otherwise the salts may eventually cause the tablets to crack apart. There are records of tablets which fairly exploded sometime after they had been removed from the ground because they had not been given proper treatment. Professor Delougaz has described fully the techniques necessary for treating clay tablets in his "The Treatment of Clay Tablets in the Field." [1]

Some instructions for the treatment of wood and metal are given by Sir Mortimer Wheeler in a chapter entitled "The Field-Laboratory." [2] He lists the various tools and chemicals necessary for first aid treatment of artifacts and skeletal material. Highly useful are his instructions for the cleaning of coins and their preservation. Coins must be cleaned immediately, for they are often necessary to help establish the dates of occupation levels. Their importance was demonstrated in the reconstruction of the history of the Dead Sea Scrolls community.

Several hundred documents or portions of documents have been recovered from the dozen caves associated with the Dead Sea Covenanter community. Not one scroll so far deciphered contains any historical information concerning this community. Yet a fairly complete history has been reconstructed from archaeological evidence, including evidence from coins. [3] The religious documents take on added significance because the historical period from which they come has been identified.

The scrolls and the scraps of leather and papyrus have been collected from the Arabs who originally found the caves. Material was also recovered from other caves which have been identified. In both cases, the written materials

---

[1] *Studies in Ancient Oriental Civilization*, No. 7 (Chicago, 1933).
[2] *Archaeology from the Earth* (London: Oxford University Press, 1954), pp. 169-73.
[3] See below Chap. 13, pp. 166-67.

were in a bad state of disrepair. None of them could be read "in situ." By far the larger number of scrolls could not even be unrolled until the leather had been made pliable. In the case of the so-called "Genesis Apocryphon" [4] several attempts were made to unroll the scroll. Dampness had badly damaged one side of the scroll; ink had chemically reacted and partially destroyed some of the leather; and white fabric inserted between some layers of the scroll had fused to the surface, or at least adhered so closely that special and extensive treatment was necessary for its removal. After many months of painstaking work both in America and in Israel the document was finally unrolled and deciphered. In some scrolls and with many scraps there are portions which need further treatment before the writing is legible. Dirt may have covered the text, or the ink may have faded completely away. Deft work can remove the dirt, and the use of infrared photography will often give readings where ordinary sight and photography fail. Amazing results have been obtained by the highly skillful team of photographers at the Palestine Archaeological Museum in Jerusalem, Jordan. Both in the Palestine Archaeological Museum and in the Shrine of the Book, Jerusalem, Israel, scrolls and scroll portions may be seen. These exhibits have been carefully prepared. The portions of leather and papyrus are mounted between glass. Precaution has been taken to exclude air or moisture which could destroy the ancient writing. It is now possible for us to read writing which came from the last three centuries prior to the Christian Era, and from the first century A.D.

In the early days of archaeological discoveries little thought was given to interpretive displays. Each object stood on its own merits, sometimes competing with other objects for its share of attention. Directors of museums were often faced with the problem of finding display space for the rapidly growing number of antiquities. The ease with which an object could be crowded into an available corner was the all-important consideration. It was only much later that consideration was given to historical and cultural groupings. By no means have all museums become instruments of education and research, but increasingly the new pattern of organization is being used. Sigfried J. De Laet tells of a Belgium museum where labels are carelessly shuffled about at every spring cleaning. He notes that one vase has had four labels showing different provenances in ten years.[5] In many of our university and national museums far more material is stored away than is displayed. Overcrowded cases and halls are seen less frequently. In addition, efforts are made to place interpretive placards on cases or brochures in the hands of the viewers, quite frequently both.

Skill in display has become one of the fine arts. Commercial supply houses now make a wide variety of cases, stands, and other equipment

---

[4] See Nahman Avigad and Yigael Yadin, editors, A Genesis Apocryphon, translated by S. S. Nardi (Jerusalem, Israel: The Magnes Press of the Hebrew University, 1956).

[5] Archaeology and Its Problems, translated by Ruth Daniel (London: Phoenix House, Ltd., 1957), p. 80.

available, so that, assuming adequate funds are available, artifacts can be displayed most meaningfully. The modern museum is a place of light and intelligible presentation. Complaint has been made that so often the facts of history have been dug from the ground only to have the information buried completely in some forbidding book (transferred from tomb to tome), or hidden successfully in some dark corner of a wretchedly disorganized museum. Marcel Brion has said, "Archaeology is the science of life." [6] Petrie is quoted by Badè as saying: "museums are ghastly charnel-houses of murdered evidence." [7]

Two museums are particularly worth mentioning even though they have nothing to do with biblical archaeology. They are noteworthy simply because imagination and skill have made their exhibits works of inspiration as well as education. These are the national museums in Manila, Philippines, and Honolulu, Hawaii. The latter takes great pains to inform the viewer about methods of modern archaeology. By chart and photograph the techniques of excavation are clearly shown. After methodology has been explained, then displays continue the story with materials from excavations. The story of life in ancient Hawaii is made intelligible. The museum in the Philippines gives major attention to chronological organization of artifacts related to Philippine history. Clearly written descriptive material relating excavation sites to artifacts is displayed. Attempts are made to avoid use of fine print. Charts are clearly printed in large type and adequately illustrated with photographs, either black and white or color as the situation démands.

The Palestine Archaeological Museum in Jerusalem, Jordan, is cited as an example because (a) it is a unique combination of international cooperation, (b) displays are organized by chronological sequence, (c) adequate interpretive material is made available to the visitor, and (d) the whole is specifically related to an area in which three major world religions (Judiasm, Christianity, Islam) have flourished. The entire building was designed so that archaeological evidence could be studied, not merely seen. The galleries have been divided into bays, each of which is given over to a specific period in the story of man. Photographs and charts enable the student to see the context and understand the significance of each exhibit. In each gallery there is a "gallery book" which the viewer may use without charge. The gallery book gives additional information concerning each object displayed. All objects are numbered as well as labeled; numbers correspond to the listings in the gallery book. Guide books to the various archaeological periods may also be purchased at the desk. There is an excellent library of books and journals as well as special rooms for students where objects from the field, especially pottery, may be handled.

The older museums, such as the British Museum in London, the Louvre

[6] Marcel Brion, The World of Archaeology, (New York: The Macmillan Company, 1962) I, 9.
[7] Badè, A Manual of Excavation in the Near East, p. 48.

in Paris, the Museum of the Ancient Orient in Istanbul, or the Museum in Cairo, have now set aside special halls, rooms, or sections for exhibits pertaining to the various countries and gradually attempts are being made to organize all exhibits in chronological sequence. The larger museums in ·the United States are in the fortunate position of having been started after the first big rush of artifacts from the Middle East was over. Under the influence of men like James Henry Breasted displays were arranged with respect to history and the history of culture rather than appeal to aesthetics. There are many museums in the United States within easy traveling distance of many millions of people. In these museums it is possible to visit the ancient world of Bible times; to see coins, similar to the "widow's mite" (Mark 12:42), that were in circulation during the days of Jesus; to get a glimpse of the grandeur of Egypt, the magnificence of Babylon and Assyria, and the exquisite beauty which graced the furniture and walls (Amos 6:4; I Kings 22:39) of the king's palace at Samaria; and to note the various written documents from many ancient lands which bear testimony to the historical setting of the Old and New Testament stories.

One large gallery and a sizeable portion of the entire second floor of the Museum in Cairo has been given over to display the enormous collection of objects found in the tomb of the Pharaoh Tut-ankh-Amon. One should certainly not visit Cairo without seeing this collection. No such display of tomb furnishings is available in any other museum.[8] Even the elaborate furnishings from the Royal Cemeteries at Ur of the Chaldees have not yet been given as fine a setting. Some of the material from Ur may be seen in the Museum in Baghdad, and it is possible that with the removal of the Museum to its new quarters more adequate space will be available. There are many specialized collections in the United States, and it is necessary to go to those museums if one would see the originals. There are, however, several museums which are now making faithful copies of artifacts available—the University of Pennsylvania and the Metropolitan Museum of New York, as well as commercial houses. The ancient world is being brought to our very doorsteps in so many ways.

The Oriental Institute at the University of Chicago has arranged its exhibits geographically, each hall being devoted to a different geographical area: Egyptian, Assyro-Babylonian, Hittite, Palestinian, et cetera. In addition to the usual displays of characteristic pottery of various periods, the Egyptian hall contains an interesting sequence of beads and a special display of the development of burial customs, including pits and cutaway models of the mastabas[9] and pyramids.

The synagogue from Dura Europus has been completely rebuilt in the

[8] This exhibit is now fully described and illustrated in Christiane Desroches Noblecourt, *Tutankhamen* (New York: Graphic Books, 1963).
[9] A "mastaba" is a superstructure of brick built over a burial pit. The term comes from the Arabic word meaning "bench." See Edwards, *The Pyramids of Egypt*, pp. 35-44, "Mastabas."

Museum at Damascus. It is now possible to stand within the ancient synagogue and to examine the paintings which adorn the walls. Such biblical scenes as Abraham's readiness to offer Isaac as a sacrifice and the struggle on Mount Carmel between Elijah and the priests of Baal are vivid. The latter story has evidently been edited, for the artist has portrayed a youth who has probably been instructed by the priests of Baal. The youth is creeping up behind the altar with a torch to set afire to the sacrifice. A pointed finger above the picture indicates divine intervention, a miracle; a poisonous snake bites the boy who presumably dies before his treacherous deed can be completed.[10] It was in this same excavation at Dura Europus that fragments of papyrus belonging to the third century B.C. were found.[11] In addition, a vellum fragment of Tatian's *Diatessaron* was recovered.[12]

The bookseller and the librarian bring the ancient world right into our homes. Modern methods of photography and printing are placing at our disposal likenesses of artifacts so realistic that these objects fairly leap from the page into our hands. No longer are writer and reader limited to transmission of thought through words. The old Chinese proverb that "a picture is worth ten thousand words" is being demonstrated daily in current publications. Such publications range from the popular to the profound, and from inexpensive paperbacks to very expensive full color plate volumes.

Volumes related to biblical archaeology may be generally classified under one of the categories noted below. The classification is typological not qualitative. An author usually indicates, either in his preface or in his outline, which of the categories will best describe his emphasis and sometimes whether or not he is being objective in his evidence or carefully selecting his evidence to support a point of view. The categories which appear to be most descriptive are:

1. *Bible Oriented.* These are the volumes which generally follow the biblical order of events and draw upon archaeology to illustrate the biblical books and customs! [13] Such a method of organization is, of necessity, highly selective. These volumes are useful for illustrative purposes and serve their stated function adequately. In general, however, the authors do not have space in which to give the larger setting of the Bible story. In addition it should be noted that it is in this category that we find some books dedicated to the

[10] See *The Excavations at Dura Europus*, edited by M. I. Rostovtzeff, et al. (8 vols.; New Haven, Conn.: Yale University Press, 1929-39); Rostovtzeff, *Dura Europos and Its Art* (New York: Oxford University Press, 1938).

[11] Jack Finegan, *Light from the Ancient Past* (Princeton, N. J.: Princeton University Press, 1946), p. 308.

[12] Dura Europus was destroyed about A.D. 256. See C. H. Kraeling, *A Greek Fragment of Tatian's Diatessaron from Dura* (London: Christopher's, 1935).

[13] An excellent bibliography, "Some Books on the Bible in the Light of Archaeology," William F. Albright, appears in BASOR (October 1962-April, 1963). Albright's bibliography deals with general biblical studies as well as those devoted solely to archaeology.

proposition that the Bible is literally accurate in all respects. None of the books appended to this chapter is committed to such a position.

2. *Bible History Oriented.* A number of writers have recognized that there is value in presenting a historical religion against a historical background. They have therefore assembled their materials and presented them in historical sequence, fitting the biblical references into the text as occasion demands. Emphasis is upon historical development. For example, in treating the period of the monarchy, there can be references to many excavations in Palestine[14] and biblical references can be taken from the so-called historical books I and II Samuel, I and II Kings, and I and II Chronicles, as well as the books of the eighth and seventh centuries B.C. prophets.

This approach is chosen by some writers because it gives them an opportunity to discuss history more fully and to draw more readily upon related historical facts. A writer, for example, may wish not merely to illustrate difficulties in the exodus from Egypt and the problems of life in the wilderness, but also to discuss some of the historical difficulties encountered as the various biblical records are compared with each other and with the archaeological evidence and the extant Egyptian records. The format of historical reference is appropriate to this kind of discussion.

The format of history appears to be an appropriate background for seeing the relatedness of the Old and New Testaments. The historian may fully recognize the significance of the symbols B.C. and A.D., but he also knows that there is continuity to history. The story of Judaism does not suddenly cease to exist at the turn of the Christian Era. It was, in fact, many centuries before the currently accepted pattern of dating was even formulated, and longer still until it was adopted. History stresses continuity while at the same time it enables us to see major breaks in tradition and the upsurge of new movements.

3. *Illustrated Bibles.* Little need be said concerning this category since its title is self-explaining. It may, however, be observed that superb volumes are being produced in this area; some, indeed, are ostentatious. The availability of excellent illustrations, made possible through color photography combined with new printing techniques which give perfect registration of colors, make fine volumes possible. Pictures of real life have replaced etchings and paintings of former years.

4. *Bible Geographies and Bible Dictionaries.* Librarians have been almost startled in recent years at the flood of publications in this category, especially at the number of Bible geographies now available in contrast to the paucity of material only a few years ago. Cartography, like other graphic arts, has taken full advantage of modern methods of reproduction. The ability to produce three-dimensional effects on a plane surface enables the

[14] Palestine is here used in the traditional sense to cover the area now divided into the countries of Israel and Jordan.

91

geographer to make us more vitally aware of landscape and topography than was possible in older texts. In addition, the modern geographer is concerned with so much more than terrain. He makes us knowledgeable concerning natural resources, products of field and industry, climate and ecology, and densities of population.

Bible dictionaries are available either in concise one-volume format or in sets of several volumes. Newer dictionaries are profusely illustrated. By and large, Bible dictionaries are considerably more up to date than Bible commentaries. There is an unfortunate lag in commentaries at two points. First, exegetes are primarily interested in language and are not always aware of the significance of discoveries in languages in which they do not have primary interest. Second, expositors are often chosen from outstanding pulpiteers, men who are skilled as religious leaders but are not primarily experts in linguistics or the more specialized aspects of archaeology. On the other hand, editors of dictionaries will usually select writers of dictionary articles on the basis of their specialized knowledge. An editor of a Bible dictionary will of necessity draw upon a far wider circle of specialists than can normally be done for a Bible commentary. The Bible dictionary, however, does not concern itself with exposition of Bible texts or furnish illustrations from modern life or classical literature for next Sunday's sermon. Each publication serves a special purpose.

The term "Bible dictionary" is a little misleading. The modern Bible dictionary goes far beyond defining the meaning of words. It is actually an encyclopedia and a dictionary combined. Words are defined first, in good dictionary style. Then there may be several paragraphs or even columns of information, depending upon the importance of the particular term being discussed. Modern Bible dictionaries have been broadened in their usefulness because of the work of the archaeologist and photographic records of sites and excavations.

5. *Studies of Individual Countries.* An increasing number of volumes are appearing which deal with individual countries such as Egypt, Assyria and Babylonia (one geographical unit), Jordan, Israel, et cetera. The special advantage of this type of presentation is that full attention can be given to the archaeological evidence being uncovered in one particular country. Such volumes usually have many references to the related biblical record, to histories of that particular country, and to the histories of neighboring areas. The author, however, assumes responsibility primarily to relate as fully as possible the excavation and surface evidence so far available.

Excavations in all Near and Middle East countries have made us increasingly aware that Western culture is heavily dependent upon what happened in those lands many centuries ago. We are no longer content to trace origins back no further than Greco-Roman times. There is a growing number of colleges and universities which recognize that the histories of Greece and Rome are fairly late in comparison with the histories of the

Sumerians, Babylonians, Assyrians, Hurrians, Hittites, Egyptians, or Canaanites. It is true that the Bible story has its setting in many of these lands, but
so does so much of modern civilization. Modern histories of drama, law,
medicine, mathematics, astronomy, horology, writing, art, now begin with
an acknowledgement of indebtedness to lands east and south of Greece.
Some, notably histories of mathematics, give considerable attention to the
pre-Greek periods. It is because of all this that archaeology, even in its early
days, could not be merely a servant of the church, synagogue, or mosque.
It is a field of study in its own right and as such may be used by those seeking
information concerning the history of the graphic arts just as readily as it can
by those primarily interested in the history of religion. Volumes recording the
archaeological studies in individual lands are designed to be useful to an
understanding of the whole story of man.

6. *General.* With increased attention from the general reading public
in archaeology it is understandable that many books have been written
telling both of results and adventures in the field. They have been written for
many publics and various age levels. Many of them make fascinating reading.
Because of the purpose and nature of these books—to entertain as well as to
inform—startling results and tingling adventures are emphasized, while bitter
defeat and disappointing expenditure of effort and funds are often omitted.
As in all scientific investigation there is despair as well as triumph. Nevertheless these books do great service in introducing the public at large,
especially young people who are trying to decide upon a career, to a discipline
which is adding so much to our understanding of man's life upon the earth,
and especially the setting for the story of the Judaeo-Christian religion.

7. *Technical.* Within recent years there has been published a number of
significant books dealing with preparation for a career in archaeology, field
methods, the use of technical help from various sciences, et cetera. In addition, texts are available which describe the development of specific aspects
of culture or the growth of beliefs and practices as indicated in buildings.
Books have appeared on the structure of the Egyptian pyramid and related
burial practices. Others describe city management and city planning in
the ancient world. Many books discuss the art of communication in pictures,
writing, and the development of the alphabet. Still others are concerned with
such matters as changing architectural style, development of the graphic arts,
ancient shrines and temples, idols and figurines, and the all-important subject
for the archaeologist, characteristic pottery styles.

The categories listed are somewhat arbitrary and are suggested, not as a
rigid classification list, but as a general guide to the kinds of information
available to the interested reader. Many books fit more than one classification.
In the appended list not more than six or seven books are given in each
category. There are many others to be found in the bibliography on pages
209-14. These are not necessarily the best but each book is chosen because it
illustrates its category so well, as well as because it is a book which can be

93

recommended with confidence. It is devoutly hoped that by the time these words are printed still more excellent volumes will have been printed.

1. BIBLE ORIENTED

Price, Ira M., *et al. The Monuments and the Old Testament.* Rev. ed. Valley Forge, Pa.: Judson Press, 1959.

Thompson, John Arthur. *The Bible and Archaeology.* Grand Rapids, Mich.: Wm. B. Eerdmans Publishing Company, 1962.

2. BIBLE-HISTORY ORIENTED

Albright, William F. *Archaeology and the Religion of Israel.* Baltimore, Md.: Johns Hopkins Press, 1942.

————. *The Archaeology of Palestine.* Baltimore, Md.: Penguin Books, Inc., 1949.

Burrows, Millar. *What Mean These Stones?* New York: Meridian Books, Inc., 1957

Finegan, Jack. *Light from the Ancient Past.* Princeton, N.J.: Princeton University Press, 1946. 2nd ed., 1959.

Gray, John. *Archaeology and the Old Testament World.* Edinburgh: Thomas Nelson & Sons, Ltd., 1962.

McCown, C. C. *The Ladder of Progress in Palestine.* New York: Harper & Brothers, 1943.

3. ILLUSTRATED BIBLES

Avi-Yonah, Michael, and Kraeling, Emil G. editors. *Our Living Bible.* New York: McGraw-Hill Book Company, 1962.

Avi-Yonah, Michael, *et al.,* editors. *Illustrated World of the Bible.* 5 vols. New York: McGraw-Hill Book Company, 1958-61.

Cornfeld, Gaalyahu, *et al.,* editors. *Adam to Daniel.* New York: The Macmillan Company, 1961.

————. *Daniel to Paul.* New York: The Macmillan Company, 1963.

4. BIBLICAL GEOGRAPHIES AND DICTIONARIES

Baly, Denis. *The Geography of the Bible.* London: Lutterworth Press, 1957.

Buttrick, George A., editor. *Interpreter's Dictionary of the Bible.* 4 vols. Nashville: Abingdon Press, 1962.

Grollenberg, L. H., compiler. *Atlas of the Bible.* London: Thomas Nelson & Sons, 1956.

Kraeling, Emil G. *Rand McNally Bible Atlas.* Chicago: Rand McNally & Company, 1956.

Lemaire, Paulin, and Baldi, Donato, editors. *Atlas Biblique: Historie et geographie de la Bible.* Paris: S.D.E.C., 1960.

May, Herbert G., editor. *Oxford Bible Atlas.* London: Oxford University Press, 1962.

Wright, George Ernest, and Filson, Floyd V., editors. *The Westminster Historical Atlas to the Bible.* Rev. ed. Philadelphia: The Westminster Press, 1956.

5. INDIVIDUAL COUNTRIES

Ceram, C. W. (K. W. Marek). *The Secret of the Hittites*. New York: Alfred A. Knopf, Inc., 1956.

Harding, G. Lankester. *The Antiquities of Jordan*. London: Lutterworth Press, 1959.

Kenyon, Kathleen. *Archaeology in the Holy Land*. London: Ernest Benn, Ltd., 1960.

Lloyd, Seton. *Foundations in the Dust*. Middlesex, England: Penguin Books, Ltd., 1955.

Murray, Margaret A. *The Splendour That Was Egypt*. New York: Philosophical Library, Inc., 1949.

Saggs, H. F. F. *The Greatness That Was Babylon*. New York: Hawthorn Books, Inc., 1962.

6. GENERAL ARCHAEOLOGY

Allen, Agnes. *The Story of Archaeology*. London: Faber & Faber, Ltd., 1956. A good book for children.

Brion, Marcel. *The World of Archaeology*. 2 vols. New York: The Macmillan Company, 1962.

Deuel, Leo, editor. *The Treasures of Time*. Cleveland, Ohio: World Publishing Company, 1961.

Hawkes, Jacquetta, editor. *The World of the Past*. 2 vols. New York: Alfred A. Knopf, Inc., 1963.

Kenyon, Kathleen. *Beginning in Archaeology*. Rev. Ed. London: Phoenix House, Ltd., 1960.

Woolley, Leonard. *History Unearthed*. London: Ernest Benn, Ltd., 1958.

7. TECHNICAL

Brothwell, Don, and Higgs, Eric, editors. *Science in Archaeology*. New York: Basic Books, Inc., 1963.

Crawford, O. G. S. *Archaeology in the Field*. New York: Frederick A. Praeger, Inc., 1953.

Detweiler, A. Henry. *Manual of Archaeological Surveying*. New York: Stechert-Hafner Service Agency, Inc., 1948.

Dumas, Frederic. *Deep-Water Archaeology*. Translated by Honor Frost. London: Routledge & Kegan Paul, Ltd., 1962.

Franken, H. J., and Franken-Battershill, C. A. *A Primer of Old Testament Archaeology*. Leiden: E. J. Brill, Publisher, 1963.

Laet, Sigfried J. de. *Archaeology and Its Problems*. Translated by Ruth Daniel. London: Phoenix House, Ltd., 1957.

Wheeler, Mortimer. *Archaeology from the Earth*. London: Oxford University Press, 1954.

PART III

The World
in Which the Bible
Was Written

8.

INTERPRETATION OF EVIDENCE

A major change of attitude toward archaeological evidence has characterized the middle decades of the twentieth century. From the seventeenth through the nineteenth centuries professional churchmen and laity alike looked with suspicion upon the findings of the archaeologist. To be sure, nothing of consequence had been dug up in Bible lands—that was to come later—but antiquarians had been making some startling proposals which challenged the current interpretations of biblical history.

During the seventeenth century interest had arisen in England concerning evidences of early occupants of the country. As early as 1533 Henry VIII had appointed John Leland (1506-52) as his personal antiquary, but his responsibility had been to gather material from cathedrals, colleges, and religious houses. In the seventeenth century attention was given to digging in order to uncover ancient towns and villages. During this investigation much material was uncovered which we now know went back into the Stone Age. In addition many fossils were recovered. Examination of the fossils persuaded some antiquaries of two things: (a) That the earth was older than most authorities believed, and (b) there probably was animal life upon the earth prior to the advent of man. Isaac de la Peyrere, a French Calvinist, published his findings in 1655. His title, A Theological Systeme upon that presupposition that Men were Before Adam, provoked much debate. He stated, "Adam was the first and father of the Jews, not of all men." Thus he sought to harmonize the biblical record with his position concerning the age of the earth.

In the following century Compte de Buffon, who was born George Louis Leclerc, September 7, 1707, added to the furious debate. He asserted that the great flood of the biblical record could not account for fossils. There simply wasn't time during the flood for a fossil to form. He estimated that the earth was 75,000 years old, and that there had been life upon the earth for 15,000 years. But the church had accepted the computation of Ussher, Archbishop of Armagh (1581-1656), that the world had been created in the year 4004 B.C. Ussher had been supported in this by Bishop Lightfoot, who refined the date to October 23, 4004. Buffon was finally forced to recant: "I declare that I had no intention of contradicting the text of scripture: that I most firmly believe all therein about the Creation, both as to order of time and matter of fact." [1] Question had, however, been raised, and it remained.

As more and more fossils came to light there was increasing conviction that animal life existed on the earth prior to man. There was even some suggestion that life may have evolved from primitive to more complex forms, but the

---

[1] Jacquetta Hawkes, editor, The World of the Past (New York: Alfred A. Knopf, Inc., 1963), I, 26.

great debate occasioned by this position did not come to its height until the time of Darwin in the nineteenth century. In the meantime faithful church-men pointed out that since, according to the Genesis account, water was divided from the dry land on the third day of Creation, and animals were not created until the fifth day, any interpretation of fossils as evidence for succession of geological ages was contrary to scripture. In recent years biblical literalists have taught that the great flood turned everything topsy turvy and therefore geological evidence must be disregarded. This same argument was used in the seventeenth and eighteenth centuries.

With the recovery of written documents from excavations in Mesopotamia new controversies arose. After scholars had learned how to decipher and translate the ancient documents it became apparent that there were marked similarities between these documents and many of the Old Testament ac-counts. George Smith [2] was the first of many translators to point out the parallels. Now the great question was which document was dependent upon the other? There was no doubt in the minds of the faithful that the biblical word was original, for had it not been dictated by God himself? The Babylo-nians, they believed, must have copied the biblical story and perverted the record to conform to their own fallen state of polytheism. Since, however, it was generally believed that Moses had written the record from Genesis to Deuteronomy in the latter half of the fifteenth century B.C., at the earliest, and the Babylonian records were several hundred years older than the fifteenth century, the impossibility of the Babylonians copying the Hebrew record was apparent. Still the controversy goes on.

With the recovery of documents from many countries which gave details of history that coincided generally with the biblical record, great emphasis came to be placed in the nineteenth and twentieth centuries upon the credibility of the Bible. This was strengthened greatly as excavation identified towns named in the Bible and recovered to history peoples and nations which had been relegated to legend if not to myth. Suddenly there was an upsurge of writing under the general theme "the Bible is true." Noteworthy, how-ever, was the fact that some writers were highly selective in their material. A number of writers completely ignored all material which suggested any-thing prior to the fourth millennium B.C. Such material is still being pub-lished and is dangerous because of what is omitted rather than what is written.

Earlier we outlined briefly the steps by which archaeology became dis-ciplined study worthy of being classified as science. We shall not try to settle the discussion concerning whether or not archaeology should be classified as social science, exact science, or auxiliary to the fields of history and anthro-pology. We are concerned primarily with motivation and techniques, or methods. Science is characterized first of all with objectivity. Any discovery must be examined objectively without regard to the consequences for one's

[2] See above. Chap. 1, p. 17, and Chap. 2, p. 27.

presuppositions, and in the case of archaeology, regardless of what it may tell us concerning the human story. Second, scientific procedure demands that methods and techniques which are trustworthy shall be developed. In the case of archaeology the two most important measurements are (a) sequence of occupation levels and (b) the closest possible dating of those levels. There has been a phenomenal development of techniques for measurement. One publication devotes fifty-four chapters and nearly six hundred pages to the various scientific techniques related to archaeology—eight on dating, two on climate, three on soils, six on plants, twelve on animals, twelve on man, nine on artifacts, and two on prospecting, with extensive bibliographies appended to each chapter.[3]

There is little point, however, in sharpening up techniques and being scrupulously careful in gathering dependably accurate evidence if some of the evidence is later to be ignored because it does not support one's theological presuppositions or biblical interpretation. Honest handling of the evidence should certainly be a characteristic of workers in the field of religion even if it were found in no other group. Unfortunately this has not always been true, but it is increasingly becoming so.

On the other hand, it must be confessed that in our zeal to be scrupulously honest we have sometimes paid full attention to evidence of sequential development and to measureable facts but often we have disregarded testimony from man's religious experience. It is, of course, recognized that the physical sciences deal with a different body of experience than do faith and philosophy. The social sciences supposedly make room for man's religious experience; yet even here sociologists are tempted to deal with man's religious institutions and not his religion. Histories of our own country are available which inadequately discuss the part that religion has played in our history.

In his book *The Social Sources of Denominationalism* H. Richard Niebuhr stated the difficulties he faced when he tried to understand religious movements, particularly denominationalism, simply by examining theological positions. He went on to say that he needed also to examine historical and sociological factors.[4] So great was the misunderstanding among his readers, however, that Niebuhr was constrained to say in the preface of his next book: "Though the sociological approach helped to explain why the religious stream flowed in these particular channels it did not account for the force of the stream itself; . . . while it could deal with the religion which was dependent on culture it left unexplained the faith which is independent, which is aggressive rather than passive, and which molds culture instead of being molded by it."[5] Unfortunately, some of Niebuhr's readers have again mis-

[3] Don Brothwell and Eric Higgs, editors, *Science in Archaeology* (New York: Basic Books, Inc., 1963).
[4] New York: Henry Holt and Company, 1929, Preface, pp. vii, viii.
[5] *The Kingdom of God in America* (New York: Harper & Row, Publishers, 1937), p. vii-viii.

understood. They believe that he has forsaken his former position, whereas he has reaffirmed his dependence upon both social studies and theological disciplines.

In the early part of this century so much attention was given to our dependence upon the past and the careful tracing of all sociological factors which have brought us to our present religious convictions that little room was left for man's experience with God. There has been some wholesome reaction to the so-called "escalator view of history," but a retreat to former theological conservatism is not wholesome. What is needed is recognition that man's religious experience is part of his environment. No valid picture of the past or present can be presented unless all facts of life are included insofar as they are available.

There is considerable difference between assuming that it is in the nature of man to progress and in seeing that there has been change, sometimes good, sometimes bad, but change there has been. We can trace that development from one culture to another, or from generation to generation. The student of religion seeks to know the answer to why this has happened. When he finds in man's written records that man believes that changes have come in his beliefs because of his sense of relationship to God he must examine the evidence. It is part of man's environment, and he responded to it. It is impossible to evaluate the work of the Hebrew prophets except in this way.

In the pages which follow we shall be concerned with the world in which the Bible was written. Of necessity, most of the information will relate to physical environment—the location of places of biblical interest; what happened in history to the Hebrews, as well as to their neighbors; identification of tribes and nations whose identities had been forgotten or confused; and the effects upon custom and language as nations rubbed shoulders with each other. In addition, attention will be directed to the languages and literature of the nations to whom the Hebrews were neighbors. A major contribution of archaeology lies here, for as we understand the languages current in biblical times we may discover nuances of thought in the languages of the Bible which had been lost to us. Finally, some consideration must be given to the increasing number of biblical manuscripts which have been brought to light in the last few decades. The Dead Sea Caves alone have given us manuscripts which are more than a thousand years closer to the original writings than the modern world has ever been. Attention of scholars is again centered upon the problems of transmission of the text and establishment of canon.

Obviously it is not possible to deal in detail with the various topics enumerated above. This is not our purpose. We shall seek to show the importance of archaeology in each of these areas and to give enough introductory material and illustrations in each case to demonstrate its importance for biblical understanding. Footnote references will be used freely in each case so that this section of the book, at least in part, may serve as a source book for those seeking additional information.

9.

THE LOCATION OF BIBLE SITES

Edward Robinson,[1] teacher of Hebrew at Andover Theological Seminary, Massachusetts, discovered to his dismay that he could not find enough material to write a biblical geography. Such a geography was needed, and he had for years been collecting whatever information was available. He finlly recognized that a work of this kind would be possible only after he had made extensive travels in the Bible lands themselves. This was little more than a hundred years ago.

In recent years, many geographies and atlases of Bible lands have been printed.[2] The contrast between the meager information available to Robinson and that which is currently available is staggering. Most of the change is due to the work of archaeologists in cooperation with geographers. Yet there are indications that we are only at the beginning of the expansion of knowledge concerning Bible lands.

Paul W. Lapp, currently the director of the American School of Oriental Research, Jerusalem, Jordan, has stated that Palestinian archaeology is still in its childhood.[3] He calls our attention to the fact that there are approximately five thousand recorded sites and monuments in Israel and Jordan; 3,500 were known to the department of antiquities prior to division; [4] more than a thousand were catalogued by Nelson Glueck in Transjordan; [5] and more than four hundred were listed by Glueck from his work in the Negeb [6] and other parts of Israel. Lapp goes on to state that only approximately one site in every two hundred has been excavated, and even allowing for the fact that not all sites and monuments warrant any extensive examination, it may be estimated that "major excavations have till now been carried out at only two per cent of the potential sites." [7] Yet the results for our knowledge of history and geography are impressive. There is still much to be done before our information is complete, but it is scarcely appropriate to equate Palestinian archaeology with "childhood."

William F. Albright asserts that there is maturity in our knowledge. In 1952 he stated that much development had taken place in our knowledge

---

[1] See above, Chap. 2, p. 28.

[2] See above, Chap. 2, pp. 26, 28; Chap. 7, pp. 91-92 and p. 94.

[3] "Palestine: Known but Mostly Unknown," BA (December, 1963), pp. 121-34.

[4] See Supplement No. 2, Palestine Gazette Extra-ordinary, No. 1375 (November 24, 1944). A new official schedule of Israel's registered antiquities has been announced by the Israel Information Service. The new list of sites is now 2,430 compared with 1,800 listed in 1944.

[5] Glueck, "Explorations in Eastern Palestine, IV," AASOR, XXV-XVIII, Part 1 (1951), xviii-xix.

[6] Glueck, Rivers in the Desert (New York: Farrar, Straus & Cudahy, Inc., 1959), p. x.

[7] Lapp, op. cit., p. 123.

of Palestinian chronology. In the period from 1932 to 1952 "documentary and archaeological crosschecks" from countries contiguous to Palestine, "astronomical data," and radio carbon dating of organic material have brought a stability to ancient chronology which was absent prior to 1932.[8]

The same claim may be made with regard to the location of places named in the Bible. Comparison of a recent Bible atlas with one published prior to World War II will show that more places can now be identified and fewer place names are accompanied by a question mark. An archaeological map published by the Department of Antiquities of Iraq lists more than 250 archaeological sites and rock monuments. Comparable listings have been made by Jordan, Israel, Egypt, Turkey, and by the various archaeological societies.

We speak easily of the Bible world but few who use the phrase are aware of the great extent of territory embraced by the Bible record. Advertising from both Israel and Jordan is misleading when it suggests that either country is "The Land of the Bible." It is true that much of the history of Judaism prior to Christian times had its setting in Palestine, yet the story would be incomplete without reference to the Mesopotamian setting of Abraham's family, the Egyptian background of much of Genesis and Exodus, the Babylonian settlement of the Exile, to say nothing of the countries neighboring upon Palestine from which so many invasions, infiltrations, and influences came.

The location of the Old Testament stories stretches all the way from Persia in the east to islands of the Mediterranean in the west, and from Asia Minor and Armenia in the north to Ethiopia, Sinai, and Arabia in the south. An even larger map is needed for the New Testament story, for it must include Palestine, Syria, Egypt, Asia Minor, Macedonia, Greece, Italy, and the isles of the sea—and the ambitions of Paul seem to have stretched as far as Spain.

Our primary concern in this chapter, however, is with the ways in which specific cities and villages have been identified and can now be placed upon our maps with some confidence.

Dr. Albright has enumerated five basic considerations in any attempt to locate an ancient site.[9] It may be helpful to make Albright's assertions the basis of questions. (1) What is the evidence from written sources? What are the correct names of ancient places? Each reference must be carefully checked against others, and where there is contradiction, the principles of textual criticism must be applied. (2) Where do the written sources indicate that the place is located? Obviously if one is traveling east of the River

[8] Albright, "The Bible after Twenty Years of Archaeology (1932-52)," *Religion in Life* (Autumn, 1952), pp. 537 ff.

[9] George Ernest Wright and Floyd V. Filson, editors, *The Westminster Historical Atlas to the Bible* (rev. ed., Philadelphia: The Westminster Press, 1956), p. 14.

Jordan and arrives at his destination without crossing the river, then the place must be located east and not west of the river. Identification must fit all dependable descriptions of travel. (3) Do modern place names show relationship to the ancient names? A correct knowledge of relationship between languages and the laws of changing sounds is essential to such comparisons. (4) What is the archaeological evidence? Do the dates suggested by occupation levels fit the known history of the proposed identification? (5) Are there local traditions which support the identification?

None of these questions can be ignored, but it is frequently true that answers to all five questions cannot be found in every attempt at identification. It is the fourth question to which the excavator must furnish the answers. He must, however, ever be conscious of the other four questions.

The story of the good Samaritan (Luke 10:30-37) has its setting on the road from Jerusalem down to Jericho. The modern road, with its fast moving traffic, does not follow the ancient route. Tradition locates the setting in the Wadi Fara, which at its lower end is known as the Wadi Qelt. A monastery marks the traditional place of the attack.[10] The New Testament does not locate Jericho for us. This was unnecessary at the time of the writing of the Gospels.

We referred earlier to the antiquity of the Old Testament city of Jericho,[11] but tradition has recognized that New Testament Jericho was located at a different place than Old Jericho. A modern village is located immediately to the east of the mound which contains the ruins of the Old Testament city. As one goes into this village local guides will be ready to identify spots within the village with the New Testament record. For example, the sycamore tree which Zacchaeus climbed (Luke 19:4) will be pointed out. Quite apart from the fact that the tree is obviously not nineteen hundred years old, the modern village is some distance removed from the New Testament Jericho.

In 1904 John B. Calkin, could write of Herod's magnificent city with its splendid palaces,[12] and while he recognized that there was a difference between the ancient Jericho and the modern village, he was totally unaware of the fact that the New Testament Jericho was located nearly two miles from either one of them.[13] This so-called New Testament Jericho stood at the place where the Wadi Qelt opens out into the plain. It was probably begun as a Hellenistic fort to guard the entrance to the road from the valley to Jerusalem and was finally developed into a larger community during the time of the Maccabees and the Romans. Excavations were made by James L. Kelso in 1950 and by James B. Pritchard in 1951. Among the buildings uncovered was the spectacular palace of Herod, with its grand staircase and

[10] See Plate XI.
[11] See above, Chap. 5, p. 67.
[12] *Historical Geography of the Bible Lands* (Philadelphia: The Westminster Press, 1904), p. 53.
[13] See Plate XII showing (a) Old Testament Jericho, (b) modern village, and Plate XIII, Herodian Jericho.

the many reflecting pools.[14] Here is an excellent instance in which a city was relocated. The new location carried the ancient name. Excavation alone, not tradition or written sources, has been responsible for acquainting us with the actual facts of history.

The first capital of Israel was Gibeah, but it was not until the campaigns of 1922 and 1923 at Tell el-Ful (with further work in 1933) that evidence was produced by Albright to substantiate the claims made eighty years earlier by Gross that Gibeah was to be identified with Tell el-Ful.[15] Dr. Robinson, on the basis of similarity of sound, had equated Gibeah with Jeba', a nearby village.[16]

The debate was carried on through the professional journals, and an excellent history of this is given by Albright.[17] At the suggestion of Professor Dalman, and with a gift from Miss Juliana Wood of Philadelphia, Albright undertook the excavation of Tell el-Ful. The site is about three miles north of Jerusalem, east of the Nablus Road. The hill is 2,754 feet above sea level, one of the highest points in the region, being dwarfed slightly by Nebi Samwil, about three miles to the west. It is an excellent lookout point. The name Tell el-Ful means "Hill of Beans," a description of the crop which grows best on its poor soil. The area is less than two acres.

In spite of the small area and the low agriculture value of the land it was owned by sixty-six people. The rent demanded was fantastically high, four hundred Egyptian pounds. After great difficulty for Dr. Albright, settlement was finally made for seven pounds Egyptian.

The results of the excavation have settled for most scholars the location of Gibeah of Saul. The history of Tell el-Ful coincides with the history of Gibeah as recorded in the Old Testament and in the writing of Jerome in the fourth century A.D.: (1) A village established in the twelfth century B.C. and destroyed by fire, (2) a village with a fortress in the middle of the eleventh century, (3) a rebuilding of the fortress or "castle" about 1000 B.C., (4) the erection of a watchtower on the ruins of the earlier community in the late ninth or early eighth century, (5) a rebuilt watchtower and village in late pre-exilic times, (6) re-occupation by a large village in the Persian and Hellenistic periods (500-100 B.C.), and (7) a village which lasted from shortly before the turn of the Christian Era until it was destroyed probably by Titus at the time of the destruction of Jerusalem. Jerome refers to its

[14] See photo, Plate XIII. Cf. Kelso, "The First Campaign of Excavation in New Testament Jericho," BASOR (December, 1950), pp. 11 ff; and Pritchard, "The 1951 Campaign at Herodian Jericho," BASOR (October, 1951), pp. 8-17.

[15] Cf. Theologische Studien und Kritiken (1843), p. 1082.

[16] Robinson, Biblical Researches (1841). Albright notes that Robinson accepted Gross's identification in Bibliotheca Sacra (1844), p. 598, and in the second edition of Biblical Researches (1856), I, 577-79. Cf. AASOR, IV (1924), 28.

[17] Albright, AASOR, IV (1924), 28 ff. Information is to be published shortly by Paul W. Lapp concerning the current season's excavation at Tell el-Ful. The previous findings of Albright have been corroborated in all essential details of occupational history.

utter destruction.[18] There seems to be no contradiction between the archaeological evidence and the record of scripture.

If the identification is correct, then the fortress of the second period could properly be identified with the "palace" of Saul. It is a relatively small building and designed primarily for protection, not comfort. The largest room is 14 by 23 feet. One wonders how Saul, in such small quarters, could twice miss David with his spear (I Sam. 18:10-11). The small austere building says much about the nature of the monarchy at that time. Apparently Saul, chosen for his great physique and military skill, was primarily a general in battle, not a monarch upon a throne. He was active during military threat, but when danger was gone the people were content to go their own way. It was David who built up the monarchy to national power and dignity, and it was David who first called the king "the Lord's anointed"—Hebrew for Messiah (I Sam. 24:6).

Identification of the ancient Mizpah of Benjamin has also been a matter of controversy. Because of the association of Mizpah with Samuel it has most often been identified with Nebi Samwil. It had been so identified by Edward Robinson [19] in the middle of the nineteenth century, and though there were some dissenting voices,[20] the identification had generally been accepted. In 1897 Raboisson suggested that Mizpah should be identified with Tell en-Nasbeh,[21] a large, rounded limestone hill about eight miles north of Jerusalem and west of the highway which runs north to Nablus. A similar but independent suggestion was made by Conder in 1898,[22] and in 1899 Père Vincent [23] accepted Raboisson's suggestion. In 1910 Dalman and his students Baumann and Alt accepted Raboisson's position, and Phythian-Adams endorsed the position at a meeting of the Palestine Oriental Society, December 7, 1922.[24] In the summary statement by Albright, to which we have made reference, he says "the writer is convinced that the identification with Nebi Samwil is correct, after all," [25] but he does recognize at the end of this same summary that "Tell en-Nasbeh is a promising site for excavation." [26] It was at the suggestion of Dr. Albright that William F. Badè accepted the responsibility for a series of seasons of excavation at Tell en Nasbeh. Work was continued through five seasons, 1926, 1927, 1929, 1932, and 1935. It was immediately after the season of 1935 that Dr. Badè was taken ill while returning home. He died in March of the following year. Badè had done some publication, but the final report of the excavations was

[18] See C. C. McCown, *The Ladder of Progress in Palestine* (New York: Harper & Brothers, 1943), pp. 207-8.
[19] *Biblical Researches*, II, 356 ff.
[20] See Albright, AASOR, IV (1924), Appendix I, 90 ff.
[21] Raboisson, *Les Maspeh* (Paris, 1897).
[22] Conder, PEF (1898) p. 169.
[23] Vincent, *Revue Biblique* (1899), p. 316.
[24] Albright, AASOR, IV (1924), 91.
[25] *Ibid.*, p. 91.
[26] *Ibid.*, p. 111.

brought to completion by his associates, C. C. McCown, James Muilenburg, and J. C. Wampler.[27] McCown has given an excellent summary in his volume *The Ladder of Progress in Palestine.*

Dr. Badè was convinced that he had definitely identified ancient Mizpah of Benjamin, but his associates McCown and Muilenburg do not believe that the question has been settled and cannot be until Nebi Samwil has been fully excavated. Badè rested his case upon three archaeological discoveries which he believed were sustained from Old Testament records. First, the excavated remains fit very closely the history of Mizpah. Second, twenty-eight jar handles bore the same three letters which Badè and others read as M-S-P or "Mizpah." Others, including McCown, read the letters M-S-H, the meaning of which has not been established. One example of this particular handle stamp has been found at Jericho, and one at el-Jib, otherwise the stamp is found only at Tell en-Nasbeh.[28] Finally, there is the now famous "Seal of Jaazaniah" found in Tomb 19 of the western necropolis. Badè identified the owner of the seal as Jaazaniah to whom reference is made in II Kings 25:23. The biblical record states that Jaazaniah came with others to Gedaliah at Mizpah. The seal gives the name of Jaazaniah with the title of "servant" or "officer." Badè believes that the fighting cock is a good symbol for a soldier.[29]

In addition to the artifacts mentioned much other significant information was recovered from Tell en-Nasbeh. The thickness of the walls, probably to be dated at the end of the Early Iron Age or the beginning of ninth century, was surprising, sometimes as much as fifteen to twenty feet. The original height has been estimated to have been thirty-five to forty feet.

It was not until the fourth season of work that the gate of the city was found. This was because the arrangements for rental of ground to be excavated only included a small section of the mound each season. There was only one gate to the city; this was in the east wall. It was an important discovery because it is the first ancient gateway in Palestine recovered intact. The wall coming up from the south overlapped at thirty feet to the east the wall coming down from the north. Guardhouses took up part of the space, and the gate itself had a span of a little over thirteen feet. McCown indicates that the gate "faced, not toward the south and Jerusalem, but toward the northeast, toward Bethel and the Northern Kingdom of Israel." [30] Apparently McCown has misunderstood the significance of the gateway's defenses. The city stood to the west of the roadway which runs north and south. A gate in the east wall was in its most logical position for traffic going either north or south.

[27] *Tell en Nasbeh* (Jerusalem: ASOR, 1943); and cf., Muilenburg, "Mizpah," *IDB,* pp. 407-9.

[28] Pritchard, *Hebrew Inscriptions and Stamps from Gibeon* (Philadelphia: University Museum, 1959), fig. 11:1.

[29] Badè, *A Manual of Excavation in the Near East* (Berkeley, Calif.: University of California Press, 1934), "The Seal of Jaazaniah," pp. 75-77; and Badè, "The Seal of Jaazaniah," *ZAW,* V. (1933), pp. 150 ff.

[30] McCown, *op. cit.,* p. 211.

The overlap in the walls was for military defense. Any man approaching the city gate was forced by the overlapping walls to turn so that his shield arm would be ineffective. His weapon arm was exposed to the guards on the inner wall.[31]

Another feature of the gate complex is worth noting. In the space between the walls, but north of the actual gateway, there were stone benches. This was the place of business "in the gate" to which reference is frequently made in scripture. Here was the "seat of the judges" in the gate, the place where contracts were made and legally witnessed, and perhaps the place at which some of the prophetic messages were spoken. Dr. Badè confessed to some of us that his work was seriously hampered after he released an announcement to the press concerning the discovery of the gate. He was besieged with visitors, many of whom came for sentimental and not archaeological reasons. A company of rabbis presented themselves, and while Badè recited in Hebrew the story of Samuel's visit to Mizpah (I Samuel 7) tears streamed down the beards of the visitors and they joined in the recitation. At least they were convinced that they were sitting in the seat of the judges of ancient Mizpah.

Finally, we should note that Badè called attention to the cultural significance of the Seal of Jaazaniah. He cited it as evidence that the chicken, originally an east Indian jungle fowl, must have been known in Palestine at least as early as the seventh century B.C., even though it is not mentioned in the Old Testament.[32]

The story of the identification of el-Jib with Old Testament Gibeon is unique in the annals of modern archaeological research. The identification had been proposed by Edward Robinson as early as 1838. His decision was based upon the agreement of evidence from biblical descriptions, classical references, and the modern name of the community. It has sometimes been pointed out that Robinson only spent forty minutes in his examination of the mound, but it should not be forgotten that Robinson had made careful preparation before his visit, and he was convinced as he saw the site that it fitted his gathered evidence. His identification of the "Pool of Gibeon" was incorrect, however, as we shall see later.

Robinson's identification of el-Jib did not go unchallenged. Albrecht Alt [33] reexamined the evidence in 1926 and came to the conclusion that Tell en Nasbeh was ancient Gibeon and el-Jib should be identified with Beeroth. With the discoveries at Tell en-Nasbeh [34] and the publication of results in 1947 it was apparent that Alt was mistaken. In 1953 he admitted that his identification made in 1926 was incorrect and proposed that Gibeon should be identified instead with el-Bireh, but he maintained his position that el-Jib was ancient Beeroth. Because of his great standing and influence among

---

[31] See drawing 2, p. 202; cf. Kenyon: Archaeology in The Holy Land, pp. 248-50.
[32] Badè, Manual of Excavation, pp. 76-77.
[33] Alt, Palästinajahrbuch, XXII (1926), 11 ff.
[34] See above, Chap. 9, pp. 107-8.

Old Testament scholars it was recognized that the question of el-Jib's identi-fication had to be re-examined.

James B. Pritchard reports that his choice of el-Jib as a site to be excavated came out of a conversation in 1955 with G. Lankester Harding, then director of the department of antiquities, Jordan. Work was started the following summer (1956) and was continued in the summers of 1957, 1959, and 1960. In addition to reports in professional journals and through the press, Dr. Pritchard has presented the results of his four campaigns in his very readable book *Gibeon: Where the Sun Stood Still.*[35]

Four campaigns have made it possible to say with little fear of contradic-tion that Gibeon has been identified with the town of el-Jib. It is a hill 2,500 feet above sea level and about six miles north west of Jerusalem in a direct line, but eight miles by road.[36] In addition, much information has been obtained concerning the history of the community, some of which is not included in the scriptural record, and insight has been obtained concerning manufacturing processes and the trade of the community.

Its strategic military importance has been emphasized by the fact that in the struggle between the British and the Turks in 1917 this hill was an outpost and bastion of the Turks. Not only was an unexploded British shell found three feet below the surface, but the Turks had "dug in" and com-pletely destroyed the stratigraphy in one part of the hill. Archaeological excavation clearly showed that Gibeon was strongly fortified in ancient days and had been made safe against siege.

No community can long withstand siege unless it has adequate food and water. El-Jib today has no water to spare, and only careful conservation makes it possible for the village to survive. Three significant discoveries concerning the water system of ancient Gibeon were made by Pritchard and his co-workers in their first season of work. First, the large reservoir in the valley northeast of the mound was excavated under the leadership of H. Neil Richardson. This reservoir had been identified by Edward Robinson as the "pool of Gibeon." He had estimated its size to be 100 by 120 feet. It actually measures 37 by 60 feet. Excavation revealed that it had been constructed in Roman times and was 6 to 8 feet in depth. Four coats of plaster were typical-ly Roman. This reservoir did not exist in the days of the monarchy. The "Pool of Gibeon" had to be sought elsewhere.

After only three days of work in the first season the excavators made a second discovery. The cover of an ancient tunnel was found which led from inside the city wall to a spring outside the city, a distance of 148 feet in a horizontal line and to a depth of eighty feet below the street surface of the city. Tunneling had been done under the city wall through solid rock. Outside the city wall the tunnel had been made by cutting a deep trench and then covering the passageway with stone slabs and soil. Altogether ninety-

[35] Princeton, N. J.: Princeton University Press, 1962.
[36] See plate XIV, el-Jib.

three steps had been cut along the passageway. In addition, two other provisions had been made to ensure an adequate water supply. A large cistern had been shaped at the bottom of the tunnel, thirty-six feet long and fourteen feet deep. A water channel was cut back into the hill along the water course for 112 feet.[37] Protection for the city was completed by placing a solid stone door which could be closed and barred in time of attack at the lower end of the water system. Parallels to such water access tunnels are known from Jerusalem, Megiddo, Ibleam, and Gezer, in Palestine; Mycenae and Athens in Greece; and Susa in Persia.[38]

The importance of this water tunnel cannot be overestimated, but its description does not account for the references to the "pool of Gibeon." In II Sam. 2:12-17 there is an account of a conflict between the forces of Saul and David. These forces sat on opposite sides of the "pool of Gibeon." Later twelve men from each side were chosen to "play before us," actually to fight. This means that there was considerable room on either side of the pool. Neither the water tunnel nor the cistern fit the biblical description.

Again the expedition was amazingly successful. During the first season it made a third discovery concerning the ancient water supply of Gibeon. Not far from the entrance to the water access tunnel the rim of a pool was uncovered. It was assumed at first that this was probably a shallow basin not more than a few feet in depth, but as work progressed it was soon discovered that it was much bigger. By the end of the first season the workers had dug to a depth of thirty-five feet and had uncovered forty-two steps. Only the southern third of the pool had been excavated with the result that the narrowing trench made further work impossible. In the next season work again proceeded from the top. Such was the enormity of the task that the American system of working two shifts a day instead of the normal work day was put into effect. Pritchard reported that after 23,000 man hours of labor, "the bottom was finally reached at the end of August in 1957." [39] The "bottom" was eighty feet below "street level." The cutting of the rock began as a cylindrical shaft, thirty-seven feet across and thirty-five feet deep, with a stairway cut clockwise on the inside of the shaft. It then changed to a tunnel which bored through the rock to a depth of forty-five feet below the bottom of the cylinder. In the floor of the cylinder, holes had been cut to admit light to the stepped tunnel. The steps of the grand staircase were about five feet wide, and a stone balustrade 1½ feet thick was cut on the inside of the steps.

Dr. Pritchard has cautiously identified this cylindrical cut as the "pool of Gibeon." It is certainly true that the area surrounding the top of the "pool" is large enough to accommodate the body of men referred to in the biblical record, but serious question must be raised as to whether or not this opening can be designated a "pool." There is the possibility, suggested by Pritchard,

[37] See Pritchard, *Gibeon*, pp. 56 ff.
[38] See "Water shafts," *IDB*, pp. 815-16.
[39] Pritchard, *Gibeon*, pp. 67-68; see also plate XV.

that the original cut may have stopped at the thirty-five foot level and only later when the water table dropped was it found necessary to make the further cut to the lower level. This assumes, of course, that a spring or source of water once existed not lower than the thirty-five foot level, a geological improbability considering the surrounding terrain. It is, however, a question which should be checked. Pritchard noted, "Obviously certainty of identification is impossible." [40]

It is apparent from the relationship of the structures that building proceeded in the following order: (1) The great city wall, (2) the cylindrical stairway of access, and (3) the tunnel of access which was cut under the city wall, but was also turned to avoid cutting into the wall of the cylindrical stairway. From evidence at the base of the defense wall Pritchard estimated that the wall was erected not earlier than the beginning of the Iron Age, about 1200 B.C. The grand stairwell could have been cut about the same time, and the access tunnel about the tenth century.

Careful examination of the walls of the access tunnel shows that they have been smoothed by the hands of water carriers as they sought to steady themselves. This, together with the fact that the stair treads were well worn with the passage of feet, indicates long usage of the tunnel. On the other hand, the steps of the grand stairwell show relatively little usage, and apparently the project was not highly successful. The cutting, however, had provided stone for the development of the city wall. The opening was left uncovered for a half millennium and seems to have served as the city dump. The broken pots and other material recovered give much insight concerning the city's history and cultural changes. To some of these we shall refer in a later chapter.

Most important are the many jar handles which were recovered from the stairwell and which bear testimony to the community's name and the names of some of the merchants. This city manufactured wine and produced olive oil. These products were shipped to other communities. The products were shipped in large clay jars on the handles of which the names of the manufacturers were stamped. This was a well-established practice throughout Palestine.

Whether the name was stamped so that the empty container could be returned, or whether the stamped name served the same purpose as a modern label to guarantee the quality of the contents has been constantly debated. For our immediate purposes it is not necessary to solve this problem. The important fact is that the labels carried the name of the community of Gibeon. If these jars had been imported from other communities there would be many names, not one. Only the name of Gibeon appears. It has, therefore, been claimed by the excavators that el-Jib is the site of the ancient city of Gibeon. The issue now seems to be settled.

The locations enumerated so far are confined to a relatively small area in

[40] *Ibid.,* p. 160.

1. **Expanded knowledge of Hebrew history.** The bald statement in II Kings 18 that "In the fourteenth year of King Hezekiah Sennacherib king of Assyria came up against all the fortified cities of Judah and took them" is amplified by Sennacherib's own record on this six-sided clay prism in the British Museum. It lists his first eight campaigns, including the third, *c.* 701 B.C. "I then besieged Hezekiah of Judah who had not submitted to my rule and I captured forty-six of his large towns and fortresses. . . . Hezekiah himself, like a caged bird, I besieged in Jerusalem, his royal city. . . ."

3. Further information about the surrender of Lachish has been provided by later archaeological investigation of the city site itself. In 1932 the Wellcome–Marston expedition under J. L. Starkey found that the city walls as excavated closely resembled those shown in the Nineveh relief. The discovery of numbers of olive stones during the excavation (right) led to the conclusion that the siege took place in the autumn of 700 B.C., an example of the way in which archaeologists obtain information from apparently unimportant discoveries.

2. Sennacherib also celebrated his victories in Judah by decorating the walls of his palace at Nineveh with magnificent reliefs. These were uncovered by Henry Layard in the middle of the nineteenth century, a period when the success of an archaeological expedition was gauged by the spoils it brought back to European museums. In this relief Sennacherib is receiving the surrender of Lachish.

4. Both the Bible and Sennacherib's prism record that Hezekiah paid heavy tribute to the Assyrian king, including "thirty talents of gold". The Hebrew kings had long been obtaining gold from Ophir as this ostracon or inscribed potsherd of the ninth century B.C. records: "Gold of Ophir to Beth Horon, thirty shekels".

5. **Biblical parallels.** The Babylonian account of the Flood, one of the fragments translated by George Smith, who was sent to Mesopotamia to find cuneiform tablets by a London newspaper in 1873.

6. The Hammurabi Code, inscribed on a stone now in the Louvre, contains a code of laws which compare and contrast with those of the Hebrews. The upper portion of the stone shows Hammurabi, a Babylonian king, standing before the sun god, Shamash, to receive the code of laws.

7. The brick tower at Susa (Biblical Shushan) where the Hammurabi Code was found.

8. **New knowledge of ancient languages.** The first step towards deciphering an ancient language has often been the discovery of a bilingual or trilingual inscription. The most famous of these fortunate discoveries is the Rosetta stone. It contains three versions of a decree of the priests of Memphis, conferring divine honours on Ptolemy V Ephiphanes, one in the "classical" Egyptian language in hieroglyphs, one in the contemporary idiom of Egyptian in the cursive writing known as Demotic, and one in Greek, which enabled the others to be deciphered.

9. Once the first steps have been taken in deciphering a language the scholar can make use of ancient aids to interpretation such as this Assyrian dictionary which lists foreign and rare words with their common Assyrian equivalents.

10. The trilingual inscription —Persian, Babylonian and Elamite—on the Rock of Behistun was recorded by Henry Rawlinson, who risked his life many times to take squeezes of the inscription which is carved on a rock-face 350 feet above the plain. Rawlinson's knowledge of Persian enabled him to read part of the inscription and this in turn led to the decipherment and translation of Babylonian.

11–14. **Excavation techniques.** Sir Leonard Woolley carried out extensive excavations at Ur of the Chaldees—identified in 1854 from cuneiform cylinders deposited in the walls of its ziggurat (above)—and recovered this magnificent harp of 2600 B.C. The unusual shape of two holes in the ground prompted Woolley to pour in plaster-of-paris to fill the place of decayed wood and to recreate the instrument's shape. In photograph 13 (above right) the stick marking one of the holes through which the plaster was poured can still be seen in the top left-hand corner. The sound-box, with its mosaic border and gold bull's head, has been covered with wax and muslin to strengthen it for removal. (Below right.) The earth has been removed from the plaster cast, revealing the shape of the upright and its ornaments.

15. Modern archaeological techniques are well illustrated in Miss Kathleen Kenyon's work at Jericho. Here a series of carefully controlled trenches has been dug to obtain the maximum of information about the site, yet leaving undisturbed sections for the archaeologists and techniques of the future. Trench 1 (above) shows successive layers of walls and fortifications.

16. One of the magnificent plastered skulls found at Jericho.

17. A Middle Bronze Age tomb from Jericho.

18 and 19. Biblical manuscripts. Few discoveries of early manuscripts have been more sensational than that of the Dead Sea Scrolls. (Above) Wadi Qumran showing the entrance to Cave IV which contained a large quantity of manuscript material. (Below) A portion of a scroll containing Isaiah.

20. An aerial view of the ruins of the Essene settlement at Qumran.

21. The crack in the cistern steps caused by the earthquake of 31 B.C.

22-24. Recovered nations. Archaeology has provided almost all the knowledge we have of peoples who lived on the periphery of the Hebrew world—the Sumerians, the Babylonians, the Assyrians, the Nabateans, the Hittites. Most of our knowledge of the Nabateans comes from investigation of Petra, their trading city in the heart of the mountains, with its tortuous entrance through the Syk, a long winding cleft in the rocks. (Left) The façade of "The Treasury", whose glowing colour has caused the epithet "rose-red" to be applied to the whole city. (Below) The Palace Tomb. (Above right) The Temple of the Snake.

25 (below right). The Hittites were an unidentified people until scholars began to link Bible references to the monuments and sculptures found in northern Syria and throughout Turkey. This led to large-scale excavation which revealed the existence of a Hittite Empire with widespread influence and power and uncovered many magnificent monuments, such as this procession of gods at Boghazkoi, the Hittite capital.

25.

26–27. Our knowledge of Biblical personages has been expanded by archaeology. Excavations at Dhiban (Biblical Dibon) brought to light the Mesha or Moabite Stone (below) on which Mesha, king of Moab, vaunts of his victories over Ahab.

28. A limestone figure of a king found at Amman shows us what a contemporary of Ahab and Mesha looked like.

Jordan, but they are representative of other sites in Palestine. Many modern atlases and geographies carry both ancient and modern names on maps showing excavation sites as well as in the indexes; e.g., the following are some of the identifications shown in Wright and Filson, *The Westminster Historical Atlas to the Bible*, Plate XVIII, "Excavated Sites in Modern Palestine"— Tell el-Hesi (Eglon), Tell ed-Duweir (Lachish), Tell Beit Mirsim (Debir), Tell Jezer (Gezer), Beitîn (Bethel), Seilûn (Shiloh), Balâtah (Shechem), Sebastye (Samaria), Jerash (Gerasa), et cetera.[41]

In lands where writing was prevalent much earlier than it was in Palestine foundation deposits and building inscriptions have aided considerably in identifying cities. Most of these cities, however, are not specifically mentioned in scripture. Their identification is important chiefly because such identification enables us to write the histories of the countries involved much more accurately and intelligently. Some cities, such as Ur, Nineveh, Babylon, Damascus, Accad (Agade), Asshur, Erech (Uruk), Shushan (Susa), Rameses, and On, have been located by one or more of the tests outlined by Albright. To some of these we shall refer in Chapters 10 to 13. Of immediate importance for our present consideration are the discoveries made in Mesopotamia and Egypt of monuments and documents which help to clarify Palestinian geography.

From 1932 to 1938 James Leslie Starkey excavated at Tell ed-Duweir with funds provided by Sir Henry Wellcome and H. Dunscombe Colt (1932-33). Starkey had been trained by Sir Flinders Petrie and applied Petrie's methodology rigidly. In 1935 Starkey discovered a dozen sherds upon which letters had been written in good biblical Hebrew.[42] Most startling was Letter Number IV which contained the identification of the mound as ancient Lachish. The writer, a military leader in the field, had sent "a field dispatch" saying that his unit was "watching for the signals of Lachish, according to all the indications which my lord hath given, for we cannot see Azekah." The biblical record (II Kings 18:13-15) does not mention Sennacherib's capture of Lachish specifically. It is apparently included with "all the fortified cities of Judah," but the record does go on to state that King Hezekiah sent a message of capitulation to Sennacherib at Lachish and a message demanding payment of a severe penalty was sent by the Assyrian monarch from Lachish to Hezekiah in Jerusalem. Additional confirmation of the details of the biblical record is contained in "The Oriental Institute Prism of Sennacherib" which states that Hezekiah paid "30 talents of gold" to Sennacherib.[43]

---

[41] Brief descriptions of the more important sites, together with references to source materials, may be found in Kathleen Kenyon, *Archaeology in the Holy Land* (London: Ernest Benn, Ltd., 1960), pp. 304-320. Summaries may also be found in G. Lankester Harding, *The Antiquities of Jordan* (London: Lutterworth Press, 1959), pp. 54-184; and G. Frederick Owen, *Archaeology and the Bible* (Westwood, N. J.: Fleming H. Revell Company, 1961), pp. 261-327.

[42] Eighteen letters were found in 1935 and three more in 1938. Cf. H. Torczyner, *Lachish I*, "The Lachish Letters" (1938).

[43] *ANET*, p. 288.

Further confirmation of the identification came as the excavated city walls were checked with bas reliefs which had been cut into the walls of the palace of Sennacherib in Nineveh. The double walls, the defense towers, the general structure of the city's defenses shown on the Nineveh bas reliefs are in startling agreement with the structures uncovered at Tell ed-Duweir. There can be no doubt of the identification. It is apparent also from the Nineveh records on wall and tablet that the conquest of Lachish was considered by Sennacherib to be one of the most significant victories in his campaign of 701 B.C. The city, however, slowly recovered from its defeat. King Manasseh may have helped finance the rebuilding of the defenses (II Chr. 33:11-14). A new attack was launched by Nebuchadnezzar first in 597 and again from 588 to 586 B.C. At that time there was considerable fire, and the flames were fed by the olive trees taken from the city's slopes (Jer. 34:7). It was in this period that the Lachish letters noted above were written. Archaeology, in this case, has not only aided in the identification of an Old Testament city, but also has added to the historical details of the Old Testament record.

10.

EXPANDED KNOWLEDGE
OF HEBREW HISTORY

Christian classification of the books of the Old Testament designates the section Joshua through Esther as "Books of History." Jewish classification refers to the books Joshua through Kings as "Former Prophets" and the remainder of the so-called historical section, including Ruth, as "Writings." The Jewish classification is more satisfactory because it recognizes that the content is not history per se but illustrations from history used to demonstrate religious truths.

It has long been recognized by scholars that the Yahwist writer was a careful collector of historical information, in contrast to the Deuteronomic writer who was more concerned with castigating "that which was evil" in a monarch's reign than in giving the facts of history. In addition, scholars have been confronted with the problem of distinguishing between actual facts of history and what the writers and the people believed happened in history. It is becoming increasingly clear that the conquest of Palestine was not the result of one major invasion, but the result of at least one major thrust and perhaps a series of minor infiltrations. In addition, it seems likely that the saga of the deliverance from Egypt was the experience of only a portion of the tribes and was later expanded and adopted as the "deliverance of the twelve tribes." It is the function of the historian to examine the evidence and to provide us, if possible, with the facts of history.

We shall be concerned here with the relationship between history (Geschichte) and "salvation-history" (Heilsgeschichte) only insofar as it is necessary to stress that the function of the historian is to recover the facts of history. The historian may be able to say whether or not the Hebrews crossed the Red Sea (Exod. 14:10-31). The theologian interprets the dividing of the waters and the safe crossing of the Israelites as acts of God. We should note that it is the linguist and exegete who inform us whether the Hebrew should be translated "Red Sea" or "Sea of Reeds (suph)." George Ernest Wright and Reginald Fuller have titled their book *The Book of the Acts of God*.[1] Wright, who did the Old Testament section, recognized that this is the major thrust of the writers of the Old Testament. They were not historians, nor even annalists. They were religious teachers. In fact the Bible refers us for further information to the written records of kings (II Kings 20:20).

The writers of such books as Samuel and Kings also were concerned almost exclusively with a few key characters, the top leadership, the major battles, and the attitude of leaders toward Yahwism. It is only occasionally that we

[1] Garden City, N.Y.: Doubleday & Company, Inc., 1957.

glimpse what is happening to the ordinary citizens, their wives, and their slaves. Just in recent years has it been recognized that history is people and what is happening to them. In the early days of excavation an archaeologist counted himself fortunate if he uncovered a palace or a temple. Here he could expect to recover the "richest" materials. Today the excavator makes sure that he gets a cross section of a community so that he may have as complete a picture of the entire community as possible.

The recovery of the history of the Hebrew people and their neighbors has, therefore, presented some real problems to the Bible scholar because of the nature of the source materials in scripture. Add to all this imperfect chronological information and the task of the historian is compounded. Chronological problems are of two kinds. First, as we noted in the opening chapter, there was no fixed point of reference by which all dates could be computed, and therefore, dates were given in terms of the king's own reign or in relationship to natural catastrophies.[2] Isaiah dated his call "in the year that King Uzziah died"; that was a significant and precise year for Isaiah's hearers, but it is not a precise date for us until the historian has pinpointed the year of King Uzziah's death.

A second problem results from the fact that each king counted his term of office from the time that he became either king or co-regent, and of course his chronicler continued counting until the time of his death. In many cases this meant an overlap of several years with the reign of his predecessor and of his successor. The problem may be diagrammed as follows:

King A	762 _____ 731			31 yrs.
King B	740 _____ 696			44 yrs.
King C	701 _____ 670			31 yrs.
				106 yrs.
King B was co-regent for 9 years				14
King C was co-regent for 5 years				
				92 yrs.
Actual time span from 762 to 670 B.C.				92 yrs.

Earlier biblical historians failed to recognize this problem of chronology, with the result that by "dead reckoning" much longer periods were assumed. By cross checking the dates of Mesopotamian and Egyptian kings who are named as contemporaries of the biblical kings it is possible to arrive at more exact figures.

Psychologists tell us that man regularly practices "selective inattention." We learn not to hear or heed disagreeable or unwanted sounds. This applies also to knowledge. A major political campaign always gives the incumbent the opportunity to stress the successes of his administration and to forget

[2] See Chap. 1, p. 16.

116

conveniently the failures. This was true in the ancient world. Many a military record has been written which recounts the magnificent successes of the writer's army; yet when a check is made of positions at the end of the battle it is seen that the victorious army has retreated considerably. This, of course, may be interpreted, as in modern warfare, as "strategic withdrawal." Comparison of the accounts of both sides in the conflict may help us to reconstruct what actually happened.

A similar pattern of selective memory is found with individuals, particularly elderly people. I live in a section of the United States in which the establishment of cities and the erection of churches and synagogues is still within the memory of the older citizens in the communities. Young historians, therefore, count themselves fortunate when they can interview "primary sources." Yet they have discovered frequently that elderly people are unconsciously highly selective in their information. Not only do they tend to emphasize the more pleasing experiences and to forget the disagreeable, but there is also a magnification and adornment of the "good old days." It frequently happens that memory's picture of the old town hall is entirely too big to be placed on the stumps of the old foundation which has been uncovered. Checks with newspapers, diaries, minutes of meetings, photographs, et cetera, enable us to reconstruct a more faithful record of the past.

The historian recognizes that any record is a primary source for the period *in* which it is written, but only a secondary source for the period *about* which it is written. The farther the written material is removed from the period about which information is being given the less reliable it becomes unless the record is based upon credible source material. On the other hand, we may well be warned by Cyrus H. Gordon that the patriarchal records are sociologically true to the period from which they purport to come.[3] The historian must know the nature of the material with which he is dealing, but always he must check and cross check his information because he knows that no matter how dependable the source may be it is the unusual record which is completely free from error.

None of the sources referred to in the books of Samuel, Kings, and Chronicles has been found, but other historical records of equal importance have been recovered by the archaeologist. From these records it is possible to obtain help in reconstructing a history of the Hebrew people. Information is available concerning at least five areas: (1) The historicity of key figures may in some cases be established because they are listed in nonbiblical and non-Hebrew documents; (2) it is now possible to establish some specific dates in biblical history because of references made to now well-established events and persons in countries which were neighbors to the Hebrews; (3) details often omitted from the biblical stories can frequently be recovered

[3] *Introduction to Old Testament Times* (Ventnor, N. J.; Ventnor Publications, Inc., 1953), p. 102.

117

from documents contemporary to those events; (4) information is available from clay and stone tablets which enables us to understand political ties and military engagements and thus obtain a better perspective of the Hebrew record; and (5) we can now go farther in settling some basic questions concerning major events in the saga of Israel.

Before turning briefly to these five areas some definition may be helpful. A history of the Hebrews or a history of Israel differs from the ordinary history of a country for the reason that this is the history of a people, not a land, and this people moved on more than one occasion from one country to another. It is the history of a people bound together by religious ties, a people who, in spite of military and political defeat, and regardless of enslavement and vassaldom, retained an entity as a distinctive religious culture. It has been the accepted pattern to use the term "history of the Hebrews" to cover the period from the beginning of their story down to the Babylonian Exile, or even down to the end of Old Testament times. The title "history of the Jews" is used to cover the period beginning with the Babylonian Exile and continuing at least through to the foundation of Christianity, ofttimes continuing the story into modern times. The important distinction is that the term Judaism is traditionally used to designate a movement which began at the time of the Babylonian Exile. Finally we must note that there is disagreement among historians concerning the beginning point of the story of the Hebrew people. Martin Noth,[4] for example, agrees with Albrecht Alt that the true beginning of the story of Israel must be at the time of the confederation, or amphictyony, [5] of the twelve tribes in the land of Canaan. On the other hand, John Bright [6] prefers to begin the story with the migration of the Hebrew patriarchs from Mesopotamia. Both men recognize that the story of Israel is unintelligible unless seen against its environment, and both draw heavily upon the histories of the surrounding nations. Johannes Pedersen,[7] while dealing essentially with the institutions of the Hebrews, depends heavily upon historical background. In turn he is concerned to etch in the important Canaanite background and history.[8] Each of these authors tells the story of a people, not a country.

If history is concerned with individuals as well as the group, then one method of validating the trustworthiness of the record is to establish the historicity of the individuals named. This is possible in many cases of in-

---

[4] The History of Israel (2nd ed.; New York: Harper & Row, Publishers, 1960), pp. 5-6; translated from Geschichte Israels by Stanley Godman.

[5] Some Old Testament scholars are using this term to designate a confederation of tribes or clans bound together with religious ties or covenant relationship to a common deity.

[6] A History of Israel (Philadelphia: The Westminster Press, 1959), p. 17. For Bright's criticism of Noth's delimitation, see his Early Israel in Recent History Writing (Naperville, Ill.: Alec R. Allenson, Inc., 1956), pp. 34-55.

[7] Israel: Its Life and Culture (2 vols., rev. ed.; London: Oxford University, Press).

[8] Ibid., I, 1-11.

dividuals named in the Bible. First of all there is the listing in non-Hebrew records of Hebrew kings. In the inscriptions of Shalmaneser III he spoke of Ahab the Israelite, and on the Black Obelisk he recorded the tribute he received from "Jehu, son of Omri." Tiglath-pileser III received tribute from Jehoahaz and made proper note on clay tablets. This same monarch lists Menahem as one of the kings he "overwhelmed." Tiglath-pileser refers to the Northern Kingdom as "Omri-Land" and tells of the overthrow of Pekah by the people and Tiglath-pileser's appointment of Hoshea as the new king.[9] There is record of constant contact between Assyria and Israel during the ninth and the eighth centuries B.C. until the final defeat of the Northern Kingdom. During the earlier period in which the United Kingdom had been established there is no biblical record of contact with Assyria, nor is there Assyrian record. This is in agreement with the fact that during the eleventh and tenth centuries the Assyrian Empire was on the decline and no forays were made into Palestine.

It is only after the fall of the Northern Kingdom that much attention is given by Assyria to Judah. Several records include references to Kings Ahaz, Hezekiah, and Manasseh. Sennacherib's account of his attack on the city of Jerusalem has been preserved in that king's annals.[10] He tells us that he held Hezekiah prisoner in Jerusalem, like a bird in a cage, and laid seige to forty-six cities altogether. From the administrative documents of Nebuchadnezzar II we have confirmation of Jehoiachin's imprisonment in Babylon (II Kings 24:12-15) and the added information that a quota of oil was provided from the royal treasury for the prisoner.

Just as there is confirmation in clay tablets of the historicity of many biblical figures, so also there is evidence from papyri, stone, and clay that foreign kings listed in scripture were historical figures. Prior to the finding of these ancient documents such names as Sennacherib and Nebuchadnezzar were merely names, not recognizable people. Most dictionaries and encyclopedias prior to the end of the nineteenth century had little information to guide the reader. Today we have rather full histories, and the newer dictionaries containing biographies are replete with information concerning kings and queens of Babylonia, Assyria, Neo-Babylonia (Chaldea), Egypt, et cetera. Chapters fifteen through nineteen in II Kings list knowledge of or dealings with every Assyrian monarch from 745 B.C. to 669 B.C., with the exception of Sargon II, and he is mentioned in Isa. 20:1. In turn, Tiglath-pileser III, Shalmaneser V, Sargon II, Sennacherib, and Esarhaddon appear. There is reference to the fall of the city of Nineveh, capital of the Assyrians, in Nahum and in Zeph. 2:13; then historical attention is given to Nebuchadnezzar, the

---

[9] ANET, p. 284.
[10] Oriental Institute Prism of Sennacherib, and the Taylor Prism; D. D. Luckenbill, *The Annals of Sennacherib* (OIP, II, 1924); Luckenbill, Ancient Records, II, ¶¶ 233 ff.; and ANET, p. 287.
[11] ANET, p. 308.

Neo-Babylonia king (II Kings 24–25). Jeremiah frequently mentions this monarch and the books of Ezra-Nehemiah and Esther also make mention of him. Attention is next turned to Cyrus (Isa. 44:28–45:1, II Chr. 36:22, and in Ezra and Daniel), who issued a decree permitting the Jews to return to their homeland. After their return to Palestine Darius I became the important monarch in their world, and reference is made to him in the prophets Haggai and Zechariah, and also in Ezra. Darius II is named by Nehemiah and Daniel. The biblical record draws upon the history of neighboring peoples as it impinges upon their own. Just as in the case of their own history not all historical references are precisely correct, but there is no mistaking the fact that they are recording history as they know it and are drawing upon that history to illustrate their religious teachings and convictions.

Precise dating of the reigns of kings and major events in history would not seem to be too important to the general reader of the Bible, yet occasionally exact dating can be helpful to understanding. In the older textbooks the date of the fall of Nineveh is given as 606 B.C., but we now know through C. J. Gadd [12] that the city was destroyed in 612. The question may be raised, apart from desire for accuracy what difference does it make? The date is specifically related to the history of the Hebrew people. The Kingdom of Judah had been spared the destruction which came to the north because they had accepted the inevitable and became a vassal state of Assyria. In the year 609 Josiah suddenly moved out to Megiddo and met the Egyptian army. It has been assumed that he did this because of his commitment to the Assyrians. By trying to cut off the Egyptians at the Megiddo pass he would be helping the beleaguered city of Nineveh. If Nineveh had already been destroyed, however, then Josiah's action had no relationship to his vassalage to Assyria. On the contrary, Josiah seems to be aware that the country to the north which once had belonged to the United Kingdom of the Hebrews was now without recognized political control. If, therefore, he could prevent the Egyptians from moving north through the pass he could perhaps regain the territory for the Hebrews. Unfortunately he arrived too late and was unable to control the pass. He was met by the Egyptians in open country and was mortally wounded in battle (II Kings 23:28-30a). Thus ended a dream of Josiah, a dream which seems to have had its origin with his selection by the prophetic party which put him upon the throne. The dream was given encouragement by the words of Huldah the prophetess when the newly found scroll was brought to her and she gave it her approval. It was further enlarged as Josiah put into effect a great religious reform which was favored by Huldah and the prophetic party. It seems within reason to infer that Josiah became possessed of a dream to restore the kingdom to its ancient glory and extent of territory. If he could have done this he would have fulfilled at least the political aspects of messianic expectation as commonly held.

[12] *The Fall of Assyria* (London: British Academy, 1923).

S. J. De Vries in his article "Chronology of the OT" [13] has listed eight other events which are closely dated in Assyrian and Neo-Babylonian sources, and they aid considerably in establishing chronology during the period of the monarchy in the history of Israel. It was in the year 841 B.C. that Jehu paid tribute to Shalmaneser III.[14] Sennacherib records that it was in the fourth year of his reign that he beseiged Hezekiah in Jerusalem, that is in 701 B.C.[15] Of particular interest is the dating of the capture of Jerusalem by Nebuchadnezzar (Nebuchadrezzar) II on 2 Adar of his seventh year; that is March 16, 597 B.C.[16]

Assyrian records were carefully kept. The Assyrians coordinated their records with the solar year. They adopted a system of assigning to each year the name of an official, who was known as the "limmu." In addition, notation was made of outstanding political events in each year, and in some cases reference is made to an eclipse of the sun which astronomers calculate occurred on June 15, 763 B.C. Assyriologists have been able to compile a list of these named years, which they designate "eponyms," and which cover 244 years (892-648 B.C.). These records are highly dependable and have been used by Old Testament scholars to establish dates in Hebrew history, particularly during the period of the monarchy.[17]

While there is much to help us in establishing more exact dates for the period of the monarchy, the same kind of evidence is not available for other periods, especially for the years prior to the tenth century B.C., at least not to the same extent. Quite apart from the fact that we hold very different ideas and have additional knowledge concerning the age of creation and the development of the universe, the data given in the Bible are inexact, and different versions give different figures. The traditional Hebrew text (Masoretic) gives 1656 years as the time which elapsed between creation and the time of the flood, while the Septuagint says 2242, and the Samaritan Pentateuch records only 1307 years. Similarly the period from the flood to the birth of Abraham is given different lengths of time; the MT records only 290 years, the LXX says 940 years, and the Sam. 1070. Again the period from Abraham's birth to the Exodus is differently dated because of the difference given for the length of the Egyptian bondage. The LXX and Sam. each have 215 years and the MT has 430 years. Thus the total time from the birth of Abraham to the Exodus is given in the MT as 720 years and in the other

[13] *IDB*, pp. 580-99.
[14] *ANET*, p. 280; *IDB*, loc. cit., p. 585.
[15] *Ibid.*
[16] Donald J. Wiseman, *Chronicles of Chaldean Kings*, pp. 33, 73.
[17] Edwin Richard Thiele, *The Mysterious Numbers of the Hebrew Kings* (Chicago: University of Chicago Press, 1951); Thiele, "A Comparison of the Chronological Data of Israel and Judah," *Vetus Testamentum*, IV (1954), 185-95; and W. F. Albright, *The Biblical Period from Abraham to Ezra* (New York: Harper & Row, Publishers, 1963), pp. 116-18.

two as 505 years. In the period from the Judges to the time of the monarchy no time is assigned to the leadership of Joshua or that of the elders, and an incomplete figure is given for the length of Saul's reign. In addition there is a difference between the MT and the LXX for the period of Othniel's judgeship (Judg. 3:11) and for the judgeship of Eli (I Sam. 4:18), with a net difference of ten years longer being given in the MT listings.[18] Material is not available in extra-biblical texts to pinpoint dates in the periods just noted, but as we shall see later, evidence is available to give good indication of the most likely dates for the migration of Abraham, the Exodus, and the conquest of Palestine.

We have already seen that the biblical writers were teachers rather than historians. They were not concerned with details which are so essential to the writing of history. Occasionally, however, we can turn to extra-biblical documents to discover those missing details. In II Kings 20:20 there is only passing reference to Hezekiah's construction of a reservoir in the city and the conduit which supplied it. In 1880 small boys discovered an inscription which had been cut on the wall of the water tunnel which lies south of the Temple area in Jerusalem. The inscription indicates that this is the very tunnel or conduit cut by order of Hezekiah. No name or date remains but the writing is characteristic of the period of the reign of King Hezekiah. Its discovery emphasizes the careful planning of that king against seige of Jerusalem and his protection of its water supply.

The Bible's record of the career of Jehu is summarized "The time that Jehu reigned over Israel in Samaria was twenty-eight years" (II Kings 10:36). Little detail of his career is given. He was a fanatical Yahwist. He was anointed to office by a member of the prophetic party (II Kings 9:4-13), but to make his appointment effective Jehu had to liquidate his predecessor Joram. His reign, according to Kings, was one of slaughter after slaughter. He ruthlessly removed all enemies of the Yahweh religion, and his wrath fell disastrously upon leaders of the Baal cultus. Yet to have remained in office for twenty-eight years and to have preserved his country intact from the Syrians and Assyrians was no mean achievement. How this was accomplished is suggested by the famous Black Obelisk of Shalmaneser III, a monument found at Nimrud. Jehu is portrayed, head bowed to the ground, paying tribute to Shalmaneser. He brought temporary reprieve. He recognized the weakness of the Syrian alliance and the strength of the Assyrian forces. By paying tribute to Assyria he saved his country from pillage and destruction.

Solomon is both praised and censured in Holy Writ. The book of Deuteronomy uses him as an example of what the monarchy should not be; at least the abuses of the reign of Solomon seem to be the basis for the prohibitions given in Deut. 17:14-17. On the other hand, he acquired a great reputation for wisdom, and I Kings 4:29-34 lists an amazing number of works accredited

[18] For details see De Vries, *IDB*, op. cit., pp. 581-83.

to him. (See also I Kings 3:16-28.) Tradition has made him the author of Proverbs and Song of Songs. In the noncanonical writings he is credited with the Wisdom of Solomon and the Psalms of Solomon. He is popularly thought of as the great lover because the record says "Solomon loved many foreign women" (I Kings 11:1), and he is said to have had "seven hundred wives, princesses, and three hundred concubines" (I Kings 11:3). In spite of his many marriages there is very little record of his family life, little information about his wives, and almost nothing about his children. The *Interpreter's Dictionary*, in fact, has only eleven lines (in the introduction) about his family in an article entitled "Solomon" which covers seventeen columns. Yet to understand his reign we must see the political purposes of Solomon's many marriages. Extra-biblical documents recovered by the archaeologist give us much insight at this joint.

It is to be noted that up until now no extra-biblical document has been found which bears the name of Solomon. Yet many documents attest the fact that by the time of the period in which Solomon reigned marriages were contracted between the sons and daughters of kings of various nations, and such marriages were considered to be the equivalent of political treaties. In a treaty between Suppiluliumas, the Hittite king, and Mattiwaza, the Hurrian, reference is made to the marriage between the Hurrian and his first wife, a daughter of the Hittite monarch. The wording of the treaty is based upon the relatedness of the two kingdoms by marriage and especially upon the fact that future kings of the Hurrians will be descendents of the "Great King of the Hatti Land." [19]

A second document comes from the same Hittite monarch, Suppiluliumas. In this case it is a response to the Egyptian queen whose husband had died. In an earlier letter she had apparently made the proposal that Tudhaliyas, father of Suppiluliumas, send one of his sons to Egypt to become the new husband of the bereaved queen. The Hittite had naturally been suspicious at such a proposal. In the end it was agreed that such a marriage would be advantageous to both countries.[20] Unfortunately, the prince never arrived in Egypt. He was murdered on the way.[21] It is to be noted that Solomon's chief wife was an Egyptian Pharaoh's daughter (I Kings 3:1) but reference is made to his marriages with "Moabite, Ammonite, Edomite, Sidonian, and Hittite women" (I Kings 11:1). A condition of the marriage treaty was that each wife would have her own retinue and her own place of worship so that she could continue to follow the customs of her own people. It was natural, therefore, that her children should be raised in her own religious faith and not that of the Hebrews. For this Solomon was roundly condemned by the Deuteronomic editor of I Kings. He states that Solomon himself became a

[19] ANET, pp. 205-6.
[20] ANET, p. 319.
[21] ANET, p. 395. Note: There seems to be some confusion concerning whose son was sent.

devotee of foreign gods (I Kings 11:4-8). It is altogether possible that Solomon was as much interested in using foreign marriages to add to his own grandeur and reputation as he was in making political commitment to foreign powers. In any case the financial burden upon his people was such that at his death there was revolt which resulted in the divided monarchy, a breach which was never healed throughout the history of the Hebrews.

The same pattern of treaty by marriage was used by other kings, notably Omri, who arranged for the marriage of his son Ahab to "Jezebel the daughter of Ethbaal king of Sidonians" (I Kings 16:31).[22] Ahab made alliance with Judah through the marriage of Athaliah to Jehoram (II Kings 8:26).

Details of history often omitted from the biblical record are now being etched in by reference to non-biblical documents. One document will illustrate the importance of such resources. In II Kings 1:1 there is the brief statement "After the death of Ahab, Moab rebelled against Israel." Ahab died in 850 B.C. He was succeeded by Ahaziah who reigned for only one year, and he in turn was followed by Jehoram (849-842). It was during Jehoram's reign that there was rebellion by the Moabites according to II Kings 3:4-27. The biblical record indicates that the combined forces of Israel and Judah were highly victorious over the Moabites until their king, presumably Mesha, made a burnt offering of his oldest son. Then, says the Bible, "there came great wrath upon Israel; and they withdrew from him and returned to their own land" (II Kings 3:27). The Moabite Stone, found at Dibon in 1868, credits the Moabites with victory. Both sources indicate that Israel withdrew. The Moabite Stone credits victory to military strategy. The Hebrew record credits withdrawal to theological disagreement. The Moabite Stone, however, gives additional information concerning the earlier relationships between Moab and Israel. Mesha informs us that it was Omri, King of Israel, who first put Moab under subjection to Israel. No word of this is given in the Bible. In fact only one event in the seven-year reign of Omri is given; that is that he purchased the hill from Shemer and established Samaria as a fort city (I Kings 16:22a-27). The statement of Mesha has further implications for the record of Omri. It indicates that Omri was able not only to withstand the power of Syria, but even to maintain control over a people (the Moabites) who normally looked to Syria for leadership.[23] This may explain why the Assyrian records refer to the "house of Omri" long after his death. Critical use of all sources including the Bible enables us to reconstruct a historical account which is credible.

We turn finally to some help which archaeological discoveries can give concerning the vexing problems of major events in the saga of Israel. Although historians are divided in their opinion concerning the time of the beginnings of Israel as a historic group, there is general agreement that few, if any, his-

---

[22] Bright, *Early Israel in Recent History Writing*, p. 222, notes that this marriage was arranged by Omri, not by Ahab himself.
[23] *Ibid.*, pp. 222-23.

torical checks can be made on anything which happened prior to the days of Abraham. The problem of dating the patriarchs is somewhat complicated by the fact that the records themselves do not distinguish between those of individuals and those of tribal groups. Some modern writers tend to the position that most names of the patriarchs are actually names of clans and tribes which have been projected into the past and assumed to be individuals. Others assert that patriarchs are really "eponymous ancestors," individuals from whom the tribes obtained their names. In any case, it is possible to find in the patriarchal records in the Bible some knowledge of the early movements of clans and tribes which became integrally related to the nation Israel.

The general period in which the Abraham cycle of stories would most comfortably fit has been touched on briefly in an earlier chapter; [24] that is, in the nineteenth century B.C. Thousands of clay tablets have been recovered from Ugarit, Mari, and Nuzi which throw light on social customs, religious concepts, and literary patterns of the first half of the second millennium B.C. These documents show amazing parallels to what is known of the patriarchal period. In addition, we are now aware of the high level of culture which had been obtained by the middle of the second millennium. This is in sharp contrast to the popular notion that tent dwellers are ignorant, have crude manners, and lack all social graces. Even a cursory reading of the biblical accounts should disabuse us of such misinformation.

It should be noted also that the theory adopted early by Assyriologists which identified Amraphel of Gen. 14:1 with Hammurabi, sixth king of the First Dynasty of Babylon, has now generally been abandoned. Thus it is not necessary to see Abraham as contemporary with Hammurabi. When it was believed that Hammurabi ruled in the twenty-second century Abraham was dated in that century. When the king's dates were brought down into the second millennium reasons were found for dating Abraham in this later period. Hammurabi is now believed to have ruled over Babylon from 1728 to 1686 B.C.,[25] and if the proposed date of Nelson Glueck for Abraham in the nineteenth century is accepted, then the patriarch would have preceded Hammurabi by a full century. Since the biblical record does not make Abraham a contemporary of Hammurabi, there is no contradiction of Glueck's proposal. With Abraham settled in Palestine in the nineteenth century, and perhaps living on into the eighteenth, the time schedule would be correct for the third generation to move into Egypt at a time when the leadership of that country was receptive to settlement of Semites in Egypt. Egypt lost its dependence upon native leadership about 1770 B.C. and was under control by the Hyksos for about two hundred years. The term "Hyksos," usually translated "shepherd kings," designates a movement of people down through the Palestinian corridor, a movement which had no ethnic unity, but which

[24] See above, Chap. 4, pp. 56-57.
[25] Roland de Vaux, *Revue Biblique*, LIII (1946), 328 ff.

at its southern end seems to have been largely Semitic. The period from 1770 to 1570, known as the Second Intermediate Period of Egyptian history, seems to be the most appropriate setting for the Joseph stories and the settlement of his family. Then Ahmose I was able to expel the Hyksos from the country, to reunite north and south, and to establish the Eighteenth Dynasty (1570-1305). The new political climate could not tolerate foreigners, and they were either expelled or put into slavery. Thus began the period of "Egyptian Bondage" in the saga of Israel.

The problem of the date of the Exodus from Egypt and the related problem of the date of the conquest of Palestine has not been settled by archaeological discoveries. Indeed it seemed for a time that the problems had been made baffling because of contradicting evidence. Gradually, however, historical fragments are falling into position, and a recognizable pattern of events is emerging. If one begins with I Kings 6:1: "In the four hundred and eightieth year after the people of Israel came out of the land of Egypt, in the fourth year of Solomon's reign," then the date of the Exodus must be put in the fifteenth century. Solomon began to reign about 965, and the fourth year of his reign would be 962/1, and the date of the Exodus 1442/1 B.C. In spite of the fact that some archaeologists have dated the fall of such cities as Jericho about 1400 B.C., this date has caused more difficulty than solution. It is specifically stated in Exod. 1:11 that the people of Israel "built for Pharaoh store cities, Pithom and Raamses." Ramses I was ruler for only one year (1303-1302), but Ramses II was a powerful leader with a long reign (1290-1224), and one for whom it would be appropriate to build cities. He is generally believed to have been the pharaoh of the oppression. Many historians now accept the suggestion that the most probable time for the Exodus was during the reign of Ramses' successor, Mer-ne-ptah (1224-1214). Difficulty is presented, however, by the fact that Mer-ne-ptah left some hymns of victory dated about 1220, the "fifth year of his reign," in which he said that he had overcome Israel.[26] Such a date would scarcely leave room for "forty years in the wilderness."

Archaeological evidence from Palestine indicates that the last part of the thirteenth century seems to be the most logical time for the conquest. City after city shows destruction in that period. Garstang insisted that the fall of Jericho was about 1400 B.C. and has often been quoted in this connection. Miss Kenyon's excavations have shown no evidence for any occupation of the mound of Jericho at that date. Dr. and Mrs. Franken say, "the work recently done by Miss Kenyon at Jericho has proved that Garstang's reconstruction of the fall of Jericho at the arrival of Joshua was completely based on the defective methods used by Garstang at Tell es-Sultan." [27] Because of the acceptance of Garstang's date, several scholars adopted a

[26] ANET, p. 378.
[27] H. J. Franken and C. A. Franken-Battershill, A Primer of Old Testament Archaeology (Leiden: E. J. Brill, Publishers, 1963), p. 15.

theory sometimes called "the double entry hypothesis," [28] and some even associated Joshua with one phase of the conquest in 1400 and Moses with a second phase shortly before 1200 B.C.[29] However, the evidence from Gibeon should be considered to be equally as valuable as that from Jericho. Gibeon became a strongly fortified city not much earlier than 1200 B.C.,[30] and Joshua's relationships to its citizens could not have been earlier than that. A date for an invasion toward the close of the thirteenth century would agree with archaeological evidence from Gibeon as well as with that from other cities in that general region. This invasion seems to have been the major thrust. It is attested by the Book of Judges and parts of the Book of Joshua that the conquest was spread over many years. That there were constant infiltrations beginning as early as the fourteenth century seems to be attested by the Tell el-Amarna Tablets, but it appears to be erroneous to identify the major invasion by the Hebrews with the raids of the Habiru noted in the tablets. Many problems still remain. It is the hope of the historian that the archaeologist will be fortunate enough to uncover conclusive evidence which will answer completely the problems raised by the incompleteness of and the inconsistencies in the biblical accounts.

It is becoming increasingly apparent that the Hebrew people lived through days in which there was political ferment throughout the Near and Middle East. Their history was inextricably interwoven with that of their neighbors. It is, therefore, impossible to write an intelligible history of the Hebrews without taking into full consideration the histories of those neighbors. Much information has come to us concerning such familiar names as the Assyrians, Babylonians, and Egyptians. The records of other nations, however, have only recently been brought to light, and from these records have come important insights concerning their relationship to the Bible story. It is to these nations and their records which we must now turn.

---

[28] J. M. P. Smith, *AJSL*, XXII (1918), 24 ff.; T. J. Meek, *AJSL*, XXXVII (1921), 101 ff. See also C. Steuernagel, *Einwanderung der israelitischen Stämme* (1901).

[29] Frederick Victor Winnett, *The Mosaic Tradition* (Toronto: University of Toronto Press, 1949), discusses the replacement of the Joshua tradition by that of Moses.

[30] See above, Chap. 9, p. 112.

11.
RECOVERED NATIONS

A distinct advantage of the modern reader of the Bible over his grand-parents is that he has many aids and resources which enable him to understand the backgrounds against which the Bible was written. Especially important are histories and geographies which identify and describe not only the Hebrews but their neighbors. Prior to the nineteenth century the names of many tribes and nations mentioned in the Bible were largely meaningless. Even such well-known names as Egypt, Assyria, and Babylonia were names without context of history or custom. In recent years these nations have been the basis of much research, and full historical accounts of them are readily available. Indeed, courses on ancient history or the history of civilization now include these nations, as they must, in their consideration of the development of Western civilization. No longer can we be content with assuming that our roots go no deeper than Greco-Roman civilization. Information concerning these nations was first sought for the light which could possibly be thrown upon the Bible account and teachings, but now much interest is shown by students of the history of human culture and the rise of civilization.

We shall, however, be concerned in this chapter with less well-known nations, nations which are mentioned in the Bible but whose identity has only quite recently been recognized. In addition we shall need to look at nations who are not mentioned in scripture but whose story is related to that of the Hebrews. Finally, we must look at one nation which had been lost completely to the world's knowledge, for there is no mention of it either in scripture or in classical and post-classical literature. It was in fact this nation which gave many basic things to cvilization and made direct contribution to Hebrew thought and practices.

We shall look at this last-mentioned nation first because it is the oldest. Samuel N. Kramer, in fact, titles one of his books *History Begins at Sumer*.[1] He lists twenty-seven "firsts" in man's recorded history, such as first schools, the first case of "apple-polishing," the first historian, the first case of tax reduction, first biblical parallels, including the first "Job," et cetera.

The land of Sumer[2] corresponds roughly to the lower half of modern Iraq. It included the ancient basins of the Tigris and Euphrates rivers and stretched from just north of Babylon in a southeasterly direction to immediately north of the confluence of the rivers. The earliest inhabitants are identified only by the culture which has been uncovered at Tell al-Obeid. They came there about 4000 B.C. Then about 3300 new settlers came in and settled in the marshlands. These are the people we now know as

[1] Garden City, N.Y.: Doubleday & Company, Inc., 1959.
[2] Pronounced "Shu-mer."

Sumerians. Their place of origin is still unknown. Their language is unrelated to either the Semitic or the Indo-European languages, or in fact to any other known language ancient or modern. They settled in with the Obeidans and the combination produced a creative and imaginative people. They are the people who taught the world to read and to write. They compiled the first codes of law. Their system of mathematics was adopted by the Babylonians and Assyrians. Their literature and religion had great impact upon later Near and Middle Eastern nations. By 3000 B.C. they had organized themselves into a unified people. This period, known as the Early Dynastic Period, lasted for seven hundred years, then the Sumerians were conquered by the Semites we know as the Akkadians, with help from the Guti. The Semites were dominant for 200 years and about 2100 B.C. there was a Sumerian revival which lasted until 1720. In that year the Sumerians under Rim Sin were defeated by Hammurabi of Babylon. Hammurabi united the countries of Sumer and Akkad, and the Sumerians were gradually absorbed into Semitic culture through intermarriage, and they disappeared as a separate ethnic group. Their language, however, was preserved for a long time. It became the language of religion, and linguists have been helped considerably in their understanding of Sumerian because bilingual dictionaries were written showing equivalences between Babylonian and Sumerian.

It is only within the last one hundred years that we have known that the Sumerians existed and only within the last twenty-five to thirty years that any significant amount of the literature of this people was available in translation. The language is difficult to understand, and only a small percentage of scholars interested in the Near and Middle East venture into Sumerology. Because so little was known about the language, clay tablets in that language went unrecognized and untranslated. As caches of tablets were recovered from the earth they were often split between museums. Many of the tablets in some museums were in fact purchased from dealers instead of coming directly from known excavations. The result is that it is frequently necessary to visit the museums at the University of Pennsylvania in Philadelphia, the Museum of the Ancient Orient in Istanbul, Turkey, and the museums under the direction of the department of antiquities of the Republic of Iraq. We are indebted to men like Kramer who gather bits and pieces from many lands to reconstruct a single document, but a document which may throw great light upon an ancient culture. It is as if a capricious wind had scattered pieces of a jigsaw puzzle across thousands of miles and then we attempted to gather the pieces to create the picture, a picture which many times cannot be completed because some pieces are lost. Sometimes, however, it happens that several copies of the same jigsaw puzzle had been made and differently distributed. By checking the reconstructions with each other one may discover that a piece missing in this reconstruction is not missing in that one, and gaps can be reconstrued.

In 1854 the British Consul at Basra, J. E. Taylor, was commissioned by the trustees of the British Museum to examine some ruins in southern Mesopotamia. At Al Muqayyer, the "Mound of Bitumen," Taylor discovered a great pile of fired red brick, brick which had been set in bitumen, hence the Arabic name. As Taylor dug at the corners of the structure he found foundation deposit boxes in which cylinders of clay covered with cuneiform signs had been placed. These cylinders identified the place as Ur, known in the Bible as Ur of the Chaldees. The foundation deposits had been placed there by King Nabonidus, the last ruler of the Neo-Babylonian empire (555-539). Nabonidus states in the cylinder inscriptions that he had restored the ziggurat which had been built by Ur-Nammu, founder of the Third Dynasty of Ur, and his son Shulgi (sometimes read as Dungi). The identification of Ur of the Chaldees was highly important for biblical as well as historical studies because of its identification with Abraham.

If, indeed, our estimate of the date of Abraham is approximately correct, then the culture with which he was acquainted in Mesopotamia was Sumerian rather than Babylonian. The ziggurat uncovered by Taylor was an important religious structure for the Sumerians. Whatever their original home was it was apparently mountain country as is evidenced by their language and their religion. Their gods were mountain gods, and this posed a real problem for them in their new country. The lower part of Mesopotamia is exceedingly flat being nothing but an enormous alluvial plain, the deposit of the rivers on their journey to the sea. If their gods were to feel at home a mountain must be constructed. This was done by baking brick and building an artificial mountain. Brick was used because stone was not available in the immediate vicinity. Clay brick was better than mud brick because it would not crumble under the pressure of high structures. Even so, it was necessary to add strength. The ziggurat at Aqurquf, twenty kilometers west of Baghdad, shows how the reinforcement was done. After several layers of brick had been laid down matting of woven material was made to cover the last layer of brick. This was thoroughly soaked with bitumen, then building of new layers of brick began. The bitumen so thoroughly preserved the matting that it may still be seen.[3]

The original purpose of the Sumerians was to bring their gods down among men, and for this purpose a chapel was placed on top of the artificial mountain. These structures were built at each of the major cities. They were comprised of three to seven stages, with ramps or stairs linking the stages. It is now generally agreed that such a structure was the background of the biblical story of the Tower of Babel (Gen. 11:1-9) which was written perhaps at a time when one of these towers was seen in partial destruction and therefore was "unfinished." In the Hebrew story man seeks to climb up into the presence of God, and his motivation was pride, not communion.

The earliest writing of the Sumerians was pictographic. It may have be-

[3] See Plate XVII.

gun as a simple method of notation or enumeration related to business transactions. In any case, the pictures soon came to stand for the sound rather than the object, and a rebus pattern of writing was developed, not for entertainment as we now use rebus writing, but for serious communication. In time the pictures were stylized, and certain combinations of strokes or wedges were recognized to be syllables. In some cases such combinations represented whole words, or even a phrase such as our "&" or "etc." (See drawing #3.)

Writing was done on clay, which was readily available from the nearby stream beds. The writers quickly discovered that when they tried to draw a line on moist clay the result left a ragged tear on the surface. They therefore developed the neat, clean method of pressing marks into the clay. The stylus used was a reed which when pressed down onto the clay left an inverted pyramid or elongated triangle. This wedge-shaped or "cuneiform" writing was continued in Mesopotamia for many hundreds of years. If Abraham ever saw any writing it would have been cuneiform on clay or occasionally on stone monuments. It is possible that on his journey to Egypt he may have seen Egyptian hieroglyphic, another type of pictographic writing, for the Egyptians began to write shortly after the Sumerians.

With the invention of writing schools became a necessity. Training of scribes became an important function of special schools in Sumeria. Practice tablets of students have been found. Their business was to learn to write and to read and to take down dictation. Just as the modern stenographer must learn many symbols accurately and know how to spell correctly, so the ancient writer had to learn long lists of signs and the correct spelling of long lists of words; there was no "shorthand" system of taking dictation, however. From the word lists, which are classified by types (such as names of trees, et cetera), we have much information concerning everyday life.

The schools were private, except for the special schools for the priests which were operated by the temples. That students paid large fees for instruction is evidenced by the fact that only the sons of well-to-do government officials or businessmen were enrolled.[4] The organization was simple. There was a school "father" or schoolmaster and an assistant schoolmaster known as "big brother." Other faculty members were in charge of specialized subjects such as drawing, Sumerian language, et cetera. One other officer was "the man with the cane," for discipline seems to have been strict and severe and administered by the school rather than the parents.[5]

Mathematics was well developed—this in spite of the fact that the Sumerians used a sexagesimal system. In addition to "tens" they used sixty as a base. We still use part of that system. Our engineers measure circles and the circumference of the earth in terms of 360 degrees. Our minutes are divided

[4] Kramer, History Begins At Sumer, pp. 3-4.
[5] Ibid., pp. 4-6.

into sixty seconds and sixty minutes make up the hour. In turn two twelve hour periods make up the day and night and twelve is a fifth of sixty. Sixty is a convenient whole number by which many fractions can be expressed: Two is a thirtieth; three, a twentieth; four, a fifteenth; five, a twelfth; six, a tenth; fifteen, a fourth; et cetera. It also served as a convenience that the ten fingers had thirty joints, giving man a natural abacus or counting frame. Even in New Testament times the expression "a hundredfold, another sixty, and . . . another thirty" (Matt. 13:23), a remnant of the Sumerian system of counting, was used. The same parable is told in *The Gospel of Thomas* (Logion 9) but refers to "sixty and one hundred twenty."

The creative spirit must have been given opportunity. There was constant copying of early masterpieces, and this must have encouraged new artists, composers, and writers. In any case, many documents which may properly be called "belles-lettres" have been preserved, and these have had their influence upon later Babylonian and Assyrian literature, and indirectly upon Hebrew writings. Stories of creation include not only the formation of heaven and earth, but also the placement of cities and the boundaries between city states. Again and again we find rulers appealing to the gods on the basis of "established" boundaries which have been violated.[6] One interesting poem shows a decided difference in point of view between the Sumerians and the Hebrews. This poem of 108 lines tells of the creation by the gods of the pickax and that it was a gift of the gods to the Sumerian people.[7] Work was not a curse, as is suggested in Gen. 3:23, and the gods helped man by inventing proper tools. The creation of man was, however, an act of the gods to provide them with food, and to make work by the gods unnecessary. After several false starts in which a half a dozen "patterns" were made of sexless creatures, man was finally shaped from clay as in Gen. 2:7, and success came when "man was given breath." [8]

Of interest, too, is the story of Gilgamesh. Gilgamesh was one of the early kings, but because of his place in the Babylonian "Epic of Gilgamesh" many readers have assumed him to be a mythical being. The story of the great flood and the ark is first found in Sumerian literature, and the earliest king to be identified with the ark is Ziusudra, later known as Utnapishtim. Gilgamesh, terrified by the threat of death, sought to find Utnapishtim who was the only human who had found immortality. Utnapishtim told Gilgamesh of the way in which he learned that he was to build an ark. All of this is part of the Gilgamesh epic.[9] It is in the Assyrian account that the marked parallels to the biblical account are strongest.

[6] Samuel N. Kramer, *Sumerian Mythology* (Philadelphia: American Philosophical Society, 1944), pp. 30-75.

[7] *Ibid.*, pp. 51-53.

[8] *Ibid.*, pp. 68-73.

[9] See "The Deluge," *ANET*, pp. 42-44; J. H. Marks, "The Flood," *IDB*, pp. 278-84; Kramer, "The First Noah," in *History Begins at Sumer*, pp. 150 ff.; the Babylonian and Assyrian accounts may be found in *ANET*, 76 ff., 90 ff.

Sir Leonard Woolley claimed to have discovered indisputable evidence for the Flood at Ur.[10] Stephen Langdon claimed a similar discovery at Kish.[11] These discoveries indicate clearly that great floods were known in Mesopotamia, but since the dates of the floods noted at Ur and Kish are widely separated, these cannot be taken as evidence for the great flood of biblical record. In addition, it has been noted that the many trials through which Gilgamesh went show marked parallelism to the labors of Hercules, and the slaying of the dragonlike creature Huwawa by Gilgamesh is the theme which was picked up later in the story of Saint George and the dragon.[12]

The Sumerians were also the first people of whom we have record to gather laws into codes. It has long been recognized that there were marked similarities between the Hammurabi Code and Exodus 21–23. The Code of Hammurabi was found in fragments by the French archaeologist J. De-Morgan at Susa (biblical Shushan) in December, 1901, and January, 1902. It was restored and taken to the Louvre in Paris. Since the finding of that stele, other codes of law have been brought to light. In 1947 the Code of Lipit-Ishtar, which had been recovered at Nippur much earlier, was found to be in the University of Pennsylvania Museum. Lipit-Ishtar preceded Hammurabi by more than 150 years.[13] An even earlier code was found at Tell Abu Harmal by Taha Baqir in 1948; it is known as the Eshnunna Code and may be dated about seventy years prior to Lipit-Ishtar.[14] This Code of Eshnunna held the honors as the "oldest law code" for just four years, then Kramer copied and translated the Ur-Nammu Code while at the Museum of the Ancient Orient in Istanbul. It is dated about 2050 B.C. or some fifty years prior to Eshnunna. There the matter rests, at least for the present.[15] It is most important to recognize, however, that each of these codes is literally dependent upon its predecessor.

Students of biblical law divide law into "Apodeictic" and "Casuistic." Apodeictic law, sometimes identified with the divine imperative, begins, "Thou shalt . . ." or "Thou shalt not. . . ." Casuistic law begins "If such and such is the condition, then thou shalt. . . ." It is in the area of casuistic laws that parallels with Sumerian and Babylonian laws are most frequently found. One further observation needs to be made. The law codes found are not the results of enactments of legislatures or even the formal pronouncements of law by a ruler, but they are collected instances of judgments which have

[10] *Spadework* (London: Lutterworth Press, 1953), pp. 103 ff.

[11] *IDB*, "The Flood," p. 283.

[12] Kramer, *History Begins at Sumer*, pp. 170 ff.

[13] Francis R. Steele published the text in the *American Journal of Archaeology*, LII (1948), 425-50, It is reproduced in *ANET*, pp. 159-61.

[14] Baqir, *Sumer*, IV (1948), 52 ff., and *ANET*, p. 161. Note, Kramer referred to this code as the Bilalama Code. A copy of the Eshnunna code was made available to me by the Iraq department of antiquities and is on display at the Iliff School of Theology.

[15] Kramer, *History Begins at Sumer*, pp. 50 ff.

traditionally been made. Law, from very ancient times, has depended heavily upon precedence.

The Hebrew story was strongly influenced at still another point in this case in the struggle which ensued between the defendants of the Yahweh religion and those who would adopt the alluring practices of the nature religion. Much is still to be unraveled before we know the full system of Sumerian religious thought and practices, but enough is known to recognize that the pattern of Baalism, so strong in Bible times, was already known in Sumeria. Inanna, the queen of heaven, is the wife of Dumuzu, who is known in the Bible as Tammuz (Ezek. 8:14). Inanna is afterwards identified with Ishtar, the goddess of love. Like Ishtar she made a descent to the underworld, the place of death, and the resting place of all outworn spirits of men. As she passed through the gates to the underworld she was stripped first of her jewels and then of her clothing. This probably symbolized the loss of fruit and then leaves by trees and plants at harvesttime, at least this is the later Babylonian version. Upon her return to the earth she was reinvested with clothing and jewels which symbolized the return of life at the spring of the year. The place she visited was called the land of no-return (Job 16:22), and it was only through special intervention that she was permitted to come back to earth. Men believed that through the practice of mimetic magic, by mock marriages of priests and temple women and through active participation of men and women of the community, the goddess was revived and all nature took on new life. It was a religion in which "free love" played a prominent part, and one which, therefore, it was most difficult to eradicate. Understanding of the practices of the nature religion enables us to know the vigor with which the prophets of the eighth and seventh centuries denounced it. The earliest known form of this religion is that practiced by the Sumerians.

It is doubtful if any country ever had as much influence, direct and indirect, upon the Hebrews as did the Sumerians. Much of that influence filtered down through the Babylonians, Assyrians, and the countries to the west of Mesopotamia. Such influence as that of writing, literature, and law was beneficial, but some was detrimental. Dedicated religious leadership enabled Israel to "choose the good and reject the evil."

It was through the stories about the patriarchs, particularly Abraham, that the Christian world first became acquainted with the "Sons of Heth" (K.J.V.), now better known as the Hittites. Heth is listed in Gen. 10:15 as a son of Canaan, and therefore, a grandson of Ham. This is ethnically indefensible because the Canaanites were Semites, but the Hittites were Indo-European. Since many Hittites lived within the area commonly associated with the Canaanites it was natural that early writers assumed their national or tribal relationship, especially when there was much intermarriage.

At the death of Sarah Abraham arranged for the purchase of a burial place from Ephron the Hittite (Gen. 23:3-20). Conversation was, in fact, carried on through the community of Hittites who were resident in the community of "Machpelah, east of Mamre (that is Hebron) in the land of Canaan" (Gen. 23:19). Abraham calls himself a "stranger and sojourner," but this may have been the polite conversation of business and trade. Another contact between the patriarchs and the Hittites is contained in the complaint of Rebekah to Isaac that she is weary of Hittite women and ardently desires that Jacob will not marry one of them (Gen. 27:46), but in the following verse (28:1) Isaac charged Jacob not to "marry one of the Canaanite women." There is difference here in literary sources; JE in the first instance and P in the second, but the confusion between Hittites and Canaanites is apparent in early and late literature.

According to the P record (Gen. 26:34) Esau married two Hittite women, Judith and Basemath, "and they made life bitter for Isaac and Rebekah." The tension is given in terms of the age-old difficulties which may arise among in-laws, not national rivalries or jealousies. However, there are constant refrains in the historical records of the conquest that such groups as the Canaanites and Hittites must be completely wiped out. Of the seven nations so listed (Canaanites, Hittites, Amorites, Perizzites, Hivites, Jebusites, and Girgashites) the Hittites are listed first six times and in second place nine times.[16] Only the Canaanites are given priority more often than the Hittites. Hittites, however, were apparently permitted to continue residence in Palestine. In the period of the monarchy Uriah was a soldier in David's army, and Ahimelech was an army officer (I Sam. 26:6). Solomon's horse trading involved the Hittites (I Kings 10:29), and Solomon used Hittites as workers in his corvée (I Kings 9:20). There is also indication that one of his wives was a Hittite (I Kings 11:1).

It is quite possible that Hittites became professional soldiers and hired themselves out as mercenaries. Support for this is found in II Kings 7:6, where it is indicated that military help was hired from the Hittites by Israel against the Syrians. If we are to judge by the references to Uriah and Ahimelech, such service was also available in the period of the United Kingdom.

From such references it was assumed that the Hittites were a minor people, possibly some associated clans, but certainly not a major power which could be compared with Assyria or Egypt. Archaeology had discovered nothing which threw any particular light on the story of the Hittites. Strange and large monuments had been discovered, however, all the way from Eyuk in northern Asia Minor to Hamath in Syria, and from as far east as the Euphrates and as far west as the coast of Ionia.[17] No minor power could have erected these, but the monuments were definitely not those of a power already identified. Through the brilliant proposals of William Wright, an

[16] I. J. Gelb, "Hittites," *IDB*, p. 613.
[17] Cowley, *The Hittites* (Schweich Lectures, 1918, published 1926), p. 5.

Irish missionary,[18] and Archibald Henry Sayce, the Orientalist,[19] the world of scholarship was made aware of the probable existence of a Hittite Empire. As noted above, monuments portraying figures arrayed in distinctive dress and others inscribed with strange hieroglyphs had been uncovered in many parts of Anatolia and Syria. These were shown to be the product of one distinctive culture. The interest evidenced, however, was primarily in the new hieroglyphic writing. In 1809 Johann Ludwig Burckhardt, born in Basel in 1784, disguised himself as a native of the East, adopted the name of "Sheikh Ibrahim" and traveled as a merchant in the service of the East India Company. During his 3½ years in Syria he learned many languages and traveled constantly. He is the first to record seeing in the corner of a building at Hamath an inscribed stone, "a kind of hieroglyphic writing, though it does not resemble that of Egypt." [20] The stone was not seen again until many years later. In the meantime other stones had been seen at Boghazköy, Alaja Hüyük, Yazilikaya, and elsewhere.[21] When the stones at Hamath had been rediscovered attempts were made to copy them, but the superstitions of the people delayed this work. The stone was believed to be a cure for rheumatism, just as the stone of Aleppo was believed to cure eye diseases. In the end, however, copies were made of significant inscriptions.

In the meantime references to the Hittites had been discovered in Assyrian and Egyptian documents. The name Khatti was used in Assyrian, and Kheta in Egyptian. Especially important were the references in the Tell el-Amarna Tablets, and the treaties written on the walls at Karnak and the Ramesseum in Egypt.[22] Hugo Winckler tells of his exciting discovery on August 20, 1906, at Boghazköy. From a breach driven into rubble a clay tablet was recovered. It was a copy of a letter written by Ramses II to the Hittite king Hattusilis concerning a treaty being drawn up between them, the treaty which appears on the walls at Karnak. It was written in November, 1280 B.C. Eighteen years earlier Winckler had become acquainted with parallel documents in Egypt and in Berlin.[23] According to the Hittite and Egyptian records the actual treaty was inscribed upon a silver tablet. Copies were put on monuments in Egypt and Anatolia. The treaty includes provisions for nonaggression between Egypt and the Hittites, mutual aid against enemies in case of attack on either country, extradition of citizens of either country which had fled to the other, and guarantee by each ruler that he would protect the right of succession to the throne of his treaty partner.

---

[18] *British and Foreign Evangelical Review* (1874).

[19] *Transactions of the Society of Biblical Archaeology* (1876).

[20] *Travels in Syria and the Holy Land* (London, 1822); quoted in C. W. Ceram, *The Secret of the Hittites* (New York: Alfred A. Knopf, Inc., 1956), p. 16.

[21] G. Contenau, *La Civilisation des Hittites et des Hurrites du Mitanni* (Paris, 1948), pp. 17-20, lists the chief locations.

[22] *ANET*, pp. 199-203.

[23] "Nach Boghasköi! Ein Fragment," *Der Alte Orient*, XIV, No. 3 (1913), reprinted in Deuel, *Treasures of Time* (Cleveland, Ohio: World Publishing Company, 1961), pp. 261 ff.

Through the joint efforts of archaeologists, philologists, and historians, the story of the Hittites has been pieced together and is now fairly well known. An amazing part of the story is that no strong Hittite Empire had been developed by the time of Abraham, and by the time of the founding of the Hebrew monarchy it had ceased to be. It should, however, be remembered that the records so far deciphered deal with the days of the Hittite Empire, not with the story of a people. It is generally recognized that following the dissolution of the empire many scattered clans and communities of the Hittites remained intact and continued to be known as Hittite: Kayseri, Tyana, Malatya, in Anatolia; Carchemish, Aleppo, and Hamath in North Syria.

Dr. Gelb makes the proposal [24] that there could have been confusion in Hebrew writing between the names "Hittite" and "Hurrian," there being the difference of only one letter in the names and thus leading to the confusion (the letters Tau and Resh). Amazingly enough, E. A. Speiser suggests the same possible confusion between the names "Hivite," "Hittite," and "Hurrian" or "Horite." [25] These proposals apparently assume that the confusion between letters came after the adoption of "square character" Hebrew, which was quite late. There could have been no such confusion in the earlier forms of writing.

The history of the Hittites may be divided into three periods: (1) The proto-kingdom in the middle of the eighteenth century during which the names of only two kings are known; (2) the Old Kingdom from about 1740 to 1460 under the suzerainty of thirteen kings; and, (3) the Empire from about 1460 until invasion from the Aegean early in the twelfth century and covering the reigns of another thirteen kings. It was in the days of the Empire that the Hittites were a dominant power in the Near and Middle East. The Empire was able to withstand the power of Egypt on the one hand and to overcome the forces of Mesopotamia on the other. It held the balance of power between the Egyptians and the Babylonians. When its territory in the eastern half of Asia Minor became too densely populated the surplus spilled on down the Palestinian corridor on the one hand and down into Mesopotamia on the other. The Hittites were characterized, perhaps caricatured, on Egyptian monuments with turned-up toe shoes, figure of eight shields, conical hats, and prominent noses. The latter physiological characteristic afterwards gave evidence of intermarriage between Hittites and Hebrews.

The major part of the Hittites came originally from Europe and spoke an Indo-European language. Part of the confusion concerning their story is due to the fact that the term "Hittite" is used by the Hebrews and the Assyrians to designate four groups of people: (1) A native non-Indo-European

---

[24] *IDB*, "Hittites," p. 615.
[25] "Hivite," *ibid.*; and drawing 4, p. 204.

group of people who lived in central Asia Minor, called Hattians; (2) the Nesians, centered largely around Boghazköy, who used cuneiform writing and spoke an Indo-European language; (3) the Luwians, another Indo-European language group which wrote in hieroglyphs; and (4) people who had lived in Hittite territory but who were not necessarily ethnically related.

In addition to their own forms of writing the Hittites made quite a little use of Assyrian cuneiform. It was because of their usage of the Assyrian values of cuneiform signs that it was possible for scholars to decipher Hittite and then to translate it.

Comparison of Hittite records with the biblical stories indicates many similarities in law and custom. The Hittite Law Code may have had some influence upon the Hebrew laws.[26] A major difference is that Hittite law provides for swineherding and the domestication of bees. Provision is made also for the branding of stallions and rams but not, apparently, of bulls.

Archaeology in Asia Minor continues to be a major activity. In addition to the interest of biblical scholars, Turkey has developed considerable interest in the Hittite background of Turkish history.

Older lexicons and dictionaries tell us that the "Horites" were cave dwellers. In Gen. 14:6 and Deut. 2:12 they are associated with Mount Seir, the chief mountain range in Edom. There is a Hebrew word "Hor" which means "cave" but it has nothing to do with the Hori's, better known today as "Hurrians."

The identity of these people has been recovered from extra-biblical documents, the study of biblical names, and the excavation of such widely separated places as Nuzi (near Kirkuk, Iraq), Mari (Tell el Hariri, Syria), Boghazköy (Turkey), and Ugarit (Ras Shamra, Syria). Dr. Speiser informs us that the Hurrians were more widely distributed through the ancient Near East than any other people before the Arameans.[27] They were people of high culture, certainly not cave dwellers. They were important politically from the middle of the third to the end of the second millennium B.C., and their cultural influence lasted long beyond that. They learned from the Mesopotamian culture in the third millennium and later became teachers of the Hittites. In the middle of the second millennium they overpowered Assyria. They influenced the Hebrews in two ways. First, they transmitted some of their culture through their influence upon Canaanite customs and practices, which in turn were adopted by the Hebrews. Comparisons have been made between the customs of Mari and Nuzi and the practices of the Hebrews.[28] The second influence was in the pronunciation of the Hebrew language. Hebrew differs from other Semitic languages in that there is a

[26] J. M. P. Smith, *The Origin and History of Hebrew Law* (Chicago: University of Chicago Press, 1931), pp. 246-79; "The Hittite Laws," *ANET*, pp. 188-97; and E. Neufeld, editor, *The Hittite Laws* (London: Luzac & Company, Ltd., 1951).

[27] Speiser, "Hurrians," *IDB*, pp. 664-65.

[28] Cyrus H. Gordon, "Biblical Customs and the Nuzu Tablets," *BA*, III (1940), 1-9.

softening of certain letters (b, g, d, k, p, t) under some conditions. Dr. Speiser states that this habit was borrowed from the Hurrian influence.[29]

Hurrians were the dominant element in the Mitanni Kingdom[30] and are to be identified also with the Hivites and Jebusites of the Bible. The terms "Horite" and "Hivite" were sometimes interchanged between the LXX and the MT (Isa. 17:9; Gen. 36:2; Josh. 9:7). If the city of Jebus (Jerusalem) was actually a Hurrian enclave in Palestine as is suggested by the name Araunah (II Sam. 24:16), then there was active interchange between the Hurrians and the Hebrews down to the end of the second millennium B.C. There would also seem to be confusion in tradition between Hurrians and Hittites, at least according to Ezekiel's statement concerning Jerusalem, "Your mother was a Hittite and your father an Amorite" (16:45). The influence of the Hurrians was apparently far greater than the half dozen references to them in the Bible would indicate. We shall need to look more closely at that influence in the next two chapters as we consider cultural diffusion and borrowed customs.

It is increasingly apparent that the history of one people cannot be written without considering carefully the histories of their neighbors. This is particularly true of the Hebrews, who furnished us with no formal history. As cities are excavated and recovered documents are translated source material for the history of the entire area is made available. Very little material has been recovered which refers directly to the Hebrews, but all the material is concerned with some aspect of the ancient Near East. Since the Hebrews were part of the entire area, increased knowledge of that area helps us to see the Hebrews in better perspective. This in fact is true of all the nations, for we are better able to avoid the biases which naturally are to be found in nationalistic presentations.

[29] Speiser, "Hurrians."
[30] Ungnad, *Vorderasiatische Schriftdenkmaler III* (Berlin, 1909); I. J. Gelb, *Hurrians and Subarians*, SAOC, No. 22 (1944), 52.

12.
CULTURAL DIFFUSION

As nations have lived in association with each other they have borrowed customs easily, married readily, and imitated one another's speech in pronunciation and vocabulary. The Christian calendar, often called the "common calendar," can be found in ports of call the world around.

In an Arab tent in the old land of Gilead we found the village dressmaker busily at work with her American-made sewing machine. Mixed marriages have multiplied in the twentieth century because travel is now worldwide for soldiers and airmen as well as sailors, and for civilian as well as serviceman. One is likely to hear a ricksha runner in Hong Kong, a merchant in Malaysia, or a hotel waiter in Paris using American slang phrases, just as the children down the street from one's home use them. Nor are these exchanges confined to the modern world. They have been going on since men learned to live in communication with men of different clothing, different language or different pronunciation of the same language, and different physical features. It is, therefore, not surprising that we should find evidence of this in Bible times. It would be more startling if there were no such patterns of cultural exchange. Archaeology has simply made us recognize cultural diffusion.

Regardless of the complex background of the Hebrew people, at the time of the conquest of Palestine the major group of the invaders came in from having lived in the wilderness. They were Bedouin. They were herders of sheep and goats. Cultivation of fields was relatively unknown to them. This meant that they had to change their culture from animal herding to cultivation of grain, or at least they combined the activities, and they were greatly dependent upon the Canaanites for instruction. From them they learned what to grow and how to grow it. It is possible that they borrowed tools until they learned how to make their own, although the Bible indicates that the process of sharpening iron tools was a closely guarded secret of the Philistines (I Sam. 13:20-21). They were, therefore, also dependent upon their Philistine neighbors. The significance lies in the fact that as the Hebrews borrowed agricultural methods and tools they also learned to worship the gods of agriculture. Throughout the Old Testament there is a constant outcry from the prophets against this invasion of their faith, but we have known almost nothing about the Baalism so ardently denounced. With the discovery of the clay tablets at Ras Shamra (Ugarit), we have for the first time the legends and rituals of the Baal cultus.[1] The denunciation of Amos at Bethel is occasioned by the fact that though the correct terminology of the prophetic religion was used, the thinking was in terms of Baalism. Hosea's illustrations through his children's names and the parable of the destroyed marital rela-

---

[1] See above, Chap. 6, pp. 75-78.

tionship are best understood as we recognize vocabulary parallel to that of Baalism.[2] The same kind of denunciation of apostasy was also given to the south by Jeremiah.[3] Even the village from which Jeremiah came, Anathoth, was named after the goddess Anat, now known to us as the sister-wife of Aleyan-Baal. The practice of Baalism may have been lessened in the post-Exilic period, but it was not eliminated. We know from excavation that Astarte (mother goddess) figurines were still being made, perhaps to be used as charms during childbirth.

Not much question had been raised concerning the practice of Baalism until the event on Mount Carmel when Elijah made it very clear that Yahweh, not Baal, was god of agriculture. Until then Hebrews had no thought of disloyalty as they turned to the gods of the fields. Yahweh had been associated with mountains, storms, and warfare, not with the increase of herds and crops. With the revelation by Elijah it became possible for the Hebrews to move on to absolute monotheism.[4] In this case, the Hebrews had to be freed from domination of a strong cultural pattern before they were able to develop their own particular contribution.

We noted in an earlier chapter that Solomon was accused of imitating foreign customs in marriage, administration, and building.[5] As archaeologists examined the palace of Saul at Tell el-Ful it was apparent that building skills were not as fully developed among the Hebrews as among the Phoenicians. The Bible records that Solomon contracted with Hiram of Tyre for building material and construction of the Temple and palace (I Kings 5:1-11). As early as the Fourth Dynasty of Egypt Pharaoh Snefru sent his boats to Byblos for cedar logs.[6] Excavations at Byblos (Gebal), Sidon, and Tyre indicate that Phoenician reputation for building was well deserved. The Egyptians tried desperately to retain at least nominal control over Phoenicia in order to protect their source of building timber.[7]

It was also with Phoenician help that Solomon was able to establish a fleet of ships and sail with Hiram's fleet (I Kings 10:22). The ships are called "ships of Tarshish" but since the cargoes were "gold, silver, ivory, apes, and peacocks," the ships must have sailed from Ezion-geber, not the west coast of Palestine or Phoenicia. This may mean that Hiram supplied or constructed ships in exchange for seaport privileges which would enable the Phoenicians to make contact with India easier. In any case, it is apparent that Hiram obtained harbor and port rights from Solomon. This is confirmed in I Kings 22:47-48 where we learn that "ships of Tarshish" were wrecked at

[2] Walter G. Williams, Prophets—Pioneers to Christianity (Nashville: Abingdon Press, 1956), pp. 157-58; 161-68.

[3] Jer. 9:13 ff.; 23:9-15; et cetera.

[4] Williams, Prophets—Pioneers to Christianity, pp. 61-67.

[5] See above, Chap. 10, p. 124.

[6] ANET, p. 227.

[7] A. S. Kapelrud, IDB, "Phoenicia," p. 802; P. K. Hitti, History of Syria, including Lebanon and Palestine (New York: The Macmillan Company, 1951).

Ezion-geber. These were ships of Jehoshaphat, and in this case their destination was Ophir to obtain gold. Solomon may have been heavily dependent upon Phoenician supplies and craftsmen, but he in turn could offer a valuable asset, namely an important shipping center. He could also supply copper which could be exchanged for other products in India, Arabia, and Africa. An ostracon[8] containing notice of a shipment of "thirty shekels of gold of Ophir to Beth-horon" has been found at Tell Qasile.[9] In general the Hebrews did not become great sailors except in the days of Solomon. This was due in part to the fact that there are few harbors on the west coast of Palestine, but also to the fact that the coast was controlled by the Philistines and the Phoenicians.

Just when the Hebrew people began to write is not known. Writing is found earliest among the Sumerians, who in turn taught the Babylonians and those with whom the Babylonians came into contact. There is no proof that the Egyptians learned from the Sumerians, but since writing appears in the Nile Valley immediately after its appearance in Mesopotamia it may be assumed that there was some influence. If there were strong similarity between the Sumerian signs and those of Egypt, then we would have some indication of direct borrowing. There is none. It may well be that a traveler, businessman, priest, or soldier saw the writing in Mesopotamia and took the concept of writing but not the sign forms with him. This would necessitate a new system of signs which were not directly copied from others. It is impossible in many cases to trace the transmission of ideas. Only when there is similarity of phrasing or signs is it possible to trace evidence of borrowing.

Writing was being produced on the north Syrian coast prior to the time of the conquest of Palestine. In addition, Egyptian, Babylonian, Assyrian, and Hittite writings were being widely circulated. There are references in the Bible to the writing of Moses, Joshua, and the priests of the early days of the conquest, but all these references are in writings several centuries removed from the period of Moses and his contemporaries. Little else is said in scripture about writing prior to the period of the monarchy except for references to the Book of Jashar (Joshua 10:13; II Sam. 1:18) and to the writing of Samuel (I Sam. 10:25). Since writing was a well-established institution and occupation it is surprising that more mention of it is not given in scripture.

A few references enable us to parallel practices of the Old Testament with what we know from archaeological discoveries. The prophet Isaiah seems to have been acquainted with the Mesopotamian method of writing on clay tablets. The name of his child, Maher-shalal-hash-baz, is inscribed upon such a tablet (8:1) and properly attested by witnesses putting their marks or seals upon the tablet. A similar reference is found later in the same chap-

[8] Ostracon—an inscribed sherd.
[9] *JNES* (1956); see "Ophir," *IDB*, pp. 605-6.

ter (8:16). The Mesopotamian methods of sealing a document were to roll a cylinder seal across the still wet clay and so prevent any change being made, or to put the whole thing into a clay envelope with a summary of the contents on the outside of the envelope. In either case the prophet asserted his confidence in his message and was willing to trust it to the future.

The prophet Jeremiah delivered many of his messages orally, but the time came when it was not safe for him to appear in public. He therefore dictated his message to Baruch his scribe (Jer. 36:4-8). The message was read several times, finally in the presence of the king himself. The king promptly cut the scroll to pieces and threw the fragments into the fire. Ancient scrolls were written either on leather, or on papyrus. Both were known and used in the days of Jeremiah. Since, however, the fragments were thrown into the fire with no apparent discomfort to the members of the royal court it strongly suggests that the scroll was made of papyrus, which burns with a sweet smelling odor, and not leather, the stench of which can be quite strong.

Ezekiel knew of the clay tablets of Mesopotamia and also the scrolls of Egypt. He drew a map of Jerusalem on a clay tablet and laid mock siege against it. Such a map of the city of Nippur has been found.[10] In addition, Ezekiel used an illustration of a scroll "and it had writing on the front and on the back" (Ezek. 2:9). This must have been papyrus. Leather scrolls, according to Jewish law, could be inscribed only on the shaved hair side. Papyrus scrolls could contain writing on both sides, but were not necessarily so used.

One other aspect of writing is illustrated by the practices of their neighbors. All of them wrote on stone, and many stone monuments have been recovered. One method of preserving one's name and reputation was to erect a monument of stone, perhaps with the name inscribed upon it. In II Sam. 18:18 there is record of Absalom's establishment of a pillar to be a permanent memorial of his name. Whether or not his name had been inscribed upon the pillar is not stated, however.

The writer of Job was well aware of the practice of inscribing memorials and information on stone. After declaring:

> Oh that my words were written!
> Oh that they were inscribed in a book! (Job 19:23),

Job reinforced his statement by saying:

> Oh that with an iron pen and lead
> they were graven in the rock for ever! (19:24.)

Lead filled inscriptions are known, the best of which is the famous Behistun Inscription of Darius I.[11] Methods of writing seem to have been copied quite

[10] Map NIN 18, *IDB*, "Nineveh," p. 552.
[11] See above, Chap. 6, p. 83.

easily. It is possible, also, that there was considerable traffic in writing materials. Egypt had a long-established trade in papyrus. About 1100 B.C. Wen-Amon, a messenger of the pharaoh, took 500 rolls of "finished papyrus" to Phoenicia to use as part purchase of cedar logs.[12] It should be noted, however, that whether papyrus or leather was used the regular practice was to roll up the writing. Codex, or book form, was not known until Christian times, and new evidence from Egypt strongly suggests that it was early Christian writers who popularized the cut sheet and book form. References in R.S.V. to "book" are incorrect translations. The Hebrew word "Sepher" means "writing," not book, and in most cases the translation "scroll" is to be preferred.

Finished documents were borrowed and purchased, just as writing materials were. When a purchaser obtained a document he acquired all rights. There was no such thing as copyright law or author's rights in ancient days. Quotation marks and footnote credits simply did not exist. No attempt was made to preserve the original form of a document. Documents belonged to the individual or community which obtained or purchased them. It is, therefore, not surprising to find material in scripture which we now know originated outside the Hebrew community or was strongly influenced by non-Hebrew writings.

Much debate has ensued among scholars concerning the dates of individual psalms. In many cases the very nature of the psalm makes precise dating difficult if not impossible. However, much information is now available to us which clearly indicates that the period of the composition of the psalms occupied a much longer period of time than has formerly been admitted and indicates also that there has been considerable borrowing of literary types as well as concepts from neighboring countries. Psalms were known in many parts of the ancient Near East, particularly in Mesopotamia and Syria. Hymns of praise and prayers of lamentation were used regularly in the temples.[13] At the other end of the Fertile Crescent a hymn to the sun god Aton was composed during the reign of Amenhotep IV (1380-1362), who preferred to be known as Akhenaton. In spite of the fact that this pharaoh's religious innovations were completely destroyed, this prayer hymn was preserved. It was later edited and modified and now appears in our Bible as Psalm 104.[14]

On the north Syrian coast psalms composed in the same literary pattern as biblical psalms were in existence as early as the fourteenth century B.C. Literary evidence is clear that the Hebrews were influenced by these early patterns.[15] From Palestine itself there is now archaeological evidence that psalms were still being composed in the days of Jesus and down to the time

[12] ANET, pp. 25-29.
[13] ANET, pp. 383-92.
[14] "The Hymn to the Aton" may be found in ANET, pp. 369-71; see also above Chap. 6, p. 80.
[15] John Hastings Patton, Canaanite Parallels in the Book of Psalms, (Baltimore, Md.: John Hopkins Press, 1944).

immediately prior to the destruction of the Qumran community in A.D. 68.[16]

Proverbs are easily borrowed from one culture to another. Kramer calls our attention to Sumerian proverbs which have been handed on to the later generations in many cultures.[17] Of great interest to Old Testament readers are the proverbs reportedly found at Thebes and entitled, "The Instructions of Amen-em-opet."[18] These have been edited and accommodated to Palestinian culture and now appear in the book of Proverbs (22:17–24:22). In the Hebrew text the expression "thirty sayings" (22:20) has no significance. The Egyptian collection is divided into thirty chapters and in the thirtieth chapter is written:

> See thou these thirty chapters:
> They entertain; they instruct.[19]

An otherwise obscure phrase is thus explained. In addition, we are aware on the one hand of the high quality of Egyptian thought; on the other we recognize that Hebrew writers and collectors were not imprisoned within their own culture but were vitally aware of the excellent writings of their political neighbors.

The Book of Job has been recognized to be one of the great masterpieces of all time. Emil Kraeling has likened the writing of the book to the building of a great cathedral, the production of centuries.[20] We might add that, like a beautiful building, the materials for its construction have been brought from many lands. This in no way invalidates or even challenges the uniqueness and grandeur of the biblical answer to the questions of God's and man's relationship to the problems of pain and suffering. It is but to recognize that men of many nations across many centuries have sought answers to life's most baffling problems.

Parallels to the Book of Job have been found in Sumerian, Babylonian, Assyrian, and Egyptian literature. No Edomite literature has yet been found, and therefore, attempts to prove connection between the Edomites and the Book of Job have no literary substantiation. Of the many cited parallels to the thought of the Book of Job only the most significant will be noted here. A Sumerian poem found at Nippur by the first University of Pennsylvania expedition (1890) has been translated by Dr. Kramer.[21] Six pieces of the ancient tablet have been recovered; four are in the University Museum in Philadelphia, and two are in Istanbul. Kramer has entitled the poem "Man and His God: A Sumerian Version of the Job Motif." It describes

---

[16] For other influences see Williams, "Liturgical Aspects in Enthronement Psalms," *JBR* (April, 1957), pp. 118-22.

[17] *History Begins at Sumer*, pp. 119-26.

[18] *ANET*, pp. 421-25.

[19] *Ibid.*, p. 424. Comparison between the Egyptian text and Prov. 22:17-24:22 is given in *ANET*, p. 424, n. 46.

[20] *The Book of the Ways of God* (New York: Charles Scribners Sons, 1939).

[21] *History Begins at Sumer*, pp. 114-18.

a man's plea to God to be relieved of his suffering. In the end the prayers were apparently answered and happiness was restored. The petitioner seems to have belonged to a family of status, but he is specifically referred to as a young man, not an elder in the community. Of special importance are the following phrases: "You have doled out to me suffering ever anew"; "Never has a sinless child been born to its mother"; and "The disease which had smitten him . . . he (God) dissipated."

Frequently cited as a parallel to Job is the Babylonian hymn "A Pessimistic Dialogue Between Master and Servant." [22] The similarities are less striking than in the Sumerian poem already noted.

An Egyptian parallel is the didactic tale and poem "A Dispute Over Suicide." [23] The document comes from the close of the third millennium B.C. Like the Hebrew book this document (or what we have of it) begins and ends with a prose section and the middle section is in poetry. It should be noted, however, that the papyrus is incomplete and the opening portion is entirely missing. Like the biblical Job, this individual seeks death, but unlike Job, he contemplates suicide. His "soul" dissuades him, apparently, because of the probability that a suicide's soul will be forever destroyed. The document is also interesting because it clearly identifies the purpose of pyramids as "last resting places."

It has been suggested by a number of writers that the essence of an old folk tale concerning Job is to be found in chapters 1-2, and 42:10-17, and that a dramatic dialogue has been inserted into the original story.[24] There are difficulties with this thesis which are too involved to be of interest here, but it is not to be denied that there was memory of an ancient hero who struggled with the problem of suffering. It was in the biblical book alone that an individual not guilty of sin was made to suffer. This was done to challenge the current Deuteronomic philosophy that "sin brings suffering; piety brings prosperity." May we again expand Kraeling's figure of the cathedral? Old buildings are often remodeled to accommodate new needs. In the same way old documents were frequently modified to accommodate new or changed theological concepts. There is much testimony that the book was controversial as is evidenced by 42:10-17, an addition which is diametrically opposed to the main thesis of the book. It should also be noted that we have no agreement between the versions. There are wide discrepancies, some of which are theological, between the transmitted Hebrew, the Septuagint and other Greek texts, and the Coptic. An early form of the Greek text was four hundred lines shorter than the Hebrew. It is anticipated that some help with the textual problem may be found in the Targum of Job, a portion of which

---

[22] ANET, pp. 437-38; also in AOT, "Ein pessimistisches Zweigesprach zwischen einem Herrn und seinem Knecht," pp. 284 ff.

[23] ANET, pp. 405-7, from Berlin Papyrus 3024.

[24] Robert H. Pfeiffer, Le Probleme du livre de Job (Master's Thesis, Geneva, 1915), pp. 10-11; cf. his Introduction to the Old Testament (rev. ed.; New York: Harper & Row, Publishers, 1948), pp. 660 ff.; and contra, Williams, "Relative Dating of Additions to Job," The Iliff Review, XVII (Winter, 1960), 11-14.

has been recovered from the Dead Sea Caves. Perhaps again the archaeologist can assist the textual critic.

The recovery of many documents from Mesopotamia and Egypt has enabled biblical scholars to examine anew the office of prophecy among the Hebrew people. No longer can it be claimed that prophecy was unique or peculiar to the Hebrews. At three distinct points insights from the literature of contiguous people are proving to be informative to biblical research: (1) Knowledge concerning the meaning of the most common noun designating the prophet; (2) information about the probable relationship of the prophet to the cultic pattern; and (3) descriptions of the functions normally associated with the office of prophet. We shall look briefly at each of these in turn.

The Hebrew noun most commonly used to name the prophet is "Nabi." It is generally translated in the Greek as "Prophetes," from which we get our English word "prophet." It has long been recognized that the Greek expression has a literal meaning, "to speak for." It is not the equivalent of the Latin "praedictus," from which the English "predict" is derived. Cognates from Akkadian now indicate that the Greek word "prophetes" has carried the true meaning of the Hebrew "Nabi." It is true that in the later days of Judaism and in early Christianity emphasis was shifted from announcement to prediction. The eighth-, seventh-, and sixth-century prophets, however, were more concerned with announcing the word from God than with predicting events of the future. In any event, prophets usually predicted the future conditionally. All depended upon man's response to God or his failure to respond. It remained for the later apocalyptists, who spoke out of a philosophy of determinism in history, to reveal or predict precise events of the future.

Such writers as Aubrey R. Johnson have produced evidence from the religious practices of nations who were neighbors to the Hebrews to show that among these people the office of prophet was officially recognized just as was that of the priest. They have proposed that such "cultic prophets" existed among the Hebrew people.[25] My own studies have persuaded me that there is validity to the suggestion, but it must be recognized that the Hebrew pattern at least made it possible for men like Amos to speak as men who were free and not subservient to a cultic pattern. Prophets, as priests in Israel, were recognized as part of the "structure" of religious leadership. The very fact that prophets held responsibility for anointing monarchs to office made official recognition imperative.[26] Official relationship, at least mutual recognition, between prophet and priest was also essential. Prophets in Israel did not seek the elimination of liturgy, but its purging and purification.

---

[25] Johnson, The Cultic Prophet in Ancient Israel (Cardiff, Wales: University of Wales Press, 1944), pp. 6 ff.

[26] Williams, Prophets—Pioneers to Christianity, particularly Chapter 4, "Prophecy as Profession," pp. 45-56.

The right to speak concerning immoral conditions was not limited to the Hebrew prophets. We find it especially active in Egypt. The prophets Ipu-wer and Nefer-Rohu (Neferti) were particularly strong in their denunciations of evil in high places and low. Ipu-wer delivered his message sometime in latter part of the third millennium B.C. A copy of his message is preserved in the Leyden Papyrus I-344, but like so many papyri, part of the text is missing.[27] The prophet complains that society is turned topsy turvey and those who were laborers in pyramid construction are now farmers, roads are not guarded, and robbers lie in ambush for travelers. Land spins around as does the potter's wheel, and maid servants make free with their tongues. The prophet longs for the day when the monarch will again be "Authority, Perception, and Justice."

The prophecy of Nefer-Rohu speaks of the Old Kingdom and the reign of Snefru (about 2650-2600 B.C.) and makes the prediction that there will be civil war, followed by deliverance under Amen-em-het I (ca. 1960 B.C.), the first ruler of the Twelfth Dynasty. This papyrus (Leningrad 1116B) was actually written in the Eighteenth Dynasty, about 500 years later. Punishment was predicted in it from a king "belonging to the south," from Upper Egypt, the son of a Nubian mother. It predicted that he would restore the fortunes of Egypt, and that his name would be "Ameni, the triumphant." Of interest is the description of Nefer-Rohu, a lector-priest, lying prostrate before the pharaoh as he delivered his prediction, and the fact that the message is being taken down by the pharaoh himself upon papyrus.[28]

Another instance of predictive prophecy is to be found in Assyrian records, from cylinder B of Ashurbanipal and dated in 648 B.C.[29] It offers the promise of the goddess Ishtar to support Ashurbanipal in his campaign against his enemy the king of Elam and her assurance to give him victory. A similar promise of victory over his enemies is made to Esarhaddon (680-669 B.C.) by the goddess Ishtar, lady of Arbela, through the prophet Ladagil-ilu. In addition the goddess promises long life, "protracted days, everlasting years." [30]

One title of the priests in Egypt was "prophet." A priest was so designated in the record of an interview with a deceased pharaoh who had been consulted as a god. This prophet, together with other attendant priests, was witness to the oracle, or sign, given by the pharaoh, Ahmose I. The deified pharaoh, addressed as Neb-pehti-Re, had been asked to decide concerning the rightful ownership of a field. It was at first proposed that the field belonged to Pai, son of Sedjemenef. There was no response from the deified pharaoh. Then it was proposed that the field belonged to the priest Pa-ser, son of

[27] A. H. Gardiner, Admonitions of an Egyptian Sage (Leipzig, 1909); James Henry Breasted, Dawn of Conscience (New York: Charles Scribners Sons, 1933), pp. 193-200; ANET, pp. 441-44.
[28] Gardiner, Journal of Egyptian Archaeology, I (1914), 100-106. ANET, "The Prophecy of Nefer-Rohu," pp. 444-49.
[29] ANET, pp. 451-52.
[30] ANET, pp. 449-50.

Mose. The response was immediate, "the god nodded very much." Since priests carried the "god," and since a priest was one of the contenders in the appeal for ownership, collusion may be indicated. The record had then been cut on a stele which was later discovered in the temple of Ramses II at Abydos; [31] the stele is now in the Cairo Museum.

A number of instances are given in scripture of revelation by means of dreams, ofttimes with a prophet supplying the meaning of the dream (Dan. 2:17-45). A stele which still stands between the forepaws of the Sphinx records a dream which came to the Pharaoh Thut-mose IV about October, of the year 1420 B.C. The stele is actually a restoration and was placed in its present position several hundred years after the time of Thut-mose IV. It tells of the day when Thut-mose was weary from hunting and took his noon day rest in the shadow of the Sphinx. During his sleep Harmakhis, the spirit in the Sphinx, appeared to Thut-mose and asked him to clear away the sand which had covered up the lower part of the Sphinx. This, apparently, the young pharaoh did. Of interest is the statement, "Look at me, my son, Thut-mose! I am thy father, Harmakhis-Khepri-Re-Atum." This seems to connect the sphinx with Chephren, builder of the second pyramid, as does the "Sports Stele" of Thut-mose III.[32] Prophecy and other means of revelation were known to many nations in the ancient Near East. The Hebrews had no monopoly in this area.

Another area in which there appears to be a relationship between the Hebrews and their neighbors is in the field of music and musical instruments. At least it is true that the modern investigator is heavily dependent for information concerning Hebrew music upon the records left by Babylonians, Assyrians, and Egyptians. Of great importance is the information which is found in pictures carved on stone showing musical instruments in use and instruments which are portrayed on coins. In addition, portions of instruments have been found in tombs and excavations. Unfortunately time and weather have destroyed instruments of wood and the skins, gut, and reed from which instruments were made.

We are concerned at this point, not with the history of music, or even with a detailed description of various musical instruments. Such information is readily available in books and articles on these subjects. We are concerned here with information which may be derived from archaeological research concerning the influence of nations upon each other in the area of music. Music, then as now, was concerned with the major aspects of life. Trumpets to sound the battle cry were as important as weapons. There was singing and dancing at social events. Vocal and instrumental music was important in

---

[31] G. Legrain, *Annales du service des antiquites de l'Egypte*, XVI (1916), 161-70; and *ANET*, p. 448.

[32] Breasted, *Ancient Records*, II, ¶¶ 810-15; and *ANET*, p. 449.

worship and in magic incantation. We have description of music frequently being used to stir up prophetic ecstasy. It is strange that with frequent reference to the shepherd there is but one place in scripture in which mention is made of the shepherd's pipe (Judg. 5:16). There is, of course, the traditional association of David the shepherd and David the musician. By tradition he has been associated with the harp, and the Negro spiritual says, "Little David, play on your harp." The account of David playing for Saul pictures him with a lyre, not a harp, and certainly not the shepherd's pipe (I Sam. 19:9). It has been the practice, however, for shepherds to play the pipe or flute. Such instruments are readily made from material available in the field. They are easily carried about, and when not in use they can be slipped into a pocket or pouch and do not interfere with activities of the shepherd.

For convenience we shall discuss the information which is available concerning discovered instruments under the headings of percussion, stringed, and wind instruments. It is necessary, however, to note that Curt Sachs[33] has suggested that Hebrew music employed a pentatonic scale, not the octave. If this is true, then harmony and counterpoint as we know it would not have been possible. There is much evidence in scripture that variety in choral music was obtained with antiphonal choirs. Variety was also possible by using the ancient counterpart of "voice speaking choirs," and by having the "dark" voices respond to the "light" voices. There seems also to have been greater emphasis upon percussion instruments rather than the tonic scale. It is, therefore, difficult to determine whether certain stringed or wind instruments were used primarily for rhythm or for pitch. It is also to be noted that the Hebrews had apparently earned a reputation as musicians, for in the Annals of Sennacherib (704-681) it is recorded not only that he made Hezekiah a prisoner in Jerusalem "like a bird in a cage," but also that in the tribute paid by Hezekiah there were included "male and female musicians." [34] Scripture indicates that the Babylonians required their Hebrew captives to "Sing us one of the songs of Zion" (Ps. 137:2-3). There is reference also to their musical instrument the lyre.

The percussion instruments were the drum, the cymbal, the sistrum, and the rattle. The Hebrew word "toph" seems to include instruments constructed by stretching a skin over a simple frame. Because of lack of information the word "toph" is variously translated "timbrel," "tabret," or "tambourine," but in modern Hebrew the word means "drum." If we are to judge from the paintings from Egypt hand drums were common and usually quite small. They had no loose metallic disks as the modern tambourine does.[35]

Cymbals were of two kinds, the harsh cymbal, which was played by the

[33] The History of Musical Instruments (New York: W. W. Norton & Company, Inc., 1940).

[34] ANET, p. 288.

[35] Erman, Life in Ancient Egypt (1896).

performer beating vertically; and the clear cymbal, which was beaten horizontally. Illustrations of both have been found on Assyrian monuments.[36]

The sistrum seems to have originated in Egypt but was accepted by the Hebrews in spite of the fact that the sistrum was associated with the goddess Hathor. The sistrum is a simple loop of metal affixed to a handle. Holes were bored in the loop through which pieces of wire were loosely inserted and bent over to prevent their becoming detached. The frame was shaken to produce a tinkling sound. Reference is made to this instrument in II Sam. 6:5 where R.S.V. translates "castanets," but the K.J.V. is wholly mistaken and translates "cornets." William F. Albright found the handle of a sistrum at Bethel. It had the Hathor head similar to those which have been found in Egypt.[37]

Rattles, bells, and gongs, have also been found,[38] but there is question concerning usage. A bell was placed on the skirt of Aaron's robe to signal his coming into the presence of the Lord (Exod. 28:34-35). Bells were used on the harness of horses as is indicated in Zech. 14:20. No other usage is mentioned in the Bible, but it is quite possible that bells were used to keep track of animals as is done today. Such uses are primarily utilitarian rather than "musical."

There were many stringed instruments including the lyre, the harp, and the zither. All stringed instruments were plucked either with the finger or with a plectrum. None were played with a bow, at least there is no reference in scripture to such usage, nor do we find any illustrations on the monuments showing the use of a bow. The Hebrew "Kinnor" has been translated "harp" but in most cases it must mean "lyre," and in modern Hebrew the word has come to mean "violin."

No such stringed instruments as lyre and harp are found in Egypt as early as the Old Kingdom. The Beni-hasan monument (ca. 1900 B.C.) shows a Semite playing a lyre. Sellers indicates that this stringed instrument was introduced to the Egyptians by the Asiatics.[39] The earliest illustration, just noted, shows a simple instrument with a few strings attached to an almost square frame being played with a plectrum, the left hand muting the unwanted sounds. A painting from an Eighteenth Dynasty tomb (ca. 1570-1310 B.C.) shows a larger instrument which stands on the floor; the player, a girl, kneels at one end with part of the frame resting on her shoulder. In this case she plucks the strings with both hands.[40] Margaret Murray calls

[36] Wellhausen, *Holy Bible, Polychrome Edition*, appendix to volume on Psalms, pp. 220-32, "Music of the Ancient Hebrews."

[37] Sellers, "Musical Instruments of Israel," *BA* (September, 1941), 34-47, figs. 12a, 12b; and *IDB*, Fig. MUS 81, "Musical Instruments," p. 471.

[38] Sellers, "Musical Instruments of Israel," fig. 13.

[39] *Ibid.*, p. 37; fig. 3.

[40] *IDB*, fig. MUS 82, "Musical Instruments," p. 471; see also figs. MUS 89, 91, pp. 474-75.

our attention to the "Blind Harper" monument in the Leyden Museum.[41] In this case the harpist plucks the strings with both hands and holds the instrument in typical harpist fashion. The frame is a simple curve with no apparent sound box. There are tuning pegs at the top of the frame. Dr. Murray also draws our attention to the illustration of the animal musicians on an eighteenth dynasty papyrus in the Turin Museum.[42] Here the animal orchestra is led by a donkey playing the harp. A lion plays the lyre and appears to be singing; a crocodile plays another stringed instrument, possibly a lute; and a monkey plays the double oboe, not the flute as Miss Murray suggests.

We have already noted the harp which was recovered from Ur in Mesopotamia.[43] Other instances of the use of the harp are to be noted on the monuments. A band including three harpists is carved on a monument at Susa, a band which is playing to King Ashurbanipal of Assyria.[44] It will be noted that each harp has its sound box at the top, not the bottom. The step from lyre to harp seems to have been taken in both Egypt and Assyria.

Dr. Sellers accepts the suggestion that the Hebrew 'asor (Ps. 33:2; 92:3; 144:9) may have been a zither, a Phoenician instrument in which ten strings were stretched upon a square frame.[45]

The best known of the wind instruments is the horn or trumpet. The horn of a ram or goat (but not a cow) was known as the "shophar," or "Qeren." It is still used ceremonially by Jews at the New Year. The horn was steamed to make it pliable and then straightened, except perhaps for a curve at the large or bell end. The instrument could also be made of metal. It was then called "chatsotserah." Moses was commanded (Num. 10:2) to make two silver trumpets. Such trumpets were carved in bas relief on the Arch of Titus in Rome. According to Josephus trumpets were about sixteen or seventeen inches in length. The trumpets were also portrayed on Jewish coins of the second century A.D.

Wellhausen notes an early Egyptian flute which is quite long.[46] It was played by blowing across the open end of the reed, and the tones were controlled with finger holes.

An Egyptian double clarinet from the Empire period has been recovered by the Oriental Institute and has actually been played. There are normally six finger holes, the upper three holes in one pipe and controlled by the fingers of one hand; the three lower holes in the second pipe and controlled by the other hand. In the model found by the Oriental Institute there are only five holes.

[41] The Splendour That Was Egypt (New York: Philosophical Library, Inc., 1949), Plate LXXIII, 2.

[42] Ibid., Plate LXXIX, 1.

[43] See above, Chap. 2, p. 34.

[44] IDB, fig. MUS 84, "Musical Instruments," p. 472.

[45] Sachs, The History of Musical Instruments, p. 118.

[46] Music of the Ancient Hebrews, p. 219.

In the Book of Daniel many musical instruments are listed (3:5, 7, 10, 15), but most of the names are non-Semitic, and none are Hebrew. All are Greek but two, which are Aramaic. In addition, many musical terms are included in titles of the psalms, the meaning of some of which are still unknown. It is hoped that with further recoveries of written records and illustrations of ancient cultures still more certainty can be brought into our knowledge of ancient Hebrew music.

Some of the earliest books on biblical archaeology called attention to the many similarities between the opening chapters of Genesis and the writings of other nations, particularly that of the Babylonians and Assyrians. In the years that have intervened between the first discovered parallels and the present time many other parallels have been identified. It has also been recognized that there are dissimilarities, that literary parallels did not necessarily entail similarity of religious beliefs. More and more attention was called to the fact that Hebrew writers used the writings of other people but that they edited them so that they could carry Hebrew conviction concerning ethical monotheism. There has been much discussion concerning the opening chapter in Genesis with the evident allusion to polytheism in 1:26, perhaps the result of imperfect editing. Careful reading of the early chapters in Genesis (1–11) does indicate to the reader that there is literary dependence upon non-Hebrew documents. This position is too well established to be denied at this late date.

Recognition of sources is one thing; the purpose of the edited material is the more important consideration. In these chapters in Genesis it is evident that the editors were coming to grips with some of the basic problems of life. The story of creation (1:1–2:4) is concerned not with "How" but "Who." There is the story and the problem, "Why does man die?" Another story is involved with the question of man's communication with man, "Why do men speak different languages?" There are the genealogies and the all-important question of the relationship between the first beings created and the purpose of God through the descendants of Abraham. There is the beginning of the story of salvation in the account of Noah. The very position of these chapters strongly suggests that they have been prepared as introductory material for the saga of Israel. For this reason, therefore, it is suggested that these chapters should no longer be classified as "primitive philosophy" borrowed from neighboring nations, but "wisdom literature" which includes ancient legendary material combined with the deepest insights of ethical monotheism.

It is the combination of the finest literary expressions with the keen insights of Hebrew religious experience which makes biblical literature the magnificent creation that it is. The Hebrews were not an ingrown people. They were part of the culture of the whole of the ancient Near East. Our debt to them is great.

13.
PARALLELS
TO BIBLICAL CUSTOMS

In the preceding chapter we gave attention to what happens when nations rub shoulders with nations—the ways in which each group's habits affect the conduct of all concerned. The theme will be continued in this chapter except that the emphasis in this chapter will be largely upon individuals rather than the group. Particular attention will be given to insights which have come through archaeology upon otherwise obscure patterns of conduct.

It was sometimes assumed in the early part of this century that in order to gain insights into the patterns of patriarchal life the best and quickest method was to live in a contemporary patriarchal society such as that of the Arabs of Palestine or Arabia. Books were written describing tent life and the wandering ways of the modern Bedouin. Undoubtedly some insights were obtained in this way. Father Roland de Vaux's book *Ancient Israel: Its Life and Institutions* has shown the value which may be derived from a careful sociological study of such society.[1] He fully recognized two disabilities of such study. First, it is a false assumption that there is a direct connection between ancient patriarchal customs of the early Hebrews and the modern Bedouin of the Near and Middle East and that no changes have taken place between then and now. We used to read frequently such phrases as "the unchanging East," "the immovable East," et cetera. The East has changed in many ways, if only to accept the conveniences of automobiles, modern fire arms, the wrist watch, and transistor radios. It was startling in the hills of Gilead to have the workman complain that the signal to stop work had been a minute or two late "according to radio time," and on another occasion to hear them discussing the tragic death of Dag Hammarskjöld in Africa, which had just been flashed on the air.

The second false assumption is that there is a simple and direct line of culture descent from patriarchal times to the Bedouin life of today, uninfluenced by any other people or any other national customs. Cultural influence is much more complicated than that. Many influences can be seen in modern society. We speak of the United States being "a melting pot," recognizing that people from many lands are assimilated into the American way of life, though we are not always willing to recognize the influences and contributions which they make to American life. The Hebrew people were influenced by many neighbors, and they in turn put their influence upon others.

Investigation concerning ancient ways is much more complicated than observing the supposed parallel pattern of one society to another will indi-

[1] New York: McGraw-Hill Book Company, 1961, translated from the French by McHugh.

154

cate. Written documents in great quantities have been recovered from neighboring nations. In these documents many words and phrases have been found which are specifically parallel to obscure or poorly understood expressions in the Old Testament.

Many of these obscurities are to be found in the records which pertain to the patriarchal period, and it is precisely this period for which significant help has been found through archaeology. Especially illuminating are the records which come from Mari (Tell el-Hariri) on the River Euphrates; from Nuzi (Yorghan Tepe) just south of Kirkuk, Iraq, on the Adhaim River, a tributary of the Tigris; and from Ugarit (Ras Shamra) on the north Syrian coast. Some twenty thousand documents were found at Mari, several thousand at Nuzi, and several hundred at Ugarit. All of them were written in cuneiform, date from the middle centuries of the second millennium B.C., and are generally contemporary with the patriarchal period of the Hebrews.[2]

Marriage and family life are central in any society. Among the Semites, including the Hebrews, the purpose of marriage was not companionship but the ongoing of the family and clan. For this reason provisions were made in marriage contracts for the contingency that the wife might be unable to produce children, provisions for procedures which seem strange to modern Western civilization.

When Sarah remained childless she gave Hagar, her maid, an Egyptian, to Abraham as a temporary wife (Gen. 16:1-3), and to this union Ishmael was born. In a Nuzi adoption tablet, Shennima was adopted by Shuriha-ilu, a circumstance to which we shall refer later, but in addition to adoption he was also to be married to Kelim-ninu, Shuriha-ilu's daughter.[3] Provision was made that if Kelim-ninu gave birth to children Shennima would not be free to marry another wife. If she was unable to bear children, however, then she had the responsibility of procuring a "woman of the land of Lullu," perhaps a slave woman, to be the proxy wife of Shennima. Further provision was made that if such a proxy wife had to be provided, and if offspring resulted to that union, then Kelim-ninu could not send such children away. Similar provision was recognized among the Hebrews; in spite of Sarah's jealousy of Hagar she could not dismiss her, but she made things so uncomfortable for Hagar that she fled (Gen. 16:5-6). The record tells us that Hagar was sent back by an angel of the Lord (16:9), but jealousy was not to be stayed. After the birth of Isaac Sarah dismissed Hagar and her son, much to Abraham's displeasure. He finally consented to the dismissal only after he was convinced that he had received God's approval (21:9-14).

By tradition Arabs are the descendants of Ishmael and through him con-

---

[2] On Mari see M. Noth, *Mari und Israel* (1953): Albright, *BASOR* (February, 1940), pp. 23 ff., 30 ff., 78; and Mendenhall, *BA*, XI (1948), 1-19; on Nuzi see E. Chiera and E. A. Speiser, *AASOR*, VI (1926), 75-90; C. H. Gordon, "Biblical Customs and the Nuzu Tablets," *BA*, III (1940), 1-12; on Ugarit see above, Chap. 6, pp. 75-78.

[3] *ANET*, p. 220.

sider themselves to be the legal descendants of Abraham. Again and again we were made aware of this in the Near and Middle East, particularly in Jordan. They said, "We are descendants of Abraham's firstborn. We have been dispossessed. The law of the tent has been violated." Right or wrong, they make their appeal to history and to tradition.

In the second generation after Abraham a variation of the pattern of children by proxy was used by the wives of Jacob. Jacob married both Leah and Rachel. Leah bore four sons (Gen. 29:31-35), but Rachel was childless. She gave her maid Bilhah to Jacob, saying, "Here is my maid Bilhah; go in to her, that she may bear children upon my knees, and even I may have children through her" (Gen. 30:3, Italics added). Two sons were born to that union. In turn, Leah was disturbed because no more children came to her, and Rachel had now become the favorite wife. Rachel said, "With mighty wrestling I have wrestled with my sister, and have prevailed" (30:8). Leah therefore gave Zilpah, her maidservant, to Jacob as wife. When children came to this union it was Leah who named them, and their names indicated her supreme pleasure at this new turn of events.

Still another pattern was used in ancient society to preserve the family name and responsibility. Prior to the birth of either Ishmael or Isaac Abram's slave servant Eliezer had been adopted as a son. Abram said, "I continue childless, and the heir of my house is Eliezer of Damascus" (15:2). He continued, "Behold, thou [God] hast given me no offspring; and a slave born in my house will be my heir" (15:3). Again we are indebted to the Nuzi documents for illustration through a parallel situation. An important duty of a son was to bury the dead father with dignity and honor and to tend the burial place so that the needs of the deceased could be cared for. Provisions for the carrying out of such duties in the event that there was no son was made by legal adoption of a son who accepted these responsibilities and as a reward became legal inheritor of the property. Shennima, mentioned previously, became a son of Shuriha-ilu by adoption. This is mentioned first, and his marriage to Shuriha-ilu's daughter, by which he became a son-in-law, is listed second. Provision is made that if Shuriha-ilu should have a son of his own that son would inherit a double share of the estate, but Shennima would still inherit one share. It is specifically provided that he could not be disinherited, nor could Shuriha-ilu adopt another son.[4] No provision seems to have been made for Eliezer in the event that a son was born to Abram—simply the notation, "This man shall not be your heir."

Cyrus H. Gordon has called our attention to the Nuzi adoption tablet which is parallel to the case of Jacob who apparently became the adopted son of Laban as well as his son-in-law.[5] It is not stated in scripture that Laban made such an adoption, but parallels to Nuzi adoption provisions are

[4] Albright, *Archaeology of Palestine and the Bible* (Westwood, N.J.: Fleming H. Revell Company, 1935), pp. 137-39.
[5] "Biblical Customs and the Nuzu Tablets," pp. 5-7.

startling and suggestive. At the time of Jacob's marriage to the daughters of Laban there is no mention of sons of Laban, (Gen. 29), but there is reference to them twenty years later (31:1). When Jacob finally decided to leave Laban he informed Leah and Rachel of his decision and charged their father with cheating him. The wives agreed and added that Laban had cheated them also and had taken the dowry which rightfully belonged to them and left them penniless (31:15). In addition, they recognized that they no longer had any inheritance (31:14), perhaps because their brothers would now inherit Laban's estate. Before they left Rachel "stole her father's household gods" (31:19) but without telling Jacob that she had done so.[6]

Upon his discovery of the departure of Jacob and the loss of his household gods (teraphim) Laban pursued Jacob and his family. Search was made for the household gods, but they were not found. They had been hidden in a camel's saddle upon which Rachel sat. This clearly indicates that they were very small. So important were the teraphim that Jacob said to Laban, "Anyone with whom you find your gods shall not live" (31:32). In a Nuzi sale-adoption tablet arrangements were made for legal adoption of Wullu by Nashwi.[7] The usual provision was made for division of the estate in case Nashwi had a son of his own. Then it was provided that in this event Nashwi's own son should receive the household gods, otherwise the gods would go to Wullu, the adopted son. Wullu was also married to Nuhuyu, a daughter of Nashwi, with the provision that Wullu would lose the rights of inheritance if he married another wife. When Laban finally settled with Jacob he said, "The daughters are my daughters, the children are my children, the flocks are my flocks, and all that you see is mine" (31:43). These are formal words of ownership. Then a contract was made and witnessed between Jacob and Laban. It was sealed with the Covenant of Mizpah, "The Lord watch between you and me, when we are absent one from the other." But it went on to say, "If you ill-treat my daughters, or if you take wives besides my daughters, although no man is with us, remember, God is witness between you and me" (31:49-50).

Related to the pattern of children by proxy is the law of Levirate Marriage, Deut. 25:5-10. This law provided that if a man died childless his brother should have union with the widow. A son born to that union would be considered the son of the deceased, not the son of the actual father. It should be noted that the sin of Onan (Gen. 38:8-9) was not that he "practiced birth control," but that he failed in his obligation to his brother's name and memory.

Gordon suggests that while Deuteronomy states that the purpose of levirate marriage is "that his name may not be blotted out of Israel" (25:6), the practice may have had its origin in purchase of brides and family owner-

---

[6] See above, Chap. 1, p. 18.
[7] ANET, pp. 219-20.

ship of such a purchase. He refers to such provision in Nuzi.[8] The Bible indicates that there were varying interpretations of the levirate law, as in the case of Ruth. Neither the "next of kin" (who is not named) nor Boaz was brother to Ruth's deceased husband. Some remnant of the law was still remembered in the days of Jesus in spite of the Levitical law (Lev. 18:16; 20:21) forbidding such sexual relationship. Jesus was asked a question which involved controversy between the Sadducees and the Pharisees. The Sadducees posited the hypothetical situation: A man died childless, but had six brothers, each of whom in turn performed the duty of temporary husband to the widow under the levirate law. Then the question was asked, "In the resurrection, therefore, to which of the seven will she be wife?" (Matt. 22:28). The answer was clear. She remained the wife of the first brother until a son was produced in his name, but for Jesus to answer in this way would have put him in immediate controversy with the Sadducees. He used the opportunity, as he usually did in such circumstances, to speak of more significant issues—in this case, the spiritual nature of the resurrection (Matt. 22:29-33).

Some formality of uniting bride and groom is to be found in most societies. We have no knowledge of a wedding ceremony performed by a priest in Old Testament times, and even today a wedding among the Bedouin is public celebration and family arrangement, not a rite to be presided over by a religious official. Provision has now been made in some countries that marriages must be registered with local officers, often religious leaders, but this is merely a form of control by the state, not formal religious blessing of marriage.

The wedding usually consists of the groom and attendants making their way to the tent (or house) of the bride and "abducting" the bride. After this formality, during which there is much hilarity, the bride and groom are escorted to the groom's tent. A canopy, representing the tent, is still used as symbol in Jewish weddings today. Again there is much singing, and feasting is added to the celebration. How many nights we have listened into the wee hours of the morning while the local impromptu "choir" has rehearsed and rehearsed. In some communities the bride and groom are king and queen during the wedding and in the days which immediately follow. This is the counterpart of the "honeymoon."

The marriage pattern is now recognized by many scholars to be the significance of the Song of Songs. It is a collection of courting and mating songs. The groom is King Solomon, and the bride is his queen.[9] Theodor H. Gaster has suggested also that Psalm 45 may be in this same pattern, and that this psalm was intended to be a general wedding song rather than a formal composition for a king's wedding. He cites many parallels to literature from neighboring nations to substantiate his claim, particularly the literature

[8] "Biblical Customs and the Nuzu Tablets," p. 10; and Revue Biblique (1935), p. 38.
[9] N. K. Gottwald, "Song of Songs," IDB, pp. 423-24.

from Ugarit.[10] Of particular interest is the parallel between Psalm 45, Song of Songs, and the Ugaritic "Birth of the Gracious Gods," in their praise of the beauty and courage of the king or bridegroom. Gaster further notes that biblical descriptions of both Saul and David emphasize their physical perfection and beauty, a royal characteristic demanded by the people.

Surprisingly little is said in the Bible concerning the laws of inheritance. The right of the firstborn son to a double portion is affirmed in Deut. 21:17. Provision is made in the Middle Assyrian laws found at Ashur: "The oldest son shall choose and take two portions as his share and then his brothers one after the other shall choose and take theirs." [11] As we have already noted, a son born to a proxy wife could not be disinherited. The late priestly record remembers the case of the five daughters of Zelophehad (Num. 27:1-11). Their father had died without having produced any sons. The daughters pleaded with Moses that they be given inheritance to their father's estate. It was then decided that in the case of a deceased man who had no sons the rights to inheritance should pass first to daughters, then in turn to the deceased's brothers, to his uncles, and failing this to any next of kin.

Provision was not made in scripture for inheritance by widows. T. J. Meek has stated that only among the Hebrews was the inheritance right of the widow disregarded.[12] Yet the provision for Levirate marriage enabled the widow to provide for her future by giving birth to a son who would care for her; she would also benefit, at least indirectly, from his inheritance. No provision is stated concerning remarriage, except that it is expressly stated that no priest may marry a widow. On the other hand, Hebrew generosity made careful provision for the "widows and orphans." At harvesttime these indigent members of society had the rights of gleaning the fruit trees and the fields of grain. Naomi was beneficiary of this practice until she was able to benefit from Ruth's marriage to Boaz, and so was Ruth herself even though she was a foreigner. Special provision was made that a widow's clothing could not be held in pawn.[13]

An individual's name not only identified him and his family, it was believed by the ancients that a man's name was his very essence. Much attention has been given by scholars to the meanings of names, and many have been identified. In the Old Testament most of the names are not explained. In a recent study Andrew F. Key said: "except for etiological stories, the attempt at explanation is found only where the name is actually being conferred." [14] Many of the names are explained by popular etymology. Outstanding are the names "Moses" and "Hebrew." The first is an Egyptian name "Mose," meaning "son," but it is explained by the Hebrew verb

[10] Theodor H. Gaster, "Psalm 45," JBL (December, 1955), pp. 239-51.
[11] ANET, p. 185.
[12] Hebrew Origins (rev. ed.; New York: Harper & Row, Publishers, 1950), p. 77.
[13] Deut. 24:19; 24:17.
[14] "The Giving of Proper Names in the Old Testament," JBL (March, 1964), pp. 55 ff.

which means "to draw out" (Exod. 2:10)—a strange language for an Egyptian princess to use. The national name "Hebrew" apparently became a term of reproach or enmity, such as the Egyptian term "Epiru." It was not used by the Hebrews of themselves until well along into the period of the monarchy. It was then explained from the Hebrew verb which means "to cross over." Other names were similarly explained.

The very fact that some names were explained clearly indicates that names did have meanings in many cases. They reflect the relationship of the parents to God, the circumstances under which the child was born, or a special mission or characteristic of the individual. Parallels may be found in the documents of neighboring nations.

A monarch's name usually indicated his special relationship to God. Ra-Mose (Ramses) was "son of the god Ra," and Thut-Mose was "son of the god Thoth." Nebuchadrezzar (or Nebuchadnezzar) worshiped the god Nabu or Nebo, and his name signified "Nabu protect my boundary stone." The name Samuel literally means "His name is El (God)" and not, as popularly interpreted, "asked of the Lord" (I Sam. 1:20). The name Jonathan signified "Gift of God."

Lists of names can make dull reading and one can sympathize with the small boy who was heard reading from his Bible, "Skipit, begat Skipit. . . ." Yet strange names can tell us much. Names betray national backgrounds. If, for instance, we read of a party of Englishmen traveling together, and we find listed among them such individuals as Sandy McTavish and Heinrich Schmidt, we know that there has been some intrusion into the national group. Genealogical lists in the Bible indicate relationship with other people. For example, Aramaean kinsmen of Abraham are found in Genesis (22:20-24), unless these are actually names of Aramaean communities.

Names ofttimes tell of the circumstances under which the child was born. The name Samuel may indicate his parents' adoration of God or that the child was considered to be holy because his· birth followed his mother's special petition to God, as in the case of Samuel. In quite an opposite mood was the name of a child at Ugarit. We know him only because he is later listed as a contributor to the temple funds. His name seems to mean quite literally "The night the well fell in." It is not hard to guess what happened the night he was born.

Basic to the sanctity of the home is the faithful wife and mother. Severe penalties were inflicted where there were violations of the marriage vows, death being the penalty for adultery. One basic consideration was property values; if a woman's body was illegally violated then her marketable value as a wife was destroyed. She belonged to her father until she was married; then she became the possession of her husband. Little attention was paid to the wishes of the woman. In an illicit love affair, even though the woman had consented, the man was guilty if he knew that she was already betrothed or the wife of another man.

160

The consent of the father was basic to marriage. The Eshnunna Code, paragraph 27, provided that even though a man and woman had lived together as man and wife for a year, if the father had not given consent they were not legally man and wife. The same provision was made in the Hammurabi Code, paragraph 128, and in Exod. 22:16-17 there is a parallel provision: "If a man seduces a virgin who is not betrothed, and lies with her, he shall give the marriage present for her, and make her his wife. If her father utterly refuses to give her to him, he shall pay money equivalent to the marriage present for virgins." Provisions were made for the death penalty for adultery in Eshnunna Code, paragraph 28; Hammurabi Code, paragraph 130; and Hittite Code, paragraphs 197-98.[15]

Provision was, however, made to protect the family rights of the man who was taken captive in war and was therefore unable to return to his home. In the event that his wife had remarried in his absence (because he was "presumed lost") he could reclaim her upon his return. If, however, a man ran away because he "hates his town and his lord" and his wife remarried during his absence, he would have no claim on her when he returned—Eshnunna, paragraphs 29 and 30.[16]

Dr. Gordon notes a parallel between Hos. 2:4-5, and a Nuzi Tablet (N 444:19-23) in which a faithless wife is stripped naked by her own children and is driven from the house.[17] There seems to have been no such provision in such codes as Lipit Ishtar, Eshnunna, Hammurabi, or Hittite. Nor was there any law in Israel so far as the biblical record is concerned, but we do have the outbursts of Ezekiel against the two sisters who had become harlots (Ezek. 16:39; 23:26), neither of whom was a wife.

Formal contracts applied to many things beside marriage. Just as legal phrases are used regularly in modern wills and deeds of sale or transfer of property, so stereotyped phrases were used in an ancient day. Today we take oaths and affirm these in court or in the presence of a notary public by placing our hands on a Bible or by lifting our hand as an oath is made. There were parallel acts in ancient days.

We are indebted to E. A. Speiser for enabling us to see the legal implications of Isaac's statement, "Behold, I am old; I do not know the day of my death" (Gen. 27:2).[18] Isaac then instructed Esau to make the necessary provision for the cermonial meal which was eaten before the formal blessing was given. Dr. Speiser notes that Nuzi text HSS, IX, 34, included the clause "now that I have grown old," which was recognized in Nuzi circles as a legal phrase expressing a man's last will and testament.[19] Both Speiser and

[15] ANET, pp. 162, 171, 196.
[16] ANET, p. 162.
[17] "Biblical Customs and the Nuzu Tablets," p. 10. The name "Nuzu" always appears in the genitive form "Nuzi".
[18] "I Know Not the Day of My Death," JBL (December, 1955), pp. 252-56.
[19] Cyrus H. Gordon cites similar parallels. See note 17.

Gordon see close relationship between this formal statement of Isaac's and the pattern of accepting deathbed statements. Speiser says, "That a deathbed statement could be legally binding is shown conclusively by a Nuzi lawsuit.[20] In this case the plaintiff, Tarmiya, states that his dying father, Huya, had promised to give him Sululi-Ishtar to be his wife, so that like his older brothers he too would be married. The statement was taken before the judges; eyewitness testimony was given to the truth of Tarmiya's statement; and the judges ruled in favor of the plaintiff. As a result the brideprice was shared by the brothers, perhaps another way of indicating that it came out of the estate.

How much, if any, legal transaction could be reduced to writing in the patriarchal society is highly questionable. While writing was in existence, it was not common in Palestine. There is no indication in the patriarchal records of any use of writing. Therefore the spoken word took on added authority. Any formally uttered pronouncement of intent, properly attested, had legal standing, just as did a deathbed statement. Attestation could be either by witnesses or by a common oath taken in the presence of God to which, presumably, God was witness. Such an agreement was that between Jacob and Laban, already noted: "Remember," said Laban, "God is witness between you and me." [21]

It should further be noted that if Dr. Speiser's identification of the statement of Isaac as legal phraseology is correct, then the so called "blessings" are in the nature of a last will and testament.

Another form of attestation was the removal of the sandal(s). Again we are indebted to Dr. Speiser for pointing to parallels between the Hebrew and Nuzi writings.[22] In addition he has thrown real meaning into the declaration of probity in office of Samuel (I Sam. 12:2-5). The Book of Ruth relates the incident of the removal of the sandal, but the author has to note that it was an ancient practice. He does not fully explain it, however (Ruth 4:7-8). Provision was made in the Deuteronomic law, that when a man refused to perform the function of levirate husband, the widow could pull off his sandal, spit in his face, and put a name of reproach upon him (Deut. 25:9-10). Two citations are made by Speiser from the Nuzi documents. In both cases a transaction which would otherwise be illegal is made legal by transferring a pair of shoes, presumably as a symbol of purchase.[23] The situation in Ruth is at least partially understood against these parallels. The symbolism in Deuteronomy does not fit the same pattern—unless the woman, by drawing off the man's own sandal and giving it to him, is indicating her rejection of his right to function as her "Goel," or redeemer; this rejection being accompanied by spitting and a name of reproach.

[20] AASOR, XVI, 56.
[21] See also M. H. Pope, "Oaths," IDB, pp. 575-77.
[22] "Of Shoes and Shekels," BASOR (February, 1940), 15-20.
[23] Ibid., p. 17; HSS V, 76, and HSS V, 17.

The symbol of the sandal as an earnest for purchase would appear to be quite flimsy, especially since in the case of Ruth the "next of kin," not Boaz, was the one to draw off the sandal, by this signifying his unwillingness to redeem Ruth and agreeing that Boaz could assume this responsibility. May there be a hidden meaning, that by removing the sandal he was recognizing the sacredness of the vow, a symbol of standing on holy ground? Nothing has been found to validate this suggestion.

In the case of Samuel the suggestion of Speiser is quite clear. He compares the Hebrew text upon which our English translation is based with that of the Greek (Septuagint) text. In the Hebrew we read, "Whom have I defrauded? whom have I oppressed? or of whose hand have I received any bribe to blind mine eyes therewith? and I will restore it you" (12:3b K.J.V.). The R.S.V. inserts the phrase from the LXX "Testify against me" between the last question and the phrase "and I will restore it to you." The LXX text reads, "Or of whose hand have I taken a bribe and a shoe? Testify against me and I will return it to you." Misunderstanding of customs led to the change from "and a shoe [or shoes]" to "blind mine eyes." Which is correct?

Speiser suggests that since a token gift of sandals or shoes simply met a legality and had no real value, Samuel is indicating that he neither took bribes nor resorted to technicalities to circumvent the law. Dr. Speiser also suggests that the "allusion of Amos to 'the selling of the needy for a pair of shoes' can easily be appreciated." [24]

Slavery was recognized as part of the social structure in all countries of the ancient Near East. Laws governed the conditions of slavery and protected rights of slaves of various classes and their owners. Comparison of the law codes indicates that adjustments were made in accordance with economic or other conditions of the various countries.

Hebrew laws on slavery are recorded in Exodus 21, Leviticus 25, and Deuteronomy 15. Provision is made in the first and third of these for a Hebrew to be released from slavery at the end of six years. The provision in Leviticus contains the famous "proclaim liberty throughout the land to all its inhabitants" (vs. 10). It is an introduction to release from slavery in the year of jubilee, the fiftieth year (25:10). In the Hammurabi Code a free man's life was worth three years of labor, and he could in case of debt become a de facto slave for that period of time. Exod. 21:2 provides that a Hebrew sold into similar slavery would serve six years. Presumably a man's daily labor was not worth as much in Palestine, or perhaps his life was worth twice as much as in Mesopotamia. There may be further consideration that by serving six years he was freed in the Sabbath year; at least it worked out that way.

Babylonian laws indicate that there could be marriage between freeborn women and slaves. Children born to such union were protected by law and

[24] *Ibid.*, p. 18.

could not be held in slavery (Hammurabi, paragraph 175). The Hebrew code provided that if a slave came into slavery single but was married during his slavery he would go out single. The children belonged to the master. (Exod. 21:3-4). Provision was made for the man to become a permanent slave if he preferred to remain with the wife and children he had acquired during slavery (Exod. 21:5-6). The ceremony was that of putting an awl through the lobe of the slave's ear into a doorpost. This symbolized contract between the master, the slave, and the god of the doorpost or the home.[25]

As the Hebrews settled on the land and tended crops as well as animals, the observance of months and seasons became increasingly important. Days of the week were not named, except for the Sabbath. Months were determined by the movements of the moon, thus giving 29½ days to each month. This was adjusted by alternating 29- and 30-day months, making a 354-day year. In 1908 Macalister discovered a soft limestone tablet on which someone named Abi had scratched a calendar. It was found at Gezer and dates from the last part of the tenth century B.C.[26] No names are given for the months, and the list, which may have been a schoolboy's exercise, simply gives agricultural events, such as planting and harvesting, in terms of the time necessary for each.[27] George Cameron has described some of the careful observation in Babylon which was necessary to the making of correct calendars.[28] The early Babylonian noted that there was no agreement between the cycle of the moon and that of the sun. The agriculturist preferred to follow the moon calendar, as the Gezer calendar indicates, but in so doing his planting and harvesting periods would shift from year to year, since planting and harvest are subject to action of the sun. The Babylonians, therefore, inserted an extra month periodically so as to keep the sun and moon calendars in approximate relationship. The Hebrews followed this same pattern. The Egyptians preferred to round out each month to thirty days. There were twelve months of thirty days each, a total of 360 days, which was followed by a five-day period which was outside any month, but brought the year to 365 days. Even so, there was discrepancy of nearly ¼ day each year. We moderns adjust this by the method of adding an extra day in "leap year." The Egyptians carefully noted differences between the solar year and the siderial year by measuring the position of the star Sothis (Sirius) on the first day of the new year. Archaeologists have been able to use this listing of measurements to check Egyptian dates. In the "Sothic Cycle" there was a discrepancy of a full year every 1460 years between the solar and sothic calendar. This calendar was never accepted by the Hebrews.

[25] Williams, "God of the Door Post," *Iliff Review*, XII (Winter, 1955), pp. 44-45.
[26] *IDB*, fig. CAL 2, "Calendar," p. 485; and *ANET*, p. 320.
[27] Macalister, *Gezer II*, pp. 24-28, and III, plate CXXVII. The generally quoted translation is that given by Albright, *BASOR* (December, 1943), pp. 16-26. A recent article challenges the translation "hoeing up of flax" since flax is not normally grown in Palestine.
[28] Cameron, "The Babylonian Scientist and His Hebrew Colleague," *BA* (May, 1944), pp. 21-29, 32-40.

terms of the newly discovered, but short-lived, freedom. Facsimiles of these coins now appear on current issues of Israeli stamps.

With the destruction of ancient buildings the records of nations and individuals were entombed. The individual who wrote, the nation of which he was a citizen and whose records he so carefully kept, and the neighbors with whom he lived and whose letters he may have read have once again become vital and living people and countries. We recognize that they were our predecessors in so many activities and that we are indebted to them.

14.
NEW KNOWLEDGE
OF ANCIENT LANGUAGES

By the latter half of the fourth millennium B.C. man had learned to write and to read. Writing is the communication of ideas through visible signs which have been marked down. Speech is the communication of ideas through the sound of the voice. Writing is a transfer of sounds into inscribed visual symbols. Many visual means of communication have been used by man—for example, the notching of a stick to count the days or to number the cattle under the care of a herdsman. Writing as we normally think of it is the next step in communication by which there can be a steady flow of ideas. There are two main forms of such transfer of information from one person to another. The first is the use of pictures, sometimes stylized, by which thoughts and actions, but not precise words, are represented. For example, pictures can tell the story of a hunter killing deer, removing their hides, and presenting choice portions of the meat to a chieftain. Such a story can be read by one who speaks French, Chinese, Urdu, or Sioux.

A second method of writing is the use of symbols which evoke in the reader's mind specific sounds, which in turn resemble human speech. Thus the writing "speaks to us." Ignace J. Gelb calls our attention to the poetic expression of Voltaire,[1] "L'ecriture est la peinture de la voix; plus elle est ressemblante, meilleure elle est." Such a method of writing makes it possible not only to communicate thoughts to persons at distant places, but too the message can also be transmitted across many centuries. Because thoughts have been imprisoned in symbols it is possible for us to know, thousands of years later, just what was said (or at least written down) in civilizations which would otherwise be lost to us. There is the further advantage to posterity that many individuals, when faced with the prospect of imprisoning their thoughts in writing, are more orderly and circumspect in their statements (although occasionally more verbose).

One hundred fifty years ago the only ancient languages remembered in the Western world were Latin, Greek, and Hebrew. Today, our libraries have hundreds of volumes containing translations from dozens of languages which were used throughout the ancient Near and Middle East. Since the languages had been forgotten and were no longer used, the only way these languages could be known to us was through writing. Before this could be done, however, symbols on monuments had to be recognized as writing. Such perception came slowly.

For many centuries there had been several instances of ancient writing

[1] *A Study of Writing* (Chicago: University of Chicago Press, 1952), p. 13.

in full view to men, but little heed had been paid to them, and no attempt had been made to understand what the signs meant. We now know that one of the easier ways to decipher unknown writing is to obtain a document in which the same message is given in two languages, a known and an unknown. Such bilingual, and occasionally trilingual, documents or monuments are sometimes found. Such was the case in the decipherment of ancient Egyptian.

In 1799 Napoleon's workers recovered a piece of black basalt stone near Rosetta, Egypt. It measured 3 feet, 9 inches high, 2 feet, 4½ inches wide, and 11 inches thick.[2] Now known as the Rosetta Stone, the monument immediately aroused interest. It contained writing in three different forms, only one of which could be recognized—the Greek. The others were identified as Egyptian hieroglyphic, or sacred writing, and demotic, or common writing. From the Greek, which could easily be read, the stone was seen to be one which had been erected in 196 B.C. by the Egyptian priests in honor of King Ptolemy V Epiphanes (ca. 203-181 B.C.) for exempting the temples of Egypt from certain taxes. It was assumed that the three kinds of writing said the same thing and that, therefore, the monument could be used as a key to the unknown writings represented on the stone. Both assumptions were proved to be correct, and ancient Egyptian can now be read.

Initial work was done by a Swedish diplomat, Akerblad; an English physicist, Thomas Young; and a French linguist, Jean Francois Champollion. It was Champollion's brilliant work in 1818-22 which finally gave the completed solution to the decipherment of Egyptian hieroglyphs. The major clue, suggested by Young, was a recognition that the name "Ptolemy" occurred in the Greek at a corresponding position to a symbol in the hieroglyphic, an oval, barred at one end, containing several signs, ⬭. It was proposed that such a ring could be a designation of a royal leader, and this was demonstrated to be correct. These ovals are now known by the French name "cartouche," meaning an ornamental enclosure.

Bit by bit the symbols were made to recover their sense, and the whole inscription was translated. In the meantime other inscriptions were being recognized and made available. International cooperation in the field of scholarship quickly produced dictionaries and grammars of the newly deciphered language. Most important, a large body of information concerning the Egyptians and other nations throughout the whole of the Fertile Crescent was made available to historians and students of the Bible. Egypt was seen to be a great nation which made large cultural contributions, produced magnificent art and great literature, invented tools and made scientific observations in medicine, physiology, and astronomy, and was skillful in

[2] G. Frederick Owen, *Archaeology and the Bible* (Westwood, N. J.: Fleming H. Revell Company, 1961), p. 32.

many handicrafts. The Egyptians were seen to be somewhat more than oppressors and unreliable political allies of the Hebrews.

We noted earlier the importance of the inscriptions which were copied by Henry Rawlinson between 1835 and 1847 at Behistun, Iran.[4] The work of translation by Rawlinson and those associated with him had been made easier because of the discoveries of the Englishman, William Jones; the Dane, Rasmus Christian Rask; and the German, Franz Bopp. William Jones, born in London in 1746, had been primarily interested in such languages as Persian, Arabic, and Hebrew. For financial reasons he made law his career and went as a colonial magistrate to India. There he studied Sanskrit, the Hindu language of scholarship and literature. He recognized that there was a structural and family relationship between the languages he had studied, but he was unable to pursue his studies further because of pressure of official duties.[5] The suggestion of Jones was taken up by Rask (1786-1832), and still later by Bopp. Bopp introduced scientific method into comparative linguistics and published a comparative grammar of seven languages including Sanskrit, Greek, Latin, and German.[6]

The work of these three men enabled other scholars to recognize that by studying families of languages insights could be obtained on the meanings of words in those related languages. Rawlinson's knowledge of modern Persian enabled him to solve more quickly the ancient Persian. Knowledge of Hebrew and Arabic enabled Rawlinson and others to identify words in Akkadian, or Babylonian.

It was through discovering the names of King Darius and his son Xerxes that G. F. Grotefend of Germany was able to make some early and tentative identifications of cuneiform, or wedged-shaped signs. These suggestions, together with knowledge of modern Persian, enabled Rawlinson to decipher the Persian section of the Behistun inscription. In turn the Median and the Babylonian sections of the inscription were then translated.

When Rawlinson made claim that Babylonian could be translated there was much skepticism. Because of the skepticism an Irish clergyman suggested to the British Museum that a test should be made by giving an untranslated inscription to several scholars, asking them to work independently, and then checking to see if their results were comparable. The suggestion was accepted, and in 1857 copies of a historical inscription from the time of Tiglath-pileser I were given to four men—two Englishmen, Rawlinson and Edward Hincks; an Irishman, H. Fox Talbot; and J. Oppert, a Frenchman. Eventually, translations were received by "the examining committee" of the British Museum. After careful comparison of the work of the four men it was decided that the translations were in close enough agreement that it could be said that the interpretation of cuneiform was an accomplished fact. The re-

---

[4] See above, Chap. 6, p. 83.
[5] See Ceram, *The Secret of the Hittites*, p. 75.
[6] *Ibid.*, p. 76.

sults of the four translators were published by the Royal Asiatic Society in 1857.[7]

These two monuments, the Rosetta Stone, and the Behistun Rock made possible translation of material from one end of the Fertile Crescent to the other. Especially important was the solution of cuneiform because it led to the reading of many other languages. Just as the Latin alphabet is used today for the printing of many languages around the world, so the syllabic signs which had begun in Sumerian times were used to write Babylonian, Assyrian, Neo-Babylonian, Nuzi, Hittite, and other languages.

In the cases just described the nations with which the monuments were associated were known even though the writing of those nations was unknown. Let us now look at two very different situations. The first is a group of clay tablets which were found on the North Syrian coast at Ras Shamra, ancient Ugarit. The tablets were covered with simple cuneiform signs; that is, there were no complicated combinations of wedges. In addition, examination showed that there were only thirty different combinations of wedges altogether. Clearly this was not syllabic, but alphabetic writing. The problem of deciphering was compounded, however, by the fact that the excavators were faced with an unknown script in an unknown language by an unknown people. While Johannes Friedrich has declared, "Nothing can be deciphered out of nothing," [8] the fact is that what man has invented other men can solve. Two circumstances strongly suggested that the writing was Semitic: (1) The tablets had been found in territory which had been generally occupied by Semites across the centuries, and (2) the words in the inscriptions were quite short, and apparently triliteral, a characteristic of the Semitic languages.

Now the archaeologists turned to another type of aid in solving strange writing. Cryptographers know that in modern languages some letters are used much more frequently than others. For example, the most commonly used letter is "e." Tables of frequency of use of other letters have been worked out. In addition, some letters appear more frequently than others at the beginning of words, or are doubled, or have some other characteristic use. The same principles apply in ancient languages. In the Semitic languages the equivalent of the letter "l" occurs most often and regularly appears at the beginnings of words. Checking the tablets it was discovered that three upright wedges used as one sign appeared quite often and frequently at the beginning of words. Presumably this was the letter "l." Then scholars looked for a two-letter word, the second of which was "l." Perhaps this was the word "El" which means "god." Other short words were tentatively identified.

Meantime some ceremonial axes inscribed with the wedge-shaped signs

---

[7] Ira M. Price, et al., The Monuments and the Old Testament (Valley Forge, Pa.: Judson Press, 1959), pp. 61-62.
[8] Quoted by Ceram, The Secret of the Hittites, p. 99.

had been found. The inscription was identified as a typical dedication phrase which named the object and contained the words "chief priest." Eventually the entire alphabet was identified, and translation was made possible. The Ugaritic language was related closely to early Canaanite, Phoenician, and Hebrew. Identification of meanings of words was possible because of the scholar's knowledge of these other languages. Comparative linguistics helped him with vocabulary and grammatical construction. This language is now taught in many of our seminaries and universities. It is an important one because of the contents of the tablets discovered. The nature of the content of these tablets we have already listed in Chapter 6.[9]

In addition, the Ras Shamra tablets are highly important because they contain the earliest use so far discovered of an alphabet, with the exception of an occasional word or phrase as in the case of the Sinaitic inscriptions.[10] Many attempts have been made to trace the origin of the Ugaritic signs and their relationship to the various alphabets which were later developed.[11] No suggested source of origin has met with the approval of the majority of experts in the field. While working on the tablets thirty years ago I became convinced that this was an invented alphabet.[12] The forms are simple. They can be readily arranged morphologically; that is, in a scheme based upon the direction of the wedges and their number. The signs evidently are not attempts to imitate pictures. They are signs arbitrarily invented, not borrowed. The importance of invention in writing is excellently presented by Dr. Gelb in his book A Study of Writing, Chapter 4.

Equally important and less debatable is the fact that the order of the alphabet which was later accepted by the Phoenicians, Canaanites, Hebrews, and Greeks had already been worked out at Ugarit. We have already noted the alphabetic exercise tablet found at Ras Shamra.[13] It seems probable, however, that while the order of the alphabet which has come with some modification down to our own day was known earliest at Ugarit, the concept of alphabetic writing was not invented there.

Another method of identification and translation of ancient documents was used in the case of Hittite. After many monuments had been recognized as belonging to the Hittites, there still remained the problem of reading documents written in their language. No one knew what the Hittite language was or its relationship to other languages. Much information had already been obtained concerning the Hittites because of their practice of writing their official political documents in the currently popular Akkadian, the international language of the latter part of the second millennium B.C. Two other types of Hittite writings had been recovered—those which were

[9] See above, p. 77.
[10] See Martin Sprengling, The Alphabet (Chicago: University of Chicago Press, 1931).
[11] For a full discussion of the problems of the origin of the alphabet see Gelb, op. cit., pp. 120 ff.
[12] See above, Chap. 6, p. 77, note 9.
[13] Chap. 6, p. 77.

NEW KNOWLEDGE OF ANCIENT LANGUAGES

written in the cuneiform syllables but spelling unrecognizable words and sentences, and pictographic writings with no known parallels.

After the death of Hugo Winckler the German Orient Society of Berlin placed the Hittite cuneiform material from Boghazköy in the care of a group of young Assyriologists for study and transcription. Included in the group was the Czech, Bedrich Hrozny, who had been born in Poland in 1879. He was in his middle thirties when World War I broke out, and the scholar found himself in military service. Strangely enough, and perhaps with the blessing of his superior officers, Hrozny was still able to continue his research.

While working on transcription he suddenly became aware of the possibility that the Hittite language was related, not to the Semitic family of languages, but to the Indo-European. He was working on a sentence which read, "nu ninda-an ezzatteni vadar-ma ekutteni." He recognized the word "ninda" which meant bread. He assumed that if the sentence dealt with food, then perhaps it would also contain the word "eat." From his knowledge of Old High German he tentatively identified German "ezzan" with the Hittite "ezzatteni." This immediately suggested the possibility that "vadar" in Hittite might be an equivalent of German "wasser"; Old Saxon, "watar"; English, "water." Eventually he was satisfied that the Hittite sentence must be read "Now you will eat bread, further you will drink water." [14] The most significant part of the discovery was the recognition that Hittite belonged to the Indo-European family of languages. Hrozny reported his findings to the Near Eastern Society of Berlin, November 24, 1915, and in 1917 his volume *The Language of the Hittites; Its Structure and Its Membership in the Indo-European Linguistic Family* was printed in Leipzig.[15]

The decipherment of pictographic Hittite has taken much longer. Little progress had been made by the late 1920's. One important fact had been noted; namely, that Hittite picture writing had characters which were the same except that they faced in opposite directions. Then it became clear that the writer wrote one line from left to right and the next from right to left, constantly reversing as he went down the tablet, just as a field is plowed. The writing was therefore named "boustrophedon," "bull-plowing," or more literally "bull-turning." Even in reading it is especially important to know the direction in which one is supposed to go.

In 1928 Meriggi, an Italian, made some important suggestions. New interest was aroused, and about 1930 such scholars as Ignace J. Gelb, Emil O. Forrer, and Helmuth T. Bossert entered the field. In 1934 a new group of clay seals were found at Boghazköy by Kurt Bittle. Of the group of about three hundred, one third were bilingual, combining hieroglyphic and cunei-

[14] Ceram, *The Secret of the Hittites*, pp. 83-84.
[15] See also his "Über die Völker und Sprachen des alten Chatti-Landes," *Boghazkoi-Studien*, No. 5 (Leipzig, 1920). In 1947 a bilingual inscription (old Phoenician and hieroglyphic Hittite) was found by H. T. Bossert at Karatepe. Its importance for decipherment is recognized by Hittitologists. Cf. O. R. Gurney, *The Hittites* (London: Penguin Books, 1952), pp. 8, 12-13.

form writing. Scholars are now well on their way to agreement concerning the reading of hieroglyphic Hittite.

Many publications which give the reader information concerning the Hittites are available. Perhaps none is more exciting or interesting than one written by the German novelist who uses the pseudonym C. W. Ceram. Earlier he had written a best-selling book based upon careful research, *Gods, Graves, and Scholars*. So successful was this publication that the publishers suggested that he write another book dealing with archaeology. After canvassing the field of Near Eastern archaeology Ceram was convinced that no story was more exciting than that of the ancient Hittites.[16] His account is informative and thoroughly dependable, but he would be the first to admit that it could not have been written without the patient and sometimes tedious work of the specialist who discovers the secrets hidden in strange pictures and symbols. The work of the epigraphist and linguist give flesh, blood, and spirit to the skeletons unearthed by the excavator. It is from the translations of the men gifted in knowledge of ancient languages that we are able to learn of literary parallels in our Bible.

There are many other languages and scripts which have been studied and interpreted. The ones selected were chosen specifically because they indicate clearly the methods and steps by which the seemingly unintelligible can be made, not only understandable, but informative. A few examples of the insights which have come from non-Hebrew documents and which give us better understanding of biblical passages will help us to understand our indebtedness to this specialized phase of archaeology.

When the Ark of the Lord was returned to Jerusalem, David accompanied it, "and danced before the Lord" (II Sam. 6:12-14). When he returned to the house his wife Michal severely criticized him and spoke disparagingly of his conduct. The word which has been translated "dance" occurs only once in scripture and had to be translated according to the context. This same word has now been found in the Ugaritic tablets. Its meaning is "to dance," but—at least in the Ugaritic texts—the dance was a special ritualistic action of the nature religion. This may be why the regular word meaning "dance" was not used to relate this story of David, and this may well explain why his wife Michal "despised him in her heart" (II Sam. 6:16).

Another word which occurs only once in scripture, this also in the books of Samuel (I Sam. 13:21), is the word "pim." It is translated incorrectly in the K.J.V. as "file" which makes little sense. The discovery of several stone weights, each of which was inscribed with this word, indicates that it is the name of a weight, "two thirds of a shekel."[17] The account is partially translated in R.S.V. and the account tells us that the charge for sharpening plows and

---

[16] This chapter depends in part on Ceram's *The Secret of the Hittites*.

[17] Julius A. Bewer, "Notes on I Sam. 13:21; II Sam. 23:1; Ps. 48:8," *JBL* (March, 1942), p. 46, and Scott, "The Shekel Sign on Stone Weights," *BASOR* (February, 1959), pp. 32-35.

mattocks was "a pim" but doesn't tell us what a "pim" is. Now we have the necessary information, and from it we learn that the charge was twice as much for sharpening a plow as for an axe.

From the Ugaritic tablets we have help on a difficult passage in Jeremiah. In Jer. 3:13 we read the condemnation of Israel because she

> rebelled against the Lord your God
> and scattered your favors among strangers under every green tree.

The word translated "favors" should be rendered "strength" if we accept the Ugaritic "dirktu." The passage would then harmonize perfectly with other condemnations brought by Jeremiah against the devotees of Baalism. The nature religion actually sapped the strength of its devotees.

In Prov. 31:10-31 is the poem describing the good wife. Verse 21 has caused some perplexity. It reads:

> She is not afraid of snow for her household,
> for all her household are clothed in scarlet.

Commentators have raised questions concerning the significance of "scarlet," pointing out that color has little to do with warmth. G. R. Driver has called our attention to a phrase in the Ugaritic literature which brings meaning into the Proverbs description.[18] The passage cited from Ugarit describes the birth of Baal's child, a bull, to Anat. The text goes on to say that "she covered him with two [coverings]." The word covering is not in the text but is understood. The word which has been translated "scarlet" is a special form of the number "two" as indicated by the Ugaritic text. Two garments are used in this case to keep the newly born child warm. The passage in Proverbs may then be read "for all her household are clothed in double garments." Color was not the question.

Another passage in the Old Testament takes on fresh meaning when it is examined against the Ugaritic literature. When the people asked Samuel to give them a king he naturally protested because he thought that it was a criticism of his own leadership and the capabilities of his sons. In I Sam. 8:10-18 Samuel lists the various burdens that kingship would put upon the Hebrew people. I. Mendelsohn has discussed this passage in the light of our knowledge of the monarchies at Ugarit and Alalakh.[19] Mendelsohn discusses Samuel's statement under four heads: (1) Service in the army, (2) appropriation of property, (3) taxation, and (4) slavery. The first threat from a king was that of subjecting the people to service in the army (vss. 11b-12a). According to the Ugaritic records it was established pattern for kings not only to impress men into service, but to put them into two classifications, the com-

---

[18] "On a Passage in the Baal Epic (IV AB iii 24) and Proverbs xxxi 21," BASOR (February, 1947), p. 11.

[19] "Samuel's Denunciation of Kingship in the Light of the Akkadian Documents from Ugarit," BASOR (October, 1956), pp. 17-22.

moners who served as foot soldiers and the professional warriors who owned property, particularly horses. This divided society into classes, and while Mendelsohn does not discuss this, it was probably an irritation to the members of the tribes that they faced this kind of division. Kings regularly conquered or appropriated property (vs. 14). One is reminded of the story of the appropriation of Naboth's vineyard. Taxes were collected by kings by imposing a tithe on produce and cattle (vss. 14, 17a). Such taxation is attested from Ugarit. Taxes included the tithe, a grazing tax, toll from goods in transit, contributions, and fines. A "pilku" tax is also mentioned but its nature is not known.

Kings also subjected people to the corvee, a type of tax paid by working for a period of time (vss. 12b-13, 16). Solomon later used this pattern but scripture specifies that he could not use Hebrews in this kind of service. Again, there is much evidence from Ugarit that this kind of service was already in existence by the time of the conquest of Palestine by the Hebrews. From these parallels Mendelsohn infers that Samuel was drawing the attention of the people to history and to the experiences which their neighbors had had with monarchs. It has been suggested by some Bible commentators that the list of warnings in this passage in I Samuel was written much later, after the Hebrews themselves had experienced difficulty with the monarchy. Mendelsohn is correct when he says that Samuel knew well the problems of his day and the new problems which would arise if Israel became a monarchy. In this case records of an ancient people help not only in interpreting the significance of biblical statements, but also by revealing social patterns of neighboring peoples enable the critic to date the time when passages of scripture were written.

There has been much controversy over the Copper Scroll found in Cave III at Qumran. Its content centers around hidden treasures. According to some legends, treasures from the old Temple were buried in hiding places in Palestine. These stories were known for a long time prior to the discovery of the Copper Scroll and have been generally discredited. John M. Allegro takes them quite seriously in spite of the preposterous size of the treasures presumably buried. It is estimated that the weight of the sixty treasures mentioned in the twelve columns of the scroll would be not less than two hundred tons of gold and silver, plus other treasures. Allegro, who proposed the program for opening the scroll, has spent much time seeking to identify the hiding places mentioned in the scroll. In rejecting Allegro's "treasure hunt" little attention has been given to his identification of places. One is of particular interest in helping us to understand one of the oracles of Isaiah. In 22:1, 5, the prophet speaks of "the valley of vision." Allegro identifies this as part of the city of Jerusalem, perhaps a place where prophetic vision was regularly given.[20]

[20] *The Treasure of the Copper Scroll* (Garden City, N.Y.: Doubleday & Company, Inc., 1960), pp. 85 ff. Allegro and others suggest that copper was chosen for this scroll so that information would be permanently preserved.

The Dead Sea Scrolls are helpful at many points. The copies of biblical books can be compared with traditional texts. The commentaries give meaning to obscure Hebrew words by stating the meaning that various expressions had in the days of the Qumran Covenanters. In addition, there is much help from noncanonical and nonscriptural books.

The Dead Sea Scrolls include many copies of the book of Isaiah. Of great importance to the translators of the Revised Standard Version was the scroll designated I Q Isaᵃ. It was used in the making of the revision. In Isa. 21:8 the Hebrew (and the KJV) reads: "And he cried, A lion: My Lord, I stand continually upon the watchtower," which doesn't make much sense. Following the reading of the Dead Sea Scroll, the RSV says:

> Then he who saw cried:
> Upon a watchtower I stand, O Lord,
>   continually by day.

This obviously makes better sense. While the difference in English is great, the actual difference in the Hebrew text is just the transposition of two letters. The RSV is in this case supported by a tradition that is older than the KJV.

Isa. 26:8 in RSV reads:

> In the path of thy judgments,
>   O Lord, we wait for thee;
> thy memorial name
>   is the desire of our soul.

Again there is help from I Q Isaᵃ which reads: "In the paths of thy judgments, O Lord, we wait for thy name and thy law is the desire of our soul." [21] Similarly in Isa. 37:27 the reading in the Dead Sea Scroll is better than the confused figure of the traditional text, which reads:

> "like grass on the housetops,
>   blighted before it is grown."

Following the Dead Sea Scroll we would translate it to read, "like grass on the housetops, burned by the east wind."

It is on the basis of the Dead Sea Scroll reading of Isa. 23:6 that the whole lament concerning Tyre takes on added meaning. The oracle is addressed to "the ships of Tarshish" warning them that the great harbor has been destroyed. The Dead Sea Scroll in Isa. 23:6 reads "You who pass over to Tarshish, wail, O inhabitants of the coast." It is on the basis of this reading that R. B. Y. Scott proposes that verse 10 should read, "Sail away from your land, O ships of Tarshish; there is no harbor any more." [22]

[21] *IB*, V, 307.
[22] *IB*, V, 295.

In a number of cases the text of the Dead Sea copies of Bible books followed the text of the Septuagint rather than the traditional Hebrew (Masoretic) text. This is particularly true in the books of Samuel found in Cave IV. "For example," wrote Frank M. Cross, "in the few published fragments of the archaic Samuel text (4QSam^b), there are some thirteen readings in which the Qumran text agrees with the Greek against the readings of the received text, four readings in which the Qumran text agrees with the traditional text against the Septuagint." [23] In the larger Samuel manuscript (4QSam^a), according to Cross, the agreements between Qumran and the Septuagint are even more numerous. Clearly the studies which Cross is making concerning the relationships between the ancient manuscripts is of the highest significance. The time has come when the older attitude that we should turn to the versions only when something is obviously wrong with the Hebrew can no longer be held.

The question is not one of the supposed superiority of the Hebrew Bible over the Greek Bible or vice versa. Examination of each individual book must be made. Apparently in the case of the books of Samuel the Greek tradition has preserved material which has been lost to the Hebrew. One aspect of Dr. Cross's studies of Samuel is especially significant. He notes that the Chronicler "often utilized an edition of Samuel closer to the tradition of the Cave IV scroll than to that which survived in the Masoretic recension." [24]

Establishing the exact text, known as "lower criticism," is highly important. Determining when, under what circumstances, and by whom material was written is equally important. It is known as "higher criticism" or textual analysis. Since the first five books of the Bible make no claim to have been written by Moses, even though tradition has asserted that he did write them, any statement about authorship is a matter of judgment. If, on the basis of evidence, I assert that Gen. 1:1–2:4a was written by the Priestly writer, I am indicating the results of text study or "higher criticism." If my friend asserts that Moses did the writing, again on the basis of evidence, he is announcing his results of text study, although he perhaps would hesitate to use the term "higher criticism." It is to be observed that textual analysis is a method of study, in fact a combination of them. It is not a theological position, nor even an attitude, except as one seeks to be objective in study.

An amazing demonstration of the validity of textual analysis and its related field of historical criticism is to be found in the Dead Sea Scrolls. In the last part of the nineteenth century (1890) some scrolls were found in a genizah of a Cairo synagogue.[25] Among these was a document variously called the "Zadokite Fragments," the "Genizah Fragments," or the "Damascus

---

[23] *The Ancient Library of Qumran* (London: Duckworth & Company, Ltd., 1958), p. 133.

[24] *Ibid.*, p. 141.

[25] A "genizah" is a room in a synagogue which is "a last resting place" where outworn and other unused manuscripts are formally discarded.

Covenant." These fragments were studied by Schechter.[26] He recognized that the actual writing of the copy he had was not earlier than the middle ages, but that the original must have been written either in the second or first century B.C. He also stated that it had been written by a member of a religious sect he identified with the Essenes who had lived in the Judean wilderness. It was with his publication in 1910 that great controversy arose over the question of the relationship of the Essenes to John Baptist and to the Christian movement.

In the first cave examined at Qumran a document now designated the Book of Discipline is recognized to be a literary parallel to the Damascus Covenant. In addition, copies of the Damascus Covenant itself have been recovered from Qumran, including the opening section which Schechter had suggested was missing from the Cairo copy of the Damascus Covenant. In all essential points Schechter has been sustained. His analysis was correct and his proposed dates have been supported by actual evidence. The community of Qumran Covenanters fit the location and dates of the community that Schechter said must have existed. It is because of this identification that there has been the same kind of controversy recently concerning the Essenes as there was in the days of Schechter. We shall leave to the next chapter the question of the suggested influence of the Essenes upon John Baptist and Jesus. Suffice it to say at this point that no study of the Essenes can be made without careful examination of the Dead Sea Scrolls.

Theodor H. Gaster calls our attention to a Qumran tradition of some interest. In the Qumran text "The Oration of Moses" [27] there is reference to the fathers wandering until the tenth day of the seventh month. Gaster makes the suggestion that this is an anniversary of the "day God drowned Pharaoh" not the end of the forty years of wandering. He cites the same tradition among the Mandaeans.[28]

We have noted above[29] that there is question concerning the classification of the Qumran "Wars of the Children of Light and the Children of Darkness" as apocalyptic. This will depend upon the definition of apocalypticism. Too much confusion has arisen from the fact that apocalyptic literature has been identified with a pattern of writing rather than a point of view, particularly a view of history. Distinction must be made between the body of apocalypticism and the clothing in which it is presented. My colleague Martin Rist has rendered real service by defining apocalypticism in terms of its theology and philosophy, and secondarily in terms of its literary characteristics.[30]

[26] *Documents of Jewish Sectaries* (2 vols.; Cambridge, England: Cambridge University Press, 1910).
[27] D. Barthélemy and J. T. Milik, *Discoveries in the Judean Desert* (London: Oxford University Press, I, 1960), 79-80; and Theodor H. Gaster, editor and translator, *The Dead Sea Scriptures* (Garden City, N.Y.: Doubleday & Company, Inc., 1956), p. 235.
[28] *BASOR* (October, 1958), p. 33.
[29] See above, Chap. 6, p. 74.
[30] "Apocalypticism," *IDB*, pp. 157-61.

Cosmic dualism with conflict between God and Satan is central in such books as Revelation. In such books the present age is wholly in the hands of Satan or his counterpart, and the true followers of God suffer at the hands of the evil forces. The only hope for the future is divine intervention and the coming of a new heaven and a new earth which will be God-given. Man cannot "build the kingdom." Question must be raised concerning whether or not the Qumran community and its literature fit into this pattern.

The community is certainly a separated community. It broke away from main-line Judaism, not because it believed that men were essentially evil, but because it believed that the religious leaders had failed in their responsibility and had become corrupt. Under the "Teacher of Righteousness," who is nowhere identified with "Messiah," they believed that they could lead righteous lives. They were examined regularly to see whether they had moved up or down the scale of righteousness. This is clear indication that the community did not teach that man was essentially evil, but they did believe that he could become evil. Their very title, "Sons of Righteousness" or "Sons of Light," asserts their belief in the essential goodness of man.

As we examine the "War Scroll" it is again apparent that there are major differences between this war and the struggle which one sees in apocryphal literature or the New Testament Apocalypse. This war is upon the earth, and it is not cosmic, although it may have cosmic overtones. The armies are the Qumran Covenanters themselves, and their enemies are named. They are the nations who live around them. To be sure there is an indication that the angels of God fight with them and not their enemies. In the end the enemy will have been overcome with the help of God, but there is no indication that evil will have been forever vanquished and Satan dethroned. The new age is not God-given except in the sense that God and his angels fight with them. The new age will be here upon the earth and is a continuation of the age of which they have been a part. In this sense, the Qumran Covenanters have a view of good and evil and a view of history and the eschaton which is much more in harmony with the prophets than the apocalyptists.

It has, of course, been recognized that there was historically no such thing as a sudden cutting off of the prophetic point of view and an adoption of the apocalyptic. Yet the points of view are so diametrically opposed to each other that it is difficult to see how there can be any compromise of positions. There seems, however, to have been a shift in related areas of thought which eventually led to the major shift of position. There was increasing despair concerning the ability of man to bring about the new age of which he had dreamed. There was increasing emphasis upon the necessity of divine intervention. As the Hebrews identified themselves and their country with God's purposes in history some answer other than man's failure seemed to be necessary. Always there had been the constant impact of various kinds of dualistic thinking of neighboring religions. The Qumran Scrolls bear testimony to some of the changes in religious thought from prophetic to apocalyptic. One of the important studies awaiting biblical scholars is an examination of the relationship between Old Testament apocalypticism, intertestamental apocalypticism, and New Testament apocalypticism.

Archaeologists in Israel have recovered significant material from Masada, Nahal Hever, and caves south of the Wadi Murabbaat. Of particular importance is the material pertaining to the defence of Masada in April, A.D. 73, and primary source material from the Second Jewish Revolt under Ben Kosiba, A.D. 132-135.[31]

It is apparent, therefore, that extra-biblical material goes far beyond attesting historicity of biblical characters or their contemporaries in neighboring nations. There is not only added historical, geographical, and sociological information. The documents enable us to understand the language of the Bible itself, either by giving us meanings of words which have hitherto escaped our attention or by helping us to see that the word used was not a Hebrew word but one borrowed from the neighbors and used as the neighbors would have used it. Finally, these documents enable us again to appreciate the fact that the Hebrew people were not isolated. They were part of an enormous culture which spread throughout the Near and Middle East. To be sure the Hebrews had their own peculiarities, as did the other nations, but they had many things in common with other nations. As we make comparisons of their life and thought, it becomes increasingly clear that the contributions of the Hebrews was not in the way they pitched their tents or built their houses, but in the knowledge of God brought to them by men who were deeply aware of the presence of God in their lives. The Hebrews disagreed with the Greek concept "know thyself." They would not be interested that we have such concern to know them. The word of their religious leaders to them and their word to us is, "Know God."

[31] Cf. *The Israel Exploration Journal*, Vol. VII, No. 1 (1957); *The Expedition to the Judean Desert, 1960* (reprint from *BIES* 1961) pp. 5-86; *The Expedition to the Judean Desert, 1961* (reprint from *BIES*, 1962), pp. 139-243; and Y. Yadin: "The Excavation of Masada—1963/64" in *Israel Exploration Journal*, XV (1965) 1 ff., translated from *BIES* (1965).

15.

BIBLICAL AND
EXTRA-BIBLICAL MANUSCRIPTS

Ralph Waldo Emerson said, "The Hebrew and Greek Scriptures contain immortal sentences that have been bread of life to millions." [1] The central place of scripture in synagogue and church is fully recognized, and recent publication of new translations and the revision of earlier translations of the Old and New Testaments is testimony to the continuing demand of the reading public. The appearance of the New English Bible—New Testament was hailed as "the most important non-fiction publication" of 1961. [2] Similar tribute was paid to recent translation of The Torah. [3]

These translations are but reminders of the fact that Jewish and Christian Scriptures have their origin in languages which are unknown to all but a few of the readers. Translation "into the common tongue" has been an accepted responsibility of church and synagogue throughout the history of the two institutions. Men skilled in the ancient languages have served faithfully and well in providing intelligible translations for worshiping congregations.

In order that we may have a faithful translation into our own language it is first necessary to have a trustworthy copy in the original language. No original copy of any Bible book has ever been found. We have only copies which are several hundred years later than the original writings. By comparing the oldest copies, in whatever language, it is possible to obtain a document which is in harmony with the best synagogue and church traditions. In the case of the Old Testament we have had older manuscripts in Greek than we do in Hebrew, at least until recently. With the discovery of the Dead Sea Scrolls we now have copies of Old Testament books in Hebrew which are a thousand years older than any Bible books we have previously had in that language and four to five hundred years older than any copies we have had in Greek. This is one major reason why the discovery of the Dead Sea Scrolls is so important for Bible study.

In the main, the synagogue and the church have done an amazing job of transmitting faithfully the writings we call scripture. When we remember the hazards through which these writings have come we are amazed that they have fared so well. It was not until the close of the first century of the Christian Era that Judaism gave official recognition to scripture at the Council of Jamnia (Jebna). Prior to that time there had been acceptance by the people and even a quasi recognition by the leaders. Yet attempts had been made to destroy the religious literature of Judaism. The writer of I Maccabees

[1] "Address to Divinity Students," July 15, 1838.
[2] London: Oxford University and Cambridge University Presses
[3] Philadelphia: Jewish Publication Society of America; 1962.

records, "On the 15th of Chislev, in 168 B.C., he [Antiochus] erected a dreadful abomination upon the altar, . . . and wherever they found the book of the Law, they tore them up and burned them" (1:54-56). Possessers of such writing were condemned to death (1:57). Copies were preserved in spite of threats.

All such documents were handwritten, and copies were made by hand for hundreds of years. It was not until the middle of the fifteenth century A.D. that printing was invented. Claims are still made on behalf of Laurens Jansoon Coster of Haarlem, Holland, that he had a printing press with movable type as early as 1423, but these claims have not been substantiated. Johannes Gutenberg is recognized as the first man to use movable type, in 1438, at least in the Western world. It is believed that the first book to be printed with such equipment was the Mazarin Bible in Latin which was completed between 1450 and 1455. The first printed Hebrew Bible was done in 1488 at Soncino, in the duchy of Milan, Italy.

Every copy of a page from the same set of type is, of necessity, the same, barring accidents. Every handwritten copy, even though made from the same master copy, may differ. Handwriting, spelling, misunderstood or misread words, poor eyesight or hearing, and a variety of human frailties introduced differences into the copies being made. This is why it is so essential to recover every known handwritten copy of ancient manuscripts. By comparing these, a process known as "lower criticism," it is possible to recover a close approximation of the original. The necessity for such recovery has long been recognized. Early in the eighteenth century, William Whiston, an eminent mathematician, wrote: "We ought faithfully to use all the Helps and Assistances we already have in order to do so truly noble a Design as is this, of restoring the true Text of the Old Testament to its original Purity. . . ." [4] As new discoveries of manuscripts are made it becomes increasingly clear that a completely pure text is still to be established.

Not all people would agree that such scholarship is necessary. Both in the synagogue and the church there are large groups of sincere believers who cling to the dogma of literal inspiration of the Bible. Some Jews accept without question the ancient tradition that a fully vocalized text was delivered to Moses on Mount Sinai, and that the rabbis and Masoretes (guardians of tradition) have faithfully guarded and transmitted a perfect text across the centuries. In Christianity there are large groups and countless individuals who accept not only the "verbal inspiration of the Word," but who believe also that under the guidance of the Holy Spirit that Word has been faithfully transmitted to our day without change. (It should be noted, however, that there has been a noticeable shift in this last position in recent years.) A few

[4] Whiston, An Essay Towards Restoring the True Text of the Old Testament; and for Vindicating the Citations made thence in the New Testament (London, 1722), p. 333. Quoted by Bleddyn J. Roberts. The Old Testament Text and Version (Cardiff, Wales: University of Wales, 1951), p. xi.

years ago a large metropolitan newspaper carried an advertisement which displayed the advertising church's beliefs. In it one article read, "We believe in the literal inspiration of the original Scripture." The word "original" had been inserted into the historical belief of that group. It actually concedes the validity of critical scholarship. It should be noted that the terms "conservative" and "liberal" have no validity in this connection. There are outstanding scholars in both camps.

Unwillingness to recognize that some errors have crept into the biblical text is by no means new. In an excellent summary of positions held by scholars in the nineteenth and twentieth centuries, Bleddyn J. Roberts of University College of North Wales says:

Until the end of the nineteenth century, it was generally thought that the text of the Hebrew Bible had become fixed and standardized during the early Christian era. Indeed, one of the most eminent textual authorities of that century, Paul de Lagarde, stated categorically that about A.D. 130 the Hebrew text of the Old Testament was established, and a *Musterkodex*, an archetype edition, produced which became the basis of every Hebrew manuscript of the Bible since that time.[5]

He goes on to state that this position was universally accepted and is still held in many quarters. Others held a contrary position. J. M. Powis Smith stated: "It has long been held that the Masoretic text of the Hebrew Bible was fixed at a relatively early date and handed down faithfully from that time until now. But the work of Paul Kahle has brought out clearly that there was no such uniformity of text as has been supposed until a very much later period."[6] In a book review, "Studies of the Masoretes," J. M. P. Smith agrees fully with the findings of Kahle that before the text of ben Chayyim in the second Rabbinic Bible of 1524-25 there was no accepted standardized Masoretic text and that the condition of the text was previously fluid.[7]

Examination of the first copy of the Book of Isaiah found in Cave I at Qumran [8] clearly indicates 98 percent agreement between its contents and the text of Isaiah known to tradition through the Masoretic text, but in two percent of the readings there are differences. Here is further evidence to indicate that this was not an unchanging document which was perfectly transmitted across the centuries to the present day.

In his attempt to recover as perfect a text as possible the scholar has been grateful for each new discovery. Two groups of manuscripts have been made available to scholars in this century, both of them of great importance. The discovery of the Dead Sea Scrolls from Qumran we have already briefly noted.[9]

[5] *Ibid.*, p. 23.
[6] J. M. P. Smith, "The Recent History of Old Testament Interpretation," *Journal of Religion* (July, 1926), pp. 403-24.
[7] A review of Kahle, *Masoreten des Westens* in *AJSL* (April, 1928), pp. 208-9. (Note —Roberts incorrectly refers to this review as appearing in *JAOS*).
[8] Designated by scholars as "I Q ISA*."
[9] See above, Chap. 6, pp. 72-75.

The other discovery is less well known except to experts. It is a collection of Hebrew manuscripts made by a Karaite Jew named Firkowitsch, some of them Bible manuscripts from the same Old Cairo Synagogue in which the Zadokite Fragments were found.

Before we turn to the manuscripts themselves it is necessary for us to examine the circumstances which led to each of the collections. We shall look at the Qumran community first. Through the splendid work of Père de Vaux of l'Ecole Biblique in Jerusalem, contacts were made with the Ta'amireh tribesmen and the place of the caves located. Careful examination supported the dates already agreed upon. Pottery, coins, and the jars in which the scrolls were found all fitted the period from 150 B.C. to A.D. 70.

It is necessary now for us to look at the archaeological evidence for the life of the Qumran community, and then to answer the questions, What group lived in that region, and what is their relationship, if any, to Judaism and to Christianity? While there is much variety of opinion, and not a little controversy, some positions are becoming increasingly clear.

Dr. Zeitlin of Dropsie College has been quite vocal in asserting that these scrolls are forgeries from the Middle Ages. He has had a small following among Jews and Christians, but his position is becoming increasingly untenable as further evidence is produced. By far the majority of scholars accept with minor adjustments the dates proposed by Sukenik, Burrows, Trever, Brownlee, Albright, and others.

Archaeological evidence indicates that the site at Qumran and the neighboring region was occupied at four different periods. The first occupation was about the eighth century B.C. This community disappeared and had no connection with the group associated with the scrolls. A second community was established during the reign of John Hyrcanus I (135-104 B.C.) and with a short break remained a community until destroyed in June, A.D. 68. To this group we shall return in a moment. A third occupation was made by Jewish partisans during the period of the Second Jewish Revolt, A.D. 132-35, but this group seems to have had no connection with the second group. Finally, there were sporadic and temporary encampments in later times as indicated by a few Byzantine and Arabic coins.

The period in which we are interested is that from 135 B.C. to A.D. 68. In this period a group of Jews established a religious community in the Wilderness of Judea, possibly due to political and religious persecution in the troublesome days of the latter part of the second century B.C. The community operated for about one hundred years and then had to flee because of a severe earthquake in the spring of 31 B.C. Their destination is not known, but references in their literature and in some other sources would indicate that flight was made to the city of Damascus.

The Qumran community was reestablished during the reign of Herod Archelaus who reigned from 4 B.C. to A.D. 6. The community remained intact for approximately another seventy years, when it was destroyed by the

Tenth Legion of the Roman army in June, A.D. 68. About this same time Jericho and Jerusalem were also destroyed. The Roman forces occupied the site until about the close of the first century.

In addition to the cave materials, sizable buildings have been found. These buildings on the plateau above the bluffs have been known by archaeologists for many years but were dismissed as unimportant until the cave hoards suggested a hitherto undiscovered importance. The building accommodations and the cemetery indicate that the community may have consisted of a hundred or more people, with that size being increased considerably at times of religious significance.

Three aspects of the buildings and cemetery are of particular importance. First, the cemetery contains women as well as men. If, therefore, this community is an Essene group, as many believe, it would appear that this group was not wholly ascetic. Marriage was permitted. This is supported also by provisions in the Zadokite Documents, one of the rule books of the community. Second, provision was made for the storage of great quantities of water. Since there is little rainfall in that region, and since the community put great emphasis upon cleanliness, enjoining regular bathing, stored water was an absolute necessity. We shall return to this aspect of the community a little later as we consider the question of baptism.

A third aspect is provision in the community for writing. Due to very careful excavation it has been possible to recover the tables, benches, and writing tools used by the men in their "scriptorium." These are now on display at the archaeological museums in Jerusalem and Amman. Evidence is very clear that an accepted task of this community was the copying of manuscripts. Since the community placed great emphasis upon the Bible these are the works most frequently copied. Whether the community made copies of manuscripts available for use in temple or synagogue cannot at this time be determined. It is certain that the primary purpose of copying was for the benefit of the community itself.

It has been claimed by Charles T. Fritsch of Princeton Seminary in his excellent book The Qumran Community[10] that the noncanonical books Jubilees and Enoch had their origin in this very community. He marshals much evidence to support this position, but to date his position has not been accepted.

The Manual of Discipline (or Hagu) is our best source of information concerning the nature of this religious community. Other documents related to it have also been discovered and help to fill in details. Hagu indicates that the members of the community considered themselves descendants of the Zadokites, at least spiritually. They established this community out in the wilderness in order that there might be a pure community of believers. This group is similar in many ways to a modern religious sect; they have the conviction that they alone are the true believers; they have a sense of per-

[10] New York: The Macmillan Company, 1956.

secution; and they believe that the present period of suffering is rapidly drawing to a close and that God himself will lead them into an era of triumph over their enemies.

Membership in the community was closely guarded. An applicant's life was carefully watched for a period of one year before he could be considered for membership in the community. Only if his life could be guaranteed to be righteous was he admitted. He then was on probation for another year. If at the end of this long period he was still judged to be a righteous man, he could then have the privilege of acceptance into the community, and after two more years, the high honor of being one of the authorities on sacred books. This indicates not only the nature of the community, but also the reverence with which the scriptures were held by this desert group.

Levels of righteousness were recognized. Each year there was a review by the Council of the Many. Each individual was upgraded or downgraded in level of righteousness. Meantime rigid rules were observed. It is worth noting that strict respect for the leaders and for each other was maintained. For a man to stretch out and go to sleep while a leader of the community was speaking meant severe punishment with suspension of rights for thirty days. To curse the reader of the law meant expulsion for life from the community. If a person walked out of a public session three times during one sitting he was penalized for ten days. If a man were guilty of spitting in a public meeting he was penalized for thirty days. Raucous laughter was punishable, as was gesticulation with the left hand. One is reminded of the old superstition that the left hand is the hand of lies or even of cursing.

No individual in the community was permitted to interrupt another. Each spoke in turn, apparently with prior rights going to the more righteous men of the community. Slander of another could result in suspension or expulsion from the community. Emphasis was upon gentlemanly conduct and purity of purpose.

Members of the community called themselves the Sons of Truth, the Elect. The community was designated "God's Plantation" and "partners of an eternal fellowship." It was governed by an "Overseer," who was aided by the "Council of the Few." This was elected by the "Council of the Many" which was actually all the initiated members of the community. The Overseer was also aided by a special group of three priests and twelve laymen. There was a Teacher of Righteousness, and concerning this office there has been much debate. Gaster seems to be correct, however, in his view that this was a continuing office and not some ideal figure in the past. There were judges and priests, with perhaps one priest who was the equivalent of a high priest. In common with the greater part of Judaism there was messianic expectation. Two messiahs were awaited—one from the line of priests and the other from the royal households. The texts indicated early that the priestly messiah clearly had the greater authority and superior position.

It was early noted that there are strong similarities between the Manual

187

of the Discipline and a text discovered at Cairo and known variously as "The Damascus Covenant," the "Genizah Fragments," or "The Zadokite Fragments." [11] Not only are there marked similarities between the two documents, but in addition, seven copies of the Damascus Covenant have been found with the Qumran scrolls. This gives strong support to the belief that this is the community for which the Damascus Covenant was a guiding authority. Could it be that during the thirty-year period of absence from Qumran this community actually did move to Damascus? Many believe this to be so. Others believe that the word "Damascus" is not the name of the actual place of retreat but is an idealized name for some other spot in the wilderness. The former seems better to fit the facts.

With the publication of the Zadokite Fragments by Schechter the question was raised concerning the relationship between the Damascus Covenanters and the Essenes. With new copies of the fragments and the obvious connection between the Qumran community and the Damascus Covenanters, question is now raised again concerning the Essenes. Were the people of Qumran Essenes? Again the answers have varied. The general consensus of opinion is solidifying around the position that the Qumran community was a branch of the Essenes which permitted marriage. A most careful examination of the Qumran materials has been made by Dr. Fritsch in his book to which we have already referred. He gathers there the evidence from the scrolls and compares it with the materials known to us through the writings of Philo, Josephus, Hippolytus, and Pliny. It is his contention that there can be no doubt concerning the identification of the two groups. Millar Burrows in his book *The Dead Sea Scrolls* holds the question open and says, "it seems to me best not to speak of the Qumran sect as Essenes, but rather to say that the Essenes and the covenanters, with other groups of which we know little or nothing, represented the same general type." [12]

There are great similarities, but there are also differences. Similarities include high moral codes for the communities, a period of probation before acceptance, titles of leaders, respect for age and leadership, a common meal, emphasis upon brotherhood in the communities, similar penalties for infraction of rules, and parallel religious beliefs.

On the other hand, the differences are striking. The Essenes were a baptizing group. It is by no means clear that the Qumran Covenanters were baptizers, despite the large amounts of water stored. The Zadokite Fragments clearly indicate that cleansing may only be obtained in waters that run fast enough to create a ripple, a manifest impossibility in large storage basins or pools. The Essenes taught and practiced a strict diet. There is nothing comparable at Qumran. The Teacher of Righteousness is an important figure at Qumran, and the priests and Levites have key positions. None of these is impor-

[11] Cf. pp. 178-79 above.
[12] New York: The Viking Press, Inc., 1955, p. 294.

tant for the Essenes. Finally, it may be noted that the Essenes are reputed to have supported themselves with farming activities. Farming would be difficult in the Qumran community unless it were done in the plains below the cave area. Some writers have suggested that some initiates may have given their farms to the common treasury. It would seem to be better at this point to hold the whole question of identity of the two groups in abeyance until further evidence is forthcoming. If it is finally agreed that the Qumran Covenanters were Essenes, then we shall need to accept the norms of Qumran as standard description of that sect instead of those of Philo and Josephus as is now the practice of some scholars. It will then be necessary to explain deviations from the norm in Philo and Josephus, rather than vice versa as is now the pattern.

Many scholars who were quick to identify the Covenanters as Essenes have also argued strongly for influences, more or less direct, by the Qumran community upon John Baptist and upon Christianity. It has been proposed, on the one hand, that John Baptist was an initiate of the Qumran community, and on the other hand, that Jesus had great sympathy for the Essenes and that many of his ideas are paralleled at Qumran.

The strongest line of argument used to identify John Baptist as at least a sympathizer is the discovery in the Qumran material of the quotation:

> In the wilderness prepare the way of the Lord,
>   make straight in the desert a highway for our God. (Isa. 40:3.)

The interpretation given in *Hagu* indicates that such preparation means the proper study of the law. This is not the sense in which the Gospels use it. Another parallel is the matter of baptism. As has already been indicated, there is no evidence that the Qumran community was a baptizing group. They used water for purification, but only for those already admitted to the community. There is also what appears to be a polemic against the concept of baptism. "He cannot be cleared by mere ceremonies of atonement, nor cleansed by any waters of ablution, nor sanctified by immersion in lakes or rivers, nor purified by any bath." [18] This would seem to remove John Baptist from the group.

There is still the argument that John Baptist's presence in the wilderness may best be accounted for because of his interest in this wilderness group, not because of his desire to be away from the centers of civilization. In this connection I would make this suggestion, John Baptist may have been attracted to this section of the wilderness because he knew that here was a group of individuals seeking salvation. May it not be that he saw an opportunity of taking his message to a group which was looking for truth through religion?

[18] Theodor H. Gaster, *Dead Sea Scriptures*, p. 42.

The strongest denial of Jesus' sympathy for Essene teaching was given by Floyd Filson in *Presbyterian Life*, November 24, 1956. He pointed out that the Essenes were initiated by secret rites, were given secret teachings, and swore an oath that none of these teachings would be divulged to anyone. None of this is in agreement with the teachings of Jesus and his command that his teachings be shared with all mankind. Yet there are great similarities in concepts, at least between the Gospels and the Qumran literature. The parallels are most striking in the Fourth Gospel. Gaster, for example, finds more parallels in John than in all of the Synoptics. The identification of truth and light; the struggle between truth and falsehood; the contrast of light and darkness; the term "sons of light"; and phrase "men from below," used in John 8:23; or the term "son of perdition," John 17:12, are but a few of the instances cited. Other New Testament books also have close similarities, not only in theological concepts, but in matters of organization of the religious community. How then may we account for these except by direct relationship?

It must not be forgotten that Christianity had its inception in a Jewish environment. As it grew it rapidly spread throughout the Greco-Roman world with a variety of backgrounds for its development. There was no one pattern of church government or organization. Christianity in different centers developed very different forms of church government and types of ritual. That is why it is possible for denominations of decidedly different types of church government to turn to the New Testament and justify from the ancient record their particular form of church polity. It would be strange indeed if in some areas of beginning Christianity we should find no parallels between it and the sects of Judaism. It should further be noted that similarity may not necessarily mean direct dependence or influence, but that each has developed independently from the same milieu. For example, the numbers three and twelve play a large part in both Christianity and Qumran. But so did they in Judaism long before either existed. The Essenes, the Qumran Covenanters, and the Christians all have their common background in Judaism. All similarities so far cited also have their roots in this same background.

Attempts to find parallels between Jesus the teacher and the Teacher of Righteousness overlook important differences. It has been stressed that there was salvation in the Qumran community by faith in the Teacher of Righteousness. More correctly there is salvation by faith in the correct teaching of the law, not faith in the teacher. Attempts have been made to identify as one person the Teacher of Righteousness and the messiah. One must first ask, Which messiah? In any case there is no such identification. Furthermore, the Teacher of Righteousness is not the head of the community and is not one historical person, but is an office which continues whenever there shall be anyone qualified to fill that office.

Allegro, an English scholar, asserted that the Teacher of Righteousness had been crucified and that his followers expected his resurrection. He arrived at this position through what was really a series of *non sequiturs*. He was immediately challenged by those who were familiar with this literature and not merely defenders of the faith. Suffice it to say that Allegro has withdrawn much if not all of this series of statements. In the meantime, however, the public press made much of the supposed similarities and a badly informed public is still sadly confused. Dr. Zeitlin is undoubtedly correct when he charges that much discussion which should have been carried on in an atmosphere of scholarship has been carried on in newspapers with too much attempt to create sensationalism.

Frank Cross has already published several articles in which the critical value of the Qumran texts has been demonstrated. In some sections of the books of Samuel it is obvious that the traditional Hebrew text has some omissions. The Septuagint text in this case appears to be the better text. In the Qumran texts support is given to the Septuagint tradition of I and II Samuel rather than the Masoretic.

In the famous "Vision of Isaiah" (Isa. 6:1 ff.) the seraphs cry to each other. The Qumran text has "Holy, Holy," not a threefold repetition. The question may be raised, Is the threefold repetition due to a later trinitarian influence?

The committee responsible for the preparation of the Revised Standard Version was able to make use of the newly discovered text of Isaiah to good advantage. In several cases a better translation was possible because of the help received from the Qumran text.

The text of the book of Jeremiah presents especially difficult problems. The divergences between the Hebrew and the Greek traditions are many. Shorter by 2,700 word than the Hebrew text, the Greek text nevertheless contains a number of concepts for which there is no equivalent in the Hebrew. In addition the order of the chapters in the book is quite different in the two traditions. For years scholars have debated concerning the superiority of one or the other text. It is reported that one manuscript from Qumran preserves in Hebrew the form of the book of Jeremiah known to us through the Greek text. Unfortunately, this will not finally settle the problem, because another manuscript follows the traditional Masoretic pattern. These texts do show, however, that the variant traditions of Jeremiah are ancient and that both Masoretic and Septuagint texts rest upon accepted traditions.

One interesting collection of psalms arranges the poems in very different order to that known to us through the traditional Psalter. The arrangement is by metrical classification. This manuscript alone can be very useful in helping us to understand more clearly the structure of Hebrew poetry.

In the noncanonical books much information is available, and here New Testament scholars may find their greatest help. The book of Tobit is preserved in one Hebrew and two Aramaic copies. There is not perfect agreement between the manuscripts, but all of them support the Greek tradition, reports Abbe Milik.

Evidence is now available to show that the Latin and Ethiopic versions of the book of Jubilees render faithfully the original text. Five manuscripts of Jubilees have been preserved at Qumran, all in excellent Hebrew.

Light is also thrown on the complex problem of the book of Enoch of which eight copies have been found in Cave IV alone. Of the five parts of the book parts I, IV, and V occur most often and are well preserved. "The Similitudes," part II, is entirely omitted, and we would agree with Father Milik that this is surely not an accident. "Three MSS contain only Part III, the astronomical work, but in a longer edition, at once more detailed and more intelligible than of Ethiopic Enoch." [14]

These brief illustrations will indicate something of the importance of the Qumran documents for textual studies. It will be many years before the full importance can be known. The task of sorting, preparing, assembling, and classifying the small scraps in which the scrolls are so frequently found is a long and sometimes wearying one. All of this must be done, however, before translations and comparisons can be made. We are deeply indebted to an international and interfaith team of workers for their painstaking work. Many others will need to take up the task. Even so, it probably will not be within this generation that the work will be completed.

A special problem faces students of Hebrew manuscripts which is not encountered by students of Greek, Latin, German, English, et cetera. In each of the last named languages words are normally fully spelled out with complete vocalization, except in the case of accepted abbreviations. Early Hebrew was written without vocalization except for some strong vowels. In addition, words were often run together with no word divisions to separate them. For example, using English letters to illustrate, the opening sentence of the Bible would look like this: NTHBGNNNGGDCRTDTHHVNSND THRTH. We can read it because we draw upon memory. But suppose we saw a strange sentence containing the letters BD. Is this the word "bad," "bed," "bid," or "bud"? Eventually a system of vocalization has worked out —actually three systems. The systems were designated so that the established text would not be disturbed; that is, consonants were not pulled apart so the vowels could be inserted between them. Dots and dashes were put above and below the letters. Actually they remind the reader of the traditional pronunciation. Such vocalization is known as "pointing," and without these marks the text is known as "unpointed" text.

We also face a second problem. Tradition sometimes carried memory of more than one pronunciation. For example, let us suppose that in one tradition the story is told about a man going up to Jerusalem. In another tradition it is remembered that two men were going. The Hebrew text had an interesting way of preserving memory of both traditions. In English the first story would begin MN WS GNG T JRSLM; the second would have

[14] BA (December, 1956), p. 89.

MN WR GNG T JRSLM. By using the consonants of the first story and vowels of the second we would have "MEN WESE GOING," et cetera. The word "wese" is an incorrect grammatical form. The Hebrews knew this. The text therefore said, in effect, "Here are two traditions. You make the decision which is correct." The first tradition, the consonantal, is known as the "Kethib," "written"; the second is known as "Qre," "spoken, or oral." What does anyone who takes scripture literally do in a situation like this? A choice must be made.

A third problem is that of the dates of tradition. By the second century of the Christian era the Jews had generally agreed upon the working of the books of the Old Testament which seemed to them to be in closest agreement with tradition. Many Jews and Christians prefer to believe that no change has occurred since that time. Evidence, however, does not support this position. As new manuscripts come to light the variety of known readings is increased. In general, translations into English have been made from a Hebrew text known as ben Chayyim, which dates from the last of the thirteenth or the beginning of the fourteenth century. Manuscripts found in the nineteenth and twentieth centuries have made it possible to push tradition back several hundred years, and most important, to have a tradition of vocalization as well as consonants which appears to be founded upon second-century tradition. In addition, the number of manuscripts has been enlarged considerably, making possible a much larger comparison than was possible prior to this century.

One source of manuscripts is old synagogues, more particularly the room known as the "genizah," or "hiding place." Here outworn and unused manuscripts were stored. Unorthodox documents were usually burned. Whenever the genizah was full the documents were taken out and formally buried and thus were lost forever. It is only occasionally that scholars have been fortunate enough to recover genizah scrolls.

The genizah of the Old Cairo Synagogue, found in 1890, was such a discovery. Fortunately its contents had not been destroyed, but unfortunately they have been widely scattered since the genizah was opened up. They have been purchased and otherwise acquired by the museums in Oxford and Cambridge, the British Museum, the Antonin collection in Leningrad, and the Jewish Seminary in New York City.[15]

Another important collection is that which was made by Abraham b. Samuel Firkowitsch, a Karaite Jew, born in 1785 in the village of Lutsk, Volhynia, southwest Russia. He is described as "a fanatical Karaite, and also an expert forger." [16] For this reason the Firkowitsch collection has been suspect, and with good reason. Paul Kahle, in his Schweich Lectures, pointed out:

[15] Roberts, The Old Testament and Text Versions, p. 76.
[16] Ibid., p. 77.

This Karaite Jew from the Crimean Peninsula is somewhat ill famed on account of the falsifications he made on dates of gravestones and on Hebrew manuscripts in order to show that the Karaites had been settled in the Crimea for a much longer time than was previously accepted, and had had a greater importance than was usually conceded to them. But Firkowitsch has the credit of bringing together the largest collection of Hebrew manuscripts which exist in the world. The manuscripts from the two Firkowitsch Collections are in the Russian Public Library in Leningrad; the first was sold to the library by Firkowitsch himself, the second was acquired by the library in 1876 soon after his death in Tshofotkale on 26 May 1874.[17]

Kahle then called attention to two interesting comparisons. First he noted that the entire number of Hebrew manuscripts described in the catalogue of the British Museum total 161. In the Bodleian Catalogue there are listed 146 Hebrew biblical manuscripts, counting both those written on parchment and on paper. By contrast the second Firkowitsch Collection holds 1,582 written on parchment and 725 on paper.[18] Second, he noted that Kennicott in his great *Vetus Testamentum Hebraice cum variis lectionibus* (1777-1780) sought to use all available Hebrew manuscripts in Europe and "was not able to collate even as many as one-third of the number of MSS. which are today to be found in this one collection." [19]

An important edition of the Hebrew Bible is that which was edited by Rudolph Kittel and known as *Biblia Hebraica*. A third edition, begun by Kittel, was published in 1936. Shortly before his death in 1939, Kittel wrote in the foreword:

So then in this edition, in place of the text of ben Chayyim or any other Masoretic text resting on manuscripts of the thirteenth or fourteenth century A.D., there is offered for the first time the text of ben Asher, several hundred years older, in the form in which MS.L gives it. At the same time arrangements are being made for utilizing for this edition the two other standard MSS. known to belong to the family of ben Asher: that in Aleppo, and the MS. of the Prophets in the synagogue of the Karaites in Cairo.[20]

With the death of Kittel the editorial work was assigned to A. Alt and O. Eissfeldt. Alt was responsible for the Pentateuch and the Former Prophets; Eissfeldt the Later Prophets and the Hagiographa. The seventh edition, published in 1951 for the American Bible Society, had no appreciable changes except to have introductory paragraphs in English as well as in German and Latin, correct some misspellings, and add to the footnotes the deviants to be found in IQ ISA*.

[17] *The Cairo Geniza* (Schweich Lectures, 1941; London: Blackwell & Mott, Ltd., 1959), pp. 2-3.
[18] *Ibid.*, p. 3; note also his note 2 in which there is reference to more than six thousand Hebrew and Arabic MSS.
[19] *Ibid.*, p. 3.
[20] New York: The American Bible Society, 1951, p. XXVII. Kittel refers to MS.L by which he means Leningrad B 19a.

In the new edition of the Kittel *Biblia Hebraica* there is available to scholars (1) an older text than has normally been available, (2) better tradition concerning the vocalization of the text, and (3) about five times as much critical information from comparison with other manuscripts and the same kind of increase of proposed emendations based upon comparison with manuscripts in many languages.

The discovery of the Dead Sea Scrolls and the discoveries of other scrolls, particularly the collections mentioned in the preceding paragraphs, have put additional resources in the hands of scholars. It is immediately put into use as has been demonstrated. Perhaps most outstanding have been the results which have been published in the new revisions and translations of the Bible. Because of careful scholarship we can be assured that we are now closer to having the original messages of the Bible writers than we have ever been before.

CONCLUSION AND A BEGINNING

In the preceding chapters we have seen from information recovered through archaeology something of what it meant for the Hebrews to be neighbor to the people of Mesopotamia, Syria, Asia Minor, and Egypt, as well as Canaan itself. It was a great area of developing culture in which they found themselves. In his most recent publication William F. Albright identifies four main groups of religious literature as the most important ones for understanding "the origin and background of Hebrew religion": "Egyptian, Mesopotamian (Sumero-Akkadian), West Semitic (Canaanite, Aramean, South Arabian), and Hurro-Hittite." [1] He says that the significant literature of these cultures was in existence and had been developed prior to the coming of the Hebrews into Palestine. He believes also that most of the Old Testament books were written, not only later than this literature, but prior to the time of Greek influence upon the Jews, with the exception of some of the smaller books, such as Daniel.

With the availability of new and dependable information it is essential that we recognize the changed character of knowledge that is ours concerning the history, customs, geography, and languages of many people, including the Hebrews themselves. Many of the old geographies, dictionaries, commentaries, and lexicons are woefully out of date, and so are the patterns of interpretation and exegesis which were based upon them.

Before we can make parallels or comparisons of the Hebrews with any people it is imperative that we have correct information, not only about the Hebrews but also about their contemporaries and predecessors. Increasingly such material is being made available. We can now draw our facts from actual records, not from a theory of a presumed "stage of development" in a particular culture. We are also recognizing that there is much more dependable information to be derived concerning the development of languages, and therefore literary sources, from a study of languages than from an assumption that certain changes in social structure, customs, and religious beliefs and practices always followed the same pattern.

As examination is made of the biblical text to determine what if any changes have occurred to the text in transmission, we need to be completely familiar with the ancient languages and to secure the most ancient documents we can obtain. In addition, we shall recognize the increasing importance which is being attached to the versions. The ancient world moved more readily from one language to another than we have been willing to admit. Some of the nations, as Albright has pointed out, were as bilingual as some modern nations. In the later days of Judaism Greek and Aramaic were

[1] *History, Archaeology, and Christian Humanism* (New York: McGraw-Hill Book Company, Inc., 1964), p. 131.

in daily use in business, politics, and social affairs. Scholars are looking with renewed interest to these languages.

There should be significant developments in the years immediately ahead in four phases of Old Testament studies. First, Old Testament scholars face the responsibility of establishing the best possible text of the Old Testament. The present custom of accepting the MT as basic unless there are manifest errors, such as an unconstruable sentence, or an obviously misspelled word, is no longer defensible. Attention must be given to all traditions in the several languages, and from them must be drawn that text which can be demonstrated to be the closest to the text originally canonized. By this we mean the individual books as canonized, not the sources from which they were composed. These are two very different studies. Only after the most dependable text has been established can we think of making an acceptable translation into a modern tongue. Revision of a translation of MT must be recognized for what it is, a revision of one tradition.

Second, a new study of canonization is overdue.[2] The evidence from the Qumran community is clear. The canon adopted by the Council of Jamnia did not represent the whole of Palestinian Judaism; at least it did not represent the Qumran Covenanters. One cannot, of course, assume that all books found in the various libraries at Qumran had been canonized by that community, but it is a fair assumption that texts quoted in support of the messianic expectation of the community were believed to be authoritative. The Qumran Covenanters, just as did some New Testament writers, quoted from books outside the Jamnia canon, the body of Old Testament books generally accepted by Protestant Christians and Orthodox Jews. It may be that the supposed differences between Palestinian and Alexandrian Jews in attitude toward scripture were not as sharply defined as we have assumed. Such study will certainly not lead to a new process of canonization. What world body could authorize such a step, even assuming that it might be profitable? The study is important, however, because it will enable us to see that the first and most important step in the process of canonization is the judgment of the people that God is speaking to them through writings of the men of God. The later ecclesiastical approval is important, but sometimes it is but a theological rationale of a fait accompli. Once the early steps of canonization had taken place, then came the important task of establishing the precise content of the approved book. How much of this detail can be determined is problematic, but certainly investigation can give us a fuller picture than we now have.

Third, new studies are already in process on the problem of the development of Hebrew religion, but more must be done. Too many theories in the past have been assumption and sometimes not much more than guess-

---

[2] Cf. Albert C. Sundberg, Jr.: *The Old Testament of the Early Church*, Harvard Theological Studies XX (Cambridge: Harvard University Press, 1964).

work. We now have dependable information on which to draw. We can say, "This is what happened in history. Here is the evidence." When we know precisely what happened we can then move on to the next step to ascertain if possible why these things happened as they did. Much of the description in older textbooks was written from the point of view, "Then this must have happened." Perhaps it did, but we can now be on surer ground as we view actual changes.

Finally, we recognize that we have passed the day when people were startled and yet seemed to be more enthusiastic about similarities between the literature of the Hebrews and their neighbors than they were about dissimilarities or divergences. Increasingly we recognize the uniqueness of Hebrew literature as it comes out of a sense of relationship with God. It was the Hebrew people alone who moved to the place of belief in ethical monotheism and from it have sprung the great monotheistic religions of the world—Judaism, Christianity, and Islam. The concept of Covenant People with a God-designed plan of salvation is likewise unique to Judaism until adopted by Christianity. The Jews also conceived God to be the prime mover in history, not imprisoned within it, and certainly not a dethroned power or an absentee landlord.

In recent years there has been a marked trend toward Old Testament theology, much of it bad. A major reason for this trend has been to find a unity in the Old Testament which many people believe to be there but cannot otherwise explain. The trend has some value, but there are dangers. One of the major contributions of Old Testament scholarship has been to show that there was more than one religious point of view in the various sections of the Old Testament. Any unity of thought comes to its climax, at least, in the process of collecting and editing the materials which went into the Old Testament corpus. This, too, is a part of canonization.

The most disturbing aspect for me, however, is that when we talk about "theology" we shift our attention from a record of religious experience to a system of thought. The Old Testament, and for that matter the entire Bible, is seeking to communicate a record of religious experience, not to teach a "system." The prophets tell of their experiences with God. This, indeed, was their validation to office. The Gospels are on fire with the experiences of Jesus and men's experiences with him and with God through Christ. As they sought to follow out the "Great Commission" to bring others into vital experience with God they had the promise of a deepened experience, "Lo I am with you always." Theology has been and is a faithful servant of church and synagogue. It must remain a servant. It finds its reward as men are brought into living relationship with God. No system of thought, however valid, can be substituted for the experience of that relationship. This the Law and the Prophets taught.

Drawings and
Outline Maps

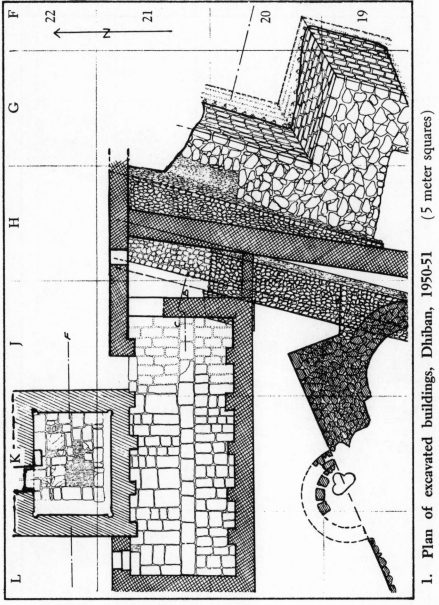

1. Plan of excavated buildings, Dhiban, 1950-51   (5 meter squares)

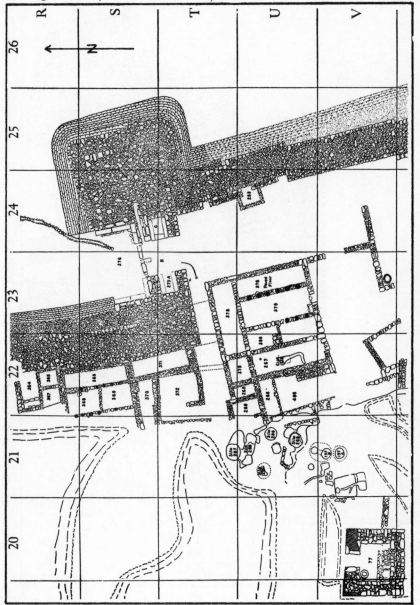

2. City gate, Tell en-Nasbeh (10 meter squares)

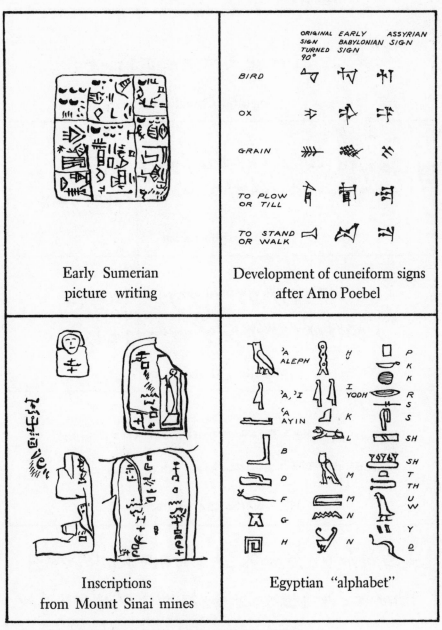

Early Sumerian
picture writing

Development of cuneiform signs
after Arno Poebel

	ORIGINAL SIGN TURNED 90°	EARLY BABYLONIAN SIGN	ASSYRIAN SIGN
BIRD			
OX			
GRAIN			
TO PLOW OR TILL			
TO STAND OR WALK			

Inscriptions
from Mount Sinai mines

Egyptian "alphabet"

3. Developments from pictographic writing

Ugaritic Cuneiform

Early Phoenician

Moabite (Mesha Stone)

אשרי האיש אשר לא הלך בעצת רשעים

ובדרך הטאים לא עמד ובמושב לצים לא ישב

Hebrew (Square Character)

Samaritan

4. Forms of alphabetic writing—West Semitic

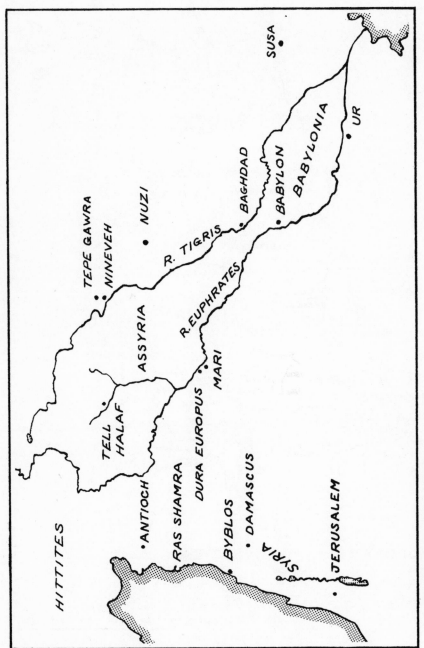

5. The ancient Near East

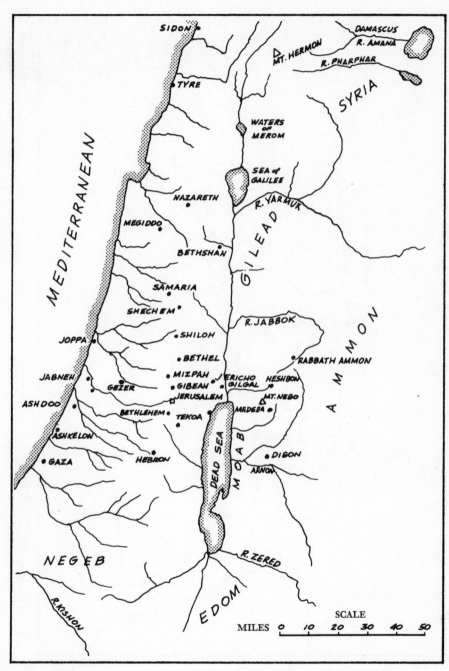

6. Palestine

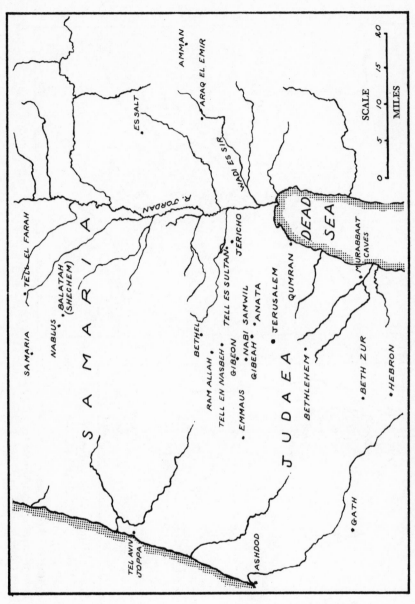

7. **Samaria and Judea—showing important excavation sites**

(map modified from Revue Biblique, plate XX, 1953)

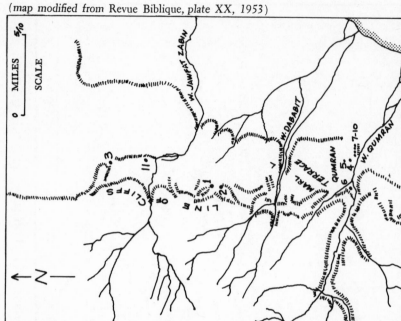

(map based on survey by F. A. Norris, 1904)

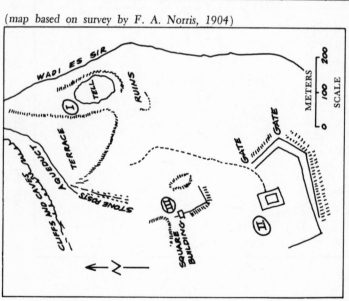

8. *Left*: **Araq el-Emir** I. Excavation "field" 1, site of ancient village II. "Field" 2, Qasr el Abd (Castle of the Slave) III. "Field" 3, Square Building

Right: **Qumran Area**— showing location of eleven caves where scrolls were found. Note: More than 200 caves have been found. Thirty of them indicate human occupation at the time of the Qumran Community

BIBLIOGRAPHY

(This listing does not include those books which appear at the end of Part II.)

Albright, William F. "Abram the Hebrew," *Bulletin of the American Schools of Oriental Research* (October, 1960).

————. *Archaeology of Palestine and the Bible.* Westwood, N.J.: Fleming H. Revell Company, 1935.

————. "The Bible After Twenty Years of Archaeology (1932-52)," *Religion in Life* (Autumn, 1952).

————. *The Biblical Period from Abraham to Ezra.* New York: Harper & Row, Publishers, 1962.

————. "The Excavation of Tell Beit Mirsim," Vol. III "The Iron Age," *Annual of the American Schools of Oriental Research* (1941-43), XXI-XXII.

————. "The Excavation of Tell Beit Mirsim," "The Pottery of the First Three Campaigns," *Annual of the American Schools of Oriental Research* (1930-31), XII.

————. "The Excavation of Tell Beit Mirsim," IA "The Bronze Age Pottery of the Fourth Campaign," *Annual of the American Schools of Oriental Research* (1931-32), XIII.

————. "Excavations at Tell el Fûl," *Annual of the American Schools of Oriental Research* (1924), IV, for 1922-23.

————. *From Stone Age to Christianity.* Baltimore: Johns Hopkins University Press, 1940.

————. "The Gezer Calendar," *Bulletin of the American Schools of Oriental Research* (December, 1943).

————. *History, Archaeology and Christian Humanism.* New York: McGraw-Hill Book Company, 1964.

————. "New Light on the History of Western Asia in the Second Millenium B.C.," *Bulletin of the American Schools of Oriental Research* (February, 1940) and (April, 1940).

————. "Some Books on the Bible in the Light of Archaeology," *Bulletin of the American Schools of Oriental Research* (October, 1962—April, 1963).

Allegro, John Marco. *The Treasure of the Copper Scroll.* Garden City, N.Y.: Doubleday & Company, Inc., 1960.

Anati, Emmanuel. *Palestine Before the Hebrews.* New York: Alfred A. Knopf, 1963.

Avigad, Nahman, and Yadin, Yigael. *A Genesis Aprocryphon.* London: Oxford University Press, 1956.

Badè, W. F. *A Manual of Excavation in the Near East.* Berkeley, Calif.: University of California Press, 1934.

————. "The Seal of Jaazaniah," *Zeitschrift für die Alttestamentliche Wissenschaft* (1933), V.

Baikie, James. "The Cradle of Civilization," *National Geographic Magazine* (February, 1916).

Barthelemy, D., and Milik, J. T. *Discoveries in the Judean Desert.* New York: Oxford University Press, 1955, I.

Bauer, Hans. *Entzifferung der Keilschrifttafeln von Ras Schamra.* Halle: M. Niemeyer, 1930.

Breasted, James H. *Ancient Records of Egypt.* New York: Russell & Russell, 1962. Reprint of 1906.

————. *Dawn of Conscience.* New York: Charles Scribner's Sons, 1933.

Bright, John. *Early Israel in Recent History Writing*. Naperville, Ill.: Alec R. Allenson, Inc., 1956.

———. *A History of Israel*. Philadelphia: The Westminster Press, 1959.

Budge, Ernest Alfred Thompson Wallis. *By Nile and Tigris*. London: John Murray, Publishers, Ltd., 1920.

———. "The Tell el-Amarna Tablets." Leo Deuel, editor. *The Treasures of Time*. Cleveland, Ohio: World Publishing Company, 1961.

Burckhardt, Johann L. *Travels in Syria and the Holy Land*. London, 1822.

Burrows, Millar. *The Dead Sea Scrolls*. New York: Viking Press, 1955.

———. *More Light on the Dead Sea Scrolls*. New York: Viking Press, 1958.

Calkin, John B. *Historical Geography of the Bible Lands*. Philadelphia: The Westminster Press, 1904.

Cameron, George G. "The Babylonian Scientist and His Hebrew Colleagues," *Biblical Archaeologist* (May, 1944).

Carter, Howard, and Mace, A. C. *The Tomb of Tut-Ankh-Amen*. 3 vols. New York: Cooper Square Publishers, Inc., 1923.

Conder, C. R., and Kitchener, H. H. *Map of Western Palestine in 26 Sheets from Surveys Conducted for the Committee of the Palestine Exploration Fund by Lieutenants C. R. Conder and H. H. Kitchener, R. E. During the Years 1872-1877*. London, 1880.

Contenau, G. *La Civilisation des Hittites et des Hurrites du Mitanni*. Paris, 1948.

Cross, Frank M., Jr. *The Ancient Library of Qumran*. Garden City, N. Y.: Doubleday & Company, Inc., 1958.

Debevoise, N. C. "A Photograph of Darius' Sculptures at Behistun," *Journal of Near Eastern Studies* (1943), II, plate II.

De Saulcy, Felicien. *Voyage en Terre Sainte*. 1865.

Dhorme, Edouard. "Le Dechiffrement des tablettes de Ras Shamra," *Journal of the Palestine Orient Society* (1931), XI.

———. "Un Nouvel Alphabet Semitique," *Revue Biblique* (1930), XXXIX.

Douglass, Andrew Ellicott. "The Secret of the Southwest Solved by Talkative Tree Rings," *National Geographic Magazine* (December, 1929).

Driver, G. R. *Canaanite Myths and Legends*. Edinburgh: T & T Clark, 1956.

———. "On a Passage in the Baal Epic (IV AB iii 24) and Proverbs xxxi 21," *Bulletin of the American Schools of Oriental Research* (February, 1947).

Dubberstein, W. H. "Prices and Interest Rates in Babylonia (625-400 B. C.)." Ph.D. dissertation, University of Chicago, 1934.

Edwards, I. E. S. *The Pyramids of Egypt*. Baltimore: Penguin Books, Inc., 1947.

Gadd, C. J. *The Fall of Assyria*. London: The British Academy, 1923.

Gardiner, A. H. *Admonitions of an Egyptian Sage*. Leipzig, 1909.

Gaster, Theodor H. *Dead Sea Scriptures in English Translation*. Garden City, N. Y.: Doubleday & Company, Inc., 1956.

———. *Thespis*. New York: Henry Schuman, Inc., Publishers, 1950.

Gelb, Ignace J. "Hittites," *The Interpreter's Dictionary of the Bible*. Nashville: Abingdon Press, 1962.

———. "Hurrians and Subarians," *Studies in Ancient Oriental Civilizations*, No. 22 (1944).

———. *A Study of Writing*. Chicago: University of Chicago Press, 1952.

Glueck, Nelson. "An Aerial Reconnaissance of the Negev," *Bulletin of the American Schools of Oriental Research* (October, 1959).

———. "Archaeological Exploration in the Negev in 1959," *Bulletin of the American Schools of Oriental Research* (October, 1960).

———. "Explorations in Eastern Palestine, IV" *Annual of the American Schools of Oriental Research* (1951), XXV-XVIII, Part 1.

————. "King Solomon's Pittsburgh," Leo Deuel, editor. *The Treasures of Time.* Cleveland, Ohio: World Publishing Company, 1961.

————. *The Other Side of the Jordan.* New York: Stechert-Hafner Service Agency, Inc., 1940.

————. *The River Jordan.* Philadelphia: The Westminster Press, 1946.

————. *Rivers in the Desert.* New York: Farrar, Strauss & Cudahy, Inc., 1959.

————. "The Seventh Season of Archaeological Exploration in the Negev," *Bulletin of the American Schools of Oriental Research* (December, 1958).

————. "The Sixth Season of Archaeological Exploration in the Negeb," *Bulletin of the American Schools of Oriental Research* (February, 1958).

Gordon, Cyrus H. "Biblical Customs and the Nuzu Tablets," *Biblical Archeologist* (1940), III.

————. *Geschichtliche Grundlagen des A. T.* Zurich, 1961.

————. *Introduction to Old Testament Times.* Ventnor, N.J.: Ventnor Publishers, 1963.

————. *Ugaritic Literature.* Rome: Pontificio Instituto Biblico, 1949.

Gottwald, N. K. "Song of Songs," *The Interpreter's Dictionary of the Bible.* Nashville: Abingdon Press, 1962.

Gray, John. *The Legacy of Canaan: The Ras Shamra Texts and Their Relevance to the Old Testament.* Leiden: E. J. Brill, Publisher, 1957.

Greenberg, Moshe. "Another Look at Rachel's Theft of the Teraphim," *Journal of Biblical Literature* (September, 1962).

Haldar, Alfred. "Habiru," *The Interpreter's Dictionary of the Bible.* Nashville: Abingdon Press, 1962.

Hamburger, H. "Money," *The Interpreter's Dictionary of the Bible.* Nashville: Abingdon Press, 1962.

Hitti, Philip K. *History of Syria, Including Lebanon and Palestine.* New York: The Macmillan Company, 1951.

Holliday, Carl. *The Dawn of Literature.* New York: The Thomas Y. Crowell Company, 1931.

Hrozny, Bedrich. "Uber die Volker und Sprachen des alten Chattilandies," *Boghakoi-Studien, No. 5.* Leipzig, 1920.

————. *The Language of the Hittites: Its Structure and Its Membership in the Indo-European Linguistic Family.* Leipzig, 1917.

Johnson, Aubrey R. *The Cultic Prophet in Ancient Israel.* Cardiff, Wales: University of Wales Press, 1944.

Josephus. *Antiquities.* ("Loeb Classical Library") New York: G. P. Putnam's Sons, 1926.

Kahle, Paul. *The Cairo Geniza.* Oxford, England: Blackwell & Mott, Ltd., 1959.

Kapelrud, Arvid S. "Phoenicia," *The Interpreter's Dictionary of the Bible.* Nashville: Abingdon Press, 1962.

Kelso, J. L. "Pottery," *The Interpreter's Dictionary of the Bible.* Nashville: Abingdon Press, 1962.

Kelso, J. L., and Thorley, J. P. "Palestinian Pottery in the Bible Times," *Biblical Archaeologist* (December, 1945).

Kenyon, Kathleen. *Digging Up Jericho.* New York: Frederick A. Praeger, Publisher, 1957.

Key, Andre W. F. "The Giving of Proper Names in the Old Testament," *Journal of Biblical Literature* (March, 1964).

Knudtzon, J. A., and Weber, O. *Die el-Amarna Tafeln.* 1915.

Kraeling, C. H. *A Greek Fragment of Tatian's Diatessaron from Dura.* London: Christopher's, 1935.

Kraeling, Emil G. *The Book of the Ways of God.* New York: Charles Scribner's Sons, 1939.

Kramer, Samuel Noah. *History Begins at Sumer.* Garden City, N. Y.: Doubleday & Company, Inc., 1959.

————. *Sumerian Mythology.* Philadelphia: American Philosophical Society, 1944.

Lapp, Paul W. "Palestine: Known But Mostly Unknown," *Biblical Archaeologist* (December, 1963).

————. *Palestinian Ceramic Chronology.* Jerusalem: American Schools of Oriental Research, 1961.

————. "The Second and Third Campaigns at Araq el-Emir," *Bulletin of the American Schools of Oriental Research* (October, 1963).

LaSor, William S. *Bibliography of the Dead Sea Scrolls.* Fuller Library Bulletin, 1958.

————. "Bibliography of the Dead Sea Scrolls," *Revue de Qumran* (1938-63), I-IV.

Legrain, G. *Annales du service des antiquites de l'Egypte* (1916), XVI.

Lerici, Carlo M. "Periscope on the Etruscan Past," *National Geographic Magazine* (September, 1959).

Luckenbill, D. D. *Ancient Records of Assyria and Babylonia.* Chicago: University of Chicago Press, 1926-27.

————. *The Annals of Sennacherib.* Chicago: Oriental Institute Publications, 1924.

Macalister, R. A. S. *A Century of Excavation in Palestine.* London: Religious Tract Society, 1925.

————. *Gezer II.* London: 1912.

McCown, C. C., *et al. Tell en-Nasbeh.* Jerusalem: American Schools of Oriental Research, 1943.

Mansoor, Menahem. *The Dead Sea Scrolls.* Grand Rapids, Mich.: Wm. B. Eerdmans, 1964.

Meek, Theophile J. *Hebrew Origins.* 2nd ed. New York: Harper & Row, Publishers, 1960.

Mendelsohn, Isaac. "Samuel's Denunciation of Kingship in the Light of the Akkadian Documents from Ugarit," *Bulletin of the American Schools of Oriental Research* (October, 1956).

Mendenhall, George E. "Mari," *Biblical Archaeologist* (1948), XI.

Mercer, S. A. B. *The Tell el-Amarna Tablets.* Toronto: Macmillan and Company, 1939.

Milik, J. T., *et al.* "Editing the Manuscript Fragments from Qumran," *Biblical Archaeologist* (December, 1956).

Neufeld, E. *The Hittite Laws.* London: Luzac & Company, Ltd., 1951.

Niebuhr, H. Richard. *The Kingdom of God in America.* New York: Harper & Row, Publishers, 1937.

————. *The Social Sources of Denominationalism.* New York: Henry Holt and Company, 1929.

Noblecourt, Christiane Desroches. *Tutankhamen.* New York: Graphic Books, 1963.

Noth, Martin. *The History of Israel.* 2nd. ed. New York: Harper & Row, Publishers, 1960.

————. *Mari und Israel.* 1963.

Olmstead, A. T. *History of Assyria.* New York: Charles Scribner's Sons, 1927.

————. *History of Palestine.* New York: Charles Scribner's Sons, 1931.

Owen, G. Frederick. *Archaeology and the Bible.* Westwood, N. J.: Fleming H. Revell Company, 1961.

Parker, Richard A., and Dubberstein, W. H. "Babylonian Chronology 626 B.C.—A.D. 45." *Studies in Ancient Oriental Civilizations*, No. 24 (1942).

Parrot, André. Series "Discovering New Worlds". London: S.C.M. Press.

Patton, John Hastings. "Canaanite Parallels in the Book of Psalms." Ph.D. Dissertation, Johns Hopkins University, 1944.

Pedersen, Johannes. *Israel: Its Life and Culture*. 4 vols.; rev. ed. London: Oxford University Press, 1959.

Pfeiffer, Robert H. "Ein pessimistisches Zweigesprach zwischen einem Herrn und seinem Knecht," *Altorientalische Texte zum alten Testament*. Edited by Hugo Gressman. Berlin, 1926.

————. *Introduction to the Old Testament*. Rev. ed. New York: Harper & Row, Publishers, 1948.

————. "Le Probleme du livre de Job." M.A. thesis, Geneva, 1915.

Pritchard, James B. *Gibeon: Where the Sun Stood Still*. Princeton, N. J.: Princeton University Press, 1962.

Raboisson. *Les Maspeh*. Paris, 1897.

Rist, Martin. "Apocalypticism," *The Interpreter's Dictionary of the Bible*. Nashville: Abingdon Press, 1962.

Roberts, B. J. *The Old Testament Text and Versions*. Cardiff, Wales: University of Wales Press, 1962.

Robinson, Edward. *Biblical Researches*. 2 vols. 1841.

Robinson, G. L. *Sarcophagus of an Ancient Civilization: Petra, Edom and the Edomites*. New York: The Macmillan Company, 1930.

Rostovtzeff, M. I., et al., editors. *The Excavations at Dura Europos*. 8 vols. New Haven, Conn.: Yale University Press, 1929-39.

Rowley, H. H. *From Joseph to Joshua*. London: Oxford University Press, 1950.

Sachs, Curt. *The History of Musical Instruments*. New York: W. W. Norton & Company, Inc., 1946.

Scott, Robert B. Y. "The Shekel Sign on Stone Weights," *Bulletin of the American Schools of Oriental Research* (February, 1959).

Sellers, O. R. "Musical Instruments of Israel," *Biblical Archaeologist* (September, 1941).

Smith, George. *Assyrian Discoveries*. London, 1875.

Smith, J. M. Powis. *The Origin and History of Hebrew Law*. Chicago: University of Chicago Press, 1931.

————. "The Recent History of Old Testament Interpretation," *Journal of Religion* (July, 1926).

————. "Studies of the Massoretes," *American Journal of Semitic Languages* (April, 1928). A review of Kahle's *Masoreten des Westens*.

Speiser, E. A. "Hivite," *The Interpreter's Dictionary of the Bible*. Nashville: Abingdon Press, 1962.

————. "Horite," *The Interpreter's Dictionary of the Bible*. Nashville: Abingdon Press, 1962.

————. "Hurrians," *The Interpreter's Dictionary of the Bible*. Nashville: Abingdon Press, 1962.

————. "I Know Not the Day of My Death," *Journal of Biblical Literature* (December, 1955).

————. "Of Shoes and Shekels," *Bulletin of the American Schools of Oriental Research* (February, 1940).

Sprengling, Martin. *The Alphabet*. Chicago: University of Chicago Press, 1931.

Steindorff, Georg, and Seele, K. C. *When Egypt Ruled the East*. Chicago: University of Chicago Press, 1942.

Steuernagel, C. *Einwanderung der israelitischen Stamme*. 1901. Berlin: C. A. Schwetschke und Sohn.

Thiele, E. R. "A Comparison of the Chronological Data of Israel and Judah," *Vetus Testamentum* (1954), IV.

———. *The Mysterious Numbers of the Hebrew Kings*. Chicago: University of Chicago Press, 1951.

Throckmorton, Peter. "Oldest Known Shipwreck Yields Bronze Age Cargo," *National Geographic Magazine* (May, 1962).

———. "Thirty-three Centuries Under the Sea," *National Geographic Magazine* (May, 1960).

Torczyner, Harry. "The Lachish Letters," *Lachish I*. New York: Oxford University Press, 1938.

Tushingham, A. D. "Excavations at Dibon in Moab," *Bulletin of the American Schools of Oriental Research* (1954), No. 133.

Van Beek, G. W. "Archaeology," *The Interpreter's Dictionary of the Bible*. Nashville: Abingdon Press, 1962.

Vaux, Roland de. *Ancient Israel: Its Life and Institutions*. New York: McGraw-Hill Book Company, 1961.

Virolleaud, Charles. "Les Inscriptions Cuneiforme de Ras Shamra," *Syria* (1929), X.

Watson, C. M. "Bonaparte's Expedition to Palestine in 1799," *Quarterly Statement of the Palestine Exploration Fund*, 1917.

Whiston, William. *An Essay Towards Restoring the True Text of the Old Testament; and for Vindicating the Citations Made Thence in the New Testament*. London, 1722.

Williams, Walter G. "God of the Door Post," *Iliff Review* (1955), XII.

———. "Liturgical Aspects in Enthronement Psalms," *Journal of the Bible and Religion* (April, 1957).

———. *Prophets—Pioneers to Christianity*. Nashville: Abingdon Press, 1956.

———. "The Ras Shamra Inscriptions and Israel's Cultural Heritage." Ph.D. Dissertation, University of Chicago, 1934.

———. "Relative Datings of Additions to Job," *Iliff Review* (Winter, 1960).

———. "The Significance of the Ras Shamra Inscriptions for the History of Hebrew Religion," *American Journal of Semitic Languages* (1934), L.

Willis, E. H. "Radiocarbon Dating," *Science in Archaeology*. Edited by Don Brothwell and Eric Higgs. New York: Basic Books, Inc., 1963.

Wilson, John Albert. *The Burden of Egypt*. Chicago: University of Chicago Press, 1951.

Winckler, Hugo. "Nach Baghaskoi! Ein Fragment," *Der Alt Orient* (1913), XIV, 3.

Winnett, Frederick V. "Excavations at Diban in Moab, 1950-51," *Bulletin of the American Schools of Oriental Research*, No. 125.

———. *The Mosaic Tradition*. Toronto: University of Toronto Press, 1949.

Wiseman, D. J. *Chronicles of Chaldean Kings*.

Woolley, Leonard. *Digging Up the Past*. New York: Charles Scribner's Sons, 1931.

———. *Spadework*. London: Lutterworth Press, 1953.

Wright, George Ernest. *Biblical Archaeology*. Philadelphia: The Westminster Press, 1961.

———. "The Pottery of Palestine from the Earliest Times to the End of the Early Bronze Age," *Annual of the American Schools of Oriental Research*, (1937).

Wright, George Ernest, and Fuller, Reginald. *The Book of the Acts of God*. Garden City, New York: Doubleday & Company, Inc., 1957.

INDEXES

INDEX OF SCRIPTURE REFERENCES

Genesis . .16, 74,
100, 104, 153
1–11 153
1:1–2:4 153, 178
1:26 153
2:7 132
3:23 132
6 74
10:15 134
11:1-9 130
14:1 125
14:6 138
15:2 156
15:3 156
16:1-3 155
16:5-6 155
16:9 155
21:9-14 155
22:20-24 . . .160
23:3-20 134
23:19 135
26:34 135
27:2 161
27:46 135
28:1 135
29 157
29:31-35 . . .156
30:3 156
30:8 156
31:1, 14, 15, 19
157
31:30 ff. 17
31:32 157
31:43 157
31:49-50 . . .157
36:2 139
38:8-9 157

Exodus . . .91, 104
1:11 126
2:10 160
14:10-31 . . .115
21 163
21:2 163
21:3-4 164
21:5-6 164
21–23 133
22:16-17 . . .161
28:34-35 . . .151

Leviticus 163
18:16 158
20:21 158
25 163
25:10 163

Numbers
10:12 152
20:4-21 51
27:1-11 159

Deuteronomy . .74,
100, 157, 162
2:12 138
15 163
17:14-17 . . .122
17:16-18 . . .52
21:17 159
24:17, 19 . .159
25:5-10 157
25:9-10 162

Joshua . .122, 127
9:7 139
10:13 142

Judges . . .80, 127
3:11 122
5:16 150

Ruth . . .115, 162
4:7 17
4:7-8 162

I & II Samuel 115,
117, 178, 191

I Samuel 91, 176
1:20 160
4:18 122
7 109
8:10-18 175
10:25 142
12:2-5 162
12.3b 163
13:20-21 . .140
13:21 174
18:10-11 . . .107
19:9 150
24:6 107
26:6 135

II Samuel 91
1:18 142
2:12-17 . . .111
6:5 151
6:12-14 174
6:16 174
18:18 143
23:1 174
24:16 139

Books of Kings 91,
115, 117, 123

I Kings
3:1 123
3:16-28 122
4:29-34 122
5:1-11 141
6:1 126
9:20-21 52, 135
9:26-28 52
10:22 141
10:26-29 . . .52
10:29 135
11:1 . .123, 135
11:3 123
11:4-8 124
16:22a-27 . .124
16:31 124
22:39 89
22:47-48 . . .141

II Kings
1:1 124
2:19-22 . . .53
3:4-27 124
3:27 124
7:6 135
8:26 124
9:4-13 122
10:36 122
15–19 119
18:13-15 . . .113
20:20 115, 122
23:28-30a . .120
24–25 120
24:12-15 . . .119
25:23 108

I & II Chronicles
91, 117

I Chronicles
4:23 58

II Chronicles
33:11-14 . . .114
36:22 120

Ezra 120
2:69 166

Ezra-Nehemiah 120

Esther 120

Job 145-46
1–2 146
2:8 58
16:22 134
19:23 143
19:24 143
42:10-17 . . .146

Psalms 74, 77,
144, 153, 191
2:9 58
22:15 58
33:2 152
45 158
48:8 174
92:3 152
104 . . . .79, 144
137:2-3 150
144:9 152

Proverbs .123, 145
22:17–24:22 145
22:20 145
26:23 58
31:10-31 . . .175
31:21 175

Song of Songs
123, 158, 159

Isaiah 15, 73, 74,
116, 184
6:1 191
8:1 142
8:16 143
17:9 139
20:1 119
21:8 177
22:1, 5 176
23:6 177
26:8 177
29:16 58
30:14 58
37:27 177
40:3 189
41:25 58
44:28–45:1 .120
45:9 58

Jeremiah .120, 191
3:13 175
9:13 ff. 141
18:1-5 58
18:3 58
19:1-13 58
23:9-15 141
34:7 114
36:4-8 143

Lamentations
4:2 58

Ezekiel
2:9 143
8:14 134
16:39 161
16:45 139
23:26 161

Daniel ...120, 153
2:17-45 149
2:41 58
3:5, 7, 10, 15
153

Hosea
2:4-5 161

Amos
6:4 89

Nahum ..119, 120

Habakkuk 74

Zephaniah
2:13 120

Haggai 120

Zechariah 120
14:20 151

I Maccabees ..182
1:54-56 183
1:57 183

Matthew
5:14 29
7:24-27 29
13:23 132
22:28 158
22:29-33 ...158
27:7-10 58

Mark
12:42 89

Luke
10:30-37 ...105
17:11-21 ...165
19:4 105

John
8:23 190
17:12 190

Romans
9:20-24 58

Revelation 180
2:27 58

INDEX OF GEOGRAPHICAL TERMS

Abydos, 39, 149
Accad; see Akkad
Agade, 113
Ain Musa, 55
Akkad, 16, 113
Alaja Huyuk, 136
Alalakh, 175
Aleppo, 136-37
Amman, 28, 68, 186
Anathoth, 141
Anatolia, 136
Anti-Lebanons, 52
Aqabah, 29
Aqurquf, 130
Arabah, 52, 55
Arabia, 104
Araq el-Emir, 19, 28, 30,
68, 85
Armenia, 104
Ashur, 159
Asia Minor, 104
Asshur, 113
Assyria, 89, 119, 120, 128,
135, 138
Athens, 111

Baalbek, 24-25
Babylon, 89, 113, 119, 125
Babylonia, 16, 119, 128
Baghdad, 27
Balatah; see Shechem
Beeroth, 109
Beer-sheba, 54
Behistun, 83, 143, 170
Beitin (Bethel), 113
Beth-horon, 142
Bethlehem, 30, 73
Bhagistan, 83
Boghazköy, 136, 138, 173
Byblos, 141

Caesarea, 69

Caesarea Philippi, 28
Cairo, 178
Calah; see Nimrud
Canaan, 134-35
Carchemish, 137
Cedars of Lebanon, 70
Chaldea, 119

Damascus, 30, 113, 185,
188
Dead Sea, 51, 53
Debir, 113
Dhiban (Dibon), 19, 24,
56, 124
Dura-Europus, 89-90

Edom, 51, 138
Eglon, 113
Egypt, 18, 25-26, 38, 76,
82, 89, 104, 113, 115,
119, 123, 125, 128, 131,
135, 148, 169
Elam, 148
el-Bireh, 109
el-Jib, 108-110, 112; see al-
so Gibeon
Erech, 113
Ethiopia, 104
et-Till, 78
Euphrates River, 76
Eyuk, 135
Ezion-geber, 52, 141

Fertile Crescent, 144

Galilee, Sea of, 69
Gebal, 141
Gerasa, 113
Gezer, 111, 113, 164
Gibeah, 106
Gibeon, 109-112, 127; see
also el-Jib

Gilead, 68, 140, 154
Gizeh, 38, 67, 81
Gomorrah, 69
Greece, 104

Hamath, 135-37
Hatti Land, 123
Hauran, 29
Hebron, 135
Hissarlik, 29

Ibleam, 111
Iraq, 27, 37, 71, 104, 128
Israel, 15, 103-4, 106, 118,
119, 124, 134-35
Israel, State of, 29, 39, 56
Istanbul, 145
Italy, 104

Jeba, 106
Jebus; see Jerusalem
Jerash, 28, 113
Jericho, 34, 53, 57, 85, 105,
108, 126-27, 186
Jericho, fall of, 126
Jericho, New Testament,
53, 105
Jericho, Plain of, 53
Jericho, Old Testament, 53,
67, 105
Jerusalem; see also Jebus,
28, 30, 43, 53-54, 60,
105, 111, 114, 119, 121-
22, 139, 143, 176, 186
Jordan, 15, 39, 53-54, 103-
4, 112
Jordan, River, 51
Jordan Valley, 52
Judah, 119-20
Judea, 28

Karnak, 136
Kayseri, 137
Khirbet Qumran, 53
Khorsabad, 27
Khufu, 81
Kirkuk, 17, 27
Kish, 133
Kuyunjik, 27

Lachish, 113
Lattaquié, 75
Lebanon, 39, 52

Macedonia, 104
Machpelah, 135
Malatya, 137
Mari, 125, 138, 155
Masada, 181
Megiddo, 32, 111, 120
Memphis, 39
Mesopotamia, 16, 25, 27, 37, 100, 104, 113, 133, 144
Mitanni Kingdom, 139
Mizpah of Benjamin; see Tell en-Nasbeh
Moab, 124
Monterozzi, 71
Mosul, 27
Mount of Olives, 30
Mycenae, 29, 37, 111

Nazareth, 28
Nebi Samwil, 106-8
Negeb, 29, 54, 56, 57, 103
Neo-Babylonia, 119
Nimrud (Calah), 27
Nineveh, 17, 27, 60, 113-14, 119-20, 143
Nippur, 133, 143, 145
Northern Kingdom; see Israel
Nuzu (Nuzi), 17, 125, 138, 155-58, 162, 171

On, 113
Ophir, 142

Palestine, 25, 28, 39, 41, 76, 79-80, 104
Persia, 83, 104
Petra, 28, 55
Phoenicia, 141, 144
Pithom, 126

Qumran, 35, 75, 145, 176, 184-85, 197

Raamses, 126
Rameses, 113
Ras Shamra, 78, 140; see also Ugarit
Red Sea, 115
Rosetta, 38, 169

Samaria, 65, 89, 113, 124
Sea of Reeds (Red Sea), 115
Sebastye, 113
Seilun, 113
Seir, Mount, 138
Shechem, 113, 166
Shemer, 124
Shiloh, 113
Shinar, 16
Shu-mer; see Sumer
Shushan, 113, 133
Sidon, 141
Sinai, 51, 104, 183
Sodom, 69
Spain, 104
Sumer, Sumeria, 16, 128, 131, 145
Susa, 111, 113, 133, 152
Syria, 29-30, 39, 79, 104, 124, 136, 144

Tanis, 39
Tell Abu Harmal, 133

Tell al-Obeid, 128
Tell Beit Mirsim, 113
Tell ed-Duweir, 113-14
Tell el-Amarna, 78-79
Tell el-Ful, 106, 141
Tell el Hariri, 138, 155
Tell el-Hesi, 29, 113
Tell el Mutesellim, 32
Tell es-Sultan, 67, 126; see also Jericho
Tell en-Nasbeh, 107-9; see also Mizpah
Tell Jezer, 113
Tell Qasile, 142
Thebes, 25, 39, 79, 145
Transjordan, 28, 29, 39, 68, 103
Troy, 37
Turkey, 37, 69, 104, 138
Tyana, 137
Tyre, 141, 177

Ugarit, 30, 76, 125, 138, 155, 159-60, 165, 171-72, 175-76; see also Ras Shamra
United Kingdom, 119-20, 135
Ur, 34, 113, 130, 133, 152
Uruk, 113

Valley of Kings, 38

Wadi Fara, 105
Wadi Qelt, 53, 105
Wadi Qumran, 53, 72

Yazilikaya, 136
Yorghan Tepe, 155
Yucatan, 70

Zagros Mountains, 83

GENERAL INDEX

agricultural, 140
Akkadians, 129, 170, 172
alphabet, 93, 171, 172
alphabetic cuneiform, 77
Amer. Acad. Relig., 43
American Bible Society, 194
American Oriental Society, 43
American Palestine Exploration Society, 41
American School of Oriental Research, 28, 41, 43, 54, 73, 75, 103

Ammonite, 51, 123
Amorites, 51, 135, 139
amphictyony, 118
"Annals of Sennacherib," 119
Antiquities, Department of, 61
apocalypse, apocalyptic, 74, 179-80
Apocrypha, 74
Apodeictic Law, 133
Arabic, 39, 50
Arameans, 52, 138
Arch of Titus, 152

Archaeological Institute of America, 43
Archaeological Society of Greece, 37
archaizing, 20
architect, 22, 64
architectual style, 93
Ark, 132, 174
artifacts, 15, 22, 49
Asholean Museum, 79
Asiatics, 151
Assyrians, 16, 120-22, 124, 127, 129, 132, 134, 136-37, 145, 148-49, 153, 171

Assyriologists, 121, 125
Astarte figurines, 58
astronomy, 104, 169

Baal cultus, Baalism, 122, 134, 140-41, 175
Babylonian, 16, 17, 23, 79, 83, 100, 127, 129-30, 132, 134, 137, 142, 145, 149-50, 153, 165, 170-71
bakshish, 62
balk, 62
baptism, 53, 186
base line, 63
basket, basket carrier, 62, 64
beads, 18, 33
Bedouin, 50, 57, 140
bees, domestication of, 138
Behistun inscription, 170
Beni-hasan monument, 151
Berlin Museum, 79
Bilalama Code; see law, codes
Black Obelisk, 119, 122
"Blind Harper," 152
Bodleian Catalogue, 194
Book of Discipline, 179
Book of Thanksgiving, The, 74
branding, 138
British Museum, 26, 27, 38, 78-79, 88, 130, 170, 194
British School of Archaeology in Egypt, 43
Bronze Age, 33
Bronze Age, Middle, 50, 57, 68
Bulak, Museum at, 39
business men, 20
Byzantine period, 19, 30, 33, 50, 68, 185

Cairo Geniza, 194
Cairo Museum, 149
calendar, 164-65
Canaanites, 79, 118, 135, 138, 140, 165, 172
canon, 102
Carbon 14 process, 19, 70
cartouche, 18, 169
Casuistic Law, 133
Cave IV, Qumran, 74
Chalcolithic Period, 32
Chalice of Antioch, 34
charcoal, 22
Chicago House, Luxor, Egypt, 43
Chicago Museum of Natural History, 34
Chicago Society of Biblical Research, 44
Church of the Holy Nativity, 25
Church of the Holy Sepulchre, 25
Christianity, 189-90
Chronicler, 178

chronology, 103, 116
cisterns, 53, 111
clay, 19
clay brick, 130
clay envelope, 143
clay tablet, 18, 27, 76, 78, 86, 118-19, 125, 129, 140, 142-43, 171
clothing, 33
cock, fighting, 108
Codex, 144
coins and coinage, 18, 20, 33, 69, 86, 152, 166, 185
Colossi of Memnon, 81
comparative grammar, 170
conquest of Palestine, 51, 115, 126
contracts, 161
cooks, 67
copper, 142
Copper Age, 33
copper scroll, 35, 176
copper smelting, 52
Coptic, 39
corvée, 52, 135
Council of Jamnia (Jebna), 182
Covenant of Mizpah, 157
Covenanters, 189
Creation, 100, 132
criticism, higher, 178
criticism, lower, 178, 183
Crusaders, 26
cultic prophets, 147
cuneiform, 20, 130-31, 138, 170-71, 173
cuneiform alphabet, 76
cuneiform syllables, 173
cylinders of clay, 130
"Cylinder B of Ashurbanipal," 148
cylinder seal, 143

Damascus Covenant, 178-79, 188
Dead Sea Caves, 102, 147
Dead Sea Scrolls, 40, 44, 53, 60, 65, 72, 75, 177-79, 182
Dead Sea Scrolls Community, 86
Deluge, The, 132
dendrochronology, 70
Deuteronomic writer, 115, 122, 123, 146, 162
Deutsche Orient-Gesellschaft, 41
Deutscher Palästina-Verein, 41
dictionaries, bilingual, 129
director, 61
doorpost, god of the, 164
drawings, 22
drugs, 165
dump dirt, 63

East India Company, 136
École Biblique et Archéologique Française, 41, 43
Edomite, 123, 145
Egyptians, 52, 54, 78-79, 104, 116, 120, 123, 126-27, 136-37, 141-42, 145-46, 149, 170, 196
Egyptian language, 38
Egyptian Museum of Antiquities, 39
Egyptian Bondage, 126
El Elohim, 77
Elamite language, 83
Elisha's fountain, 53
Enoch, Book of, 186, 192
epigraphy, 65, 66, 83, 174
Epiru, 160
eponyms, 121, 125
eponymous ancestors, 125
Eshnunna Code; see law, codes of
Essenes, 179, 186, 188-90
Ethiopic, 39
Etruscan tombs, 71
excavation, underwater, 69
Exile, 104, 118
Exodus from Egypt, 51, 122, 126

farming, 20, 32
fellah-(in), 50
field archaeology, 19, 21
field supervisor, 61, 64-65
Firkowitsch Collection, 194
Flood, Great, 17, 28, 133
floor level, 30
foreman, 62
Former Prophets, 115
fossils, 99
foundation deposit boxes, 130
furnaces, 52

gateway, ancient, 108
"Genesis Apocryphon," 87
genizah, 178, 193
"Genizah Fragments," 178
geography, biblical, 103, 113
German Orient Society, 173
Gezer calendar, 164
Gibeon, Pool of, 109-11
Gilgamesh Epic, 23, 132
Girgashites, 135
gods, household, 157
Good Samaritan, 105
gospels, 190; see also Biblical Index
grain, 18
Greco-Roman civilization, 128
Greeks, 37, 168-69, 172
gufa, 64
Guti, 129

Habiru, 80, 127
"Hagu," 74, 186, 189
"Hammurabi Code," 133, 161, 163, 165
Hattians, 138
health and medical officers, 165
Hebrews, 16, 80, 102, 115, 132, 134, 137-39, 149, 168, 172, 181
   history of Jews, 118
   history of Hebrews, 118
Hebrew language, 17, 138
Hebrew monarchy, 137
Hebrew poetry, 191
Hebrew Union College Cincinnati, 51, 56
Hebrew Univ., 40, 43, 73, 74
Heilsgeschichte, 115
Hellenistic, 33, 50
henotheism, 79
herbs and medicines, 165
Heth, Sons of; see Hittites
hieroglyph, 131, 136, 138, 169, 173
historian, 127
"History, Books of," 115
Hittites 16, 52, 123, 134-39, 161, 171-74
"Hittite Code," 161
Hittite Empire, 136-37
Hittite, pictographic, 173
Hivites, 135, 137, 139
hoeman, 62
Horite; see Hurrians
houses, 19, 29
Hurrians, 16, 136-39
Hurro-Hittite, 196
Hyksos, 125
"Hymn to Aton," 79, 144
hymns, 144, 146

Imperial Ottoman Museum, 78
Indo-European, 129, 134, 137
inheritance, laws of, 159
Iraqi Museum, 43, 129
Iron Age, 33, 108, 112; see Chart, p. 36
irrigation systems, 52-54
Islamic, 33
Israel Exploration Society, 40
Istanbul, Museum of the Ancient Orient in, 133

Jaazaniah, Seal of, 108-9
Jamnia, Council of, 197
jar handles, 108, 112
"Jashar, Book of," 142
Jebusites, 135, 139
Jewish Institute of Religion, 56

Jews, 120
"Job, Targum of," 146
Job, writer of, 143
Jordan Archaeological Museum in Amman, Jordan, 34, 40, 43
Jubilee, the fiftieth year, 163
"Jubilees, Book of," 186, 192
Judiasm, 91, 180, 190
Judaean Kingdom, 57
judges, seat of the, 109

Karaites, 194
Khatti, Kheta; see Hittites
Khirbet, 53

"Lachish Letters, The," 113-14
Latin, 168
law, codes of, 129, 133, 134
Law, Code of, Hammurabi, 161-165
Law Code, Hittite, 138, 161
law, Levitical, 158
Law, Code of Lipit-Ishtar, 133
laws, Middle Assyrian, 159
lead-filled inscriptions 143
leather, tanning of, 53
leather scrolls, 143
"Leningrad 1116B," 148
levels of occupation, 31, 57, 64
Levirate marriage, 157-59 162
Leyden Museum, 152
"Leyden Papyrus 1-344" 148
library, 27
libraries, Assyrian, 23
literal inspiration, 183
literature, 134
Louvre, 38, 88, 133
Luwians, 138

Maccabees, 105
man, creation of, 132
"Manual of Discipline, The" 74, 186-87
manuscripts, Bible, 73
map, 143
marriage, 155, 161, 163
Masoretic, Masoretes, 121, 139, 178, 183-84, 191, 194, 197
mastaba, 89
mathematics, 129, 131, 166
Mazarin Bible in Latin, 183
Median, 170
medical doctors and medicines, 165, 169
"Mesha Inscription," 81
meso-lithic, 32

Mesopotamian, 116, 142, 196
messiah, 107, 180, 187, 190
Metropolitan Museum of New York, 89
midrash-(im), 74
Moabites, 51, 123, 124
Moabite Stone, 81, 124
money; see coins
monolatry, 79
monotheism, absolute, 141, 153
Museum of the Ancient Orient in Istanbul, 88, 129
museum in Baghdad, 89
museum in Cairo, 88
museum in Damascus, 77 90
music, 149-50
musical instruments, 149

Nabateans 28, 55-56
name, 159
National Association of Biblical Instructors, 44
National Geographic Society, 70
Near Eastern Society of Berlin, 173
Neo-Babylonian sources, 121, 130, 171
Neo-lithic Age, 32, 57-58, 76
Nesians, 138
New Stone Age, 32
New Testament, 104, 132, 182, 190, 191; see also Biblical Index
notebook, 62
Nuzu tablets, 17, 161, 162
"Nuzi Tablet N444: 19-23," 161

oaths, 162
Obeidans, 129
occupation levels, 19
Old Cairo Synagogue, 185, 193
Old Testament, 74, 104, 115; see Biblical Index
"Oration of Moses" Dead Sea Scrolls, 179
Oriental Institute, 25, 38, 44, 86, 89, 152
Ostrakon, 142

paleolithic, 32, 55
Palestine Exploration Fund, 28, 29, 41, 67
Palestine Archaeological Museum in Jerusalem, 40, 43, 87, 88, 186
Palestine Oriental Society, 107
papyrus, 143, 148

Patriarch, patriarchal, 56, 117, 118, 125, 134, 135, 154-55, 162
Pentateuch, 74
Perizzites, 135
Persian, 16, 170
Persian Period, 33
Persian language, 83
Philistines, 140, 142
Phoenicians, 16, 141-42, 172
photographs, 22, 31, 50, 64-65
photographs, aerial, 71
physiology, 169
pickax, 132
pickman, 62
pictographic, 130, 131, 173
"pot-hunting," 22
pottery types, 19, 29, 43, 49, 53, 57-58, 65, 185
pot washer, 65
potter's wheel, 58, 148
prayers, 144
price charts, 21
prophets, 91, 102, 134, 140, 147-48
prophetic ecstasy, 150
prophetic party, 120, 122
prophets—medicine men, 165
Proverbs, 175
proverbs, Sumerian, 145
psalms, 144-45, 191
"Psalms of Solomon," 123
Pseudepigrapha, 74
Pyramids, 24, 25, 38, 68, 81, 89, 146, 148

Quarterly Statement of Palestine Exploration Fund, 41
Qumran scrolls, 180, 191
Qumran Covenanters, 177, 180, 186, 188, 190

Rabbinic Bible of, 1524-25, 184
radio carbon, 14, 104; see also carbon 14 process
railway, light, 63
Ramesseum, 136
rebus writing, 131
records (excavation), 22, 30, 65
religious and civil calendars, 165; see also calendar
Revolt, Second Jewish, A.D., 132-35, 185
rolling stone door, 54

Roman period, 33, 105
Rosetta Stone, 38, 169, 171
Royal Asiatic Society, 83, 171
Royal Cemeteries at Ur, 89
Russian Public Library, 194

Sabbath, 164
Sabbath year, 163
Sadducees, 158
saga of Israel, 126
salting, 62
Samaritan, 73
Samaritan Pentateuch, 121
schools, 131
schoolmaster, 131
seals, 142
Semitic, 126, 129, 134
Septuagint, 121, 139, 163, 178, 191
Serapeum, 39
sexagesimal, 131
sherds, 27, 50, 65
ships, 141
ships of Tarshish, 141
shrines, 93
Shrine of the Book Jerusalem, Israel, 87
Sidonian, 123
"Siloam Inscription," 81
Siloam Tunnel, 81
"Similitudes, The," 192
Sinaitic inscriptions, 172
slavery, 163-64
Society of Biblical Literature, 43
sociology, 101
Sothic Cycle, 164
sounding, 70
source, primary, 117
source, secondary, 117
sphinxes, 39, 68, 149
squares, excavation, 62
squeezes, 83
stamp (name), 112
stairwell, grand (Gibeon), 112
Stone Age, Old, 32, 99
stratum, stratification, 31
students, 131
Sumerians, 16, 129-34, 142, 145-46, 171
survey maps and surveyors, 49, 63
swineherding, 138
syllabic signs; see cuneiform
Syriac, 39
Syrians, 16, 122, 135
Syrian alliance, 122
Syrian Orthodox Church, 73, 75

Ta'amireh Bedouin, 72, 73, 75
Tatian's "Diatessaron," 90
"Taylor Prism," 119
Teacher of Righteousness, 180, 187, 189, 190
Tell (Telul), 29, 49
"Tell el-Amarna Tablets," 127, 136
temples, 93, 141
teraphim, 17, 157
"Thomas, Gospel of," 132
"Tobit, book of," 191
tomb clearance, 33-34
Tomb of the Kings, 54
tools, iron, 140
topographical survey, 28
Torah, The, 182
tree-ring date, 70
tunnel (el Jib), 110
Turin Museum, 152
Turks, 37, 110
Tutankhamen's tomb, 60
typology, 70

Ugaritic Language and Tablets, 140, 159, 172, 174, 175
Underwater archaeology, 69
University of Pennsylvania, 89, 129, 133, 145
Ur, Third Dynasty of, 130
urban planning, 52
Urn Tomb, 55
"Ur-Nammu Code," see law, codes of

Valley of the Kings, 60

wadi, 51
"Wars of the Children of Light and the Children of Darkness, The," 74, 179-80
water boy, 66
water engineering, 56, 110-11
wedding, 158
weights, stone, 174
wheat, 19
Winged Bull, 86
Wisdom of Solomon, 123
writing, 130, 134, 142, 162, 168

Yahwism, 115, 122

"Zadokite Fragments," 178, 185, 186, 188
ziggurat, 130

INDEX OF NAMES

Aaron, 151
Abbas Pasha, Khedive, 39
Abraham, Abram, 15, 34, 57, 90, 104, 121-22, 125, 130-31, 134, 137, 155-56, 160
Absalom, 143
Agamemnon, 37
Ahab, 119, 124
Ahaz, 119
Ahaziah, 124
Ahimelech, 135
Ahmose I, 126, 148
Akerblad, 169
Akhenaton, 79, 80, 144
Akhetaton, 79
Albanese, L., 76
Albright, William F., 59, 63, 73, 80, 90, 103-4, 106-7, 113, 121, 155-56, 164, 185, 196
Aleyan-Baal, 141
Allegro, John M., 35, 176, 190
Alt, Albrecht, 107, 109, 118, 194
Amen-em-het I, 148
Amen-em-opet, 145
Amenhotep III, 79
Amenhotep IV, 79, 144
Amos, 140, 147, 163
Amraphel, 125
Anat, Anath, 77, 141, 175
Antiochus IV, 166
Apis, 39
Aqhat, 77
Araunah, 139
Aristobulus I, 166
Asherah, 77
Ashurbanipal, 23, 27, 148, 152
Ashurnasirpal, 27
Astarte, 77, 141
Athaliah, 124
Aton, 144
Avigad, Nahman, 87

Baal, 77, 90, 175
Badè, William F., 64, 88, 107-9
Baikie, James, 23
Baqir, Taha, 38, 133
Barthélemy, D., 179
Baruch, 143
Basemath, 135
Bass, G. F., 69
Bauer, Hans, 76
Bell, Gertrude, 37
Belzoni, Giovanni Battista, 38
ben Asher, 194
ben Chayyim, 193, 194

Bewer, Julius A., 174
Bilhah, 156
Bittle, Kurt, 173
Bliss, Frederick J., 29
Boaz, 158, 159, 163
Bopp, Franz, 170
Bossert, Helmuth T., 173
Botta, P. E., 25, 27
Breasted, James Henry, 80, 82, 89, 148-49
Bright, John, 118, 124
Brion, Marcel, 87
Brothwell, Don, 101
Brownlee, Wm., 185
Buckingham, James Silk, 28
Budge, Sir Wallace, 78-79
Burckhardt, Johann Ludwig (Sheikh Ibrahim), 28, 38, 55, 136
Burrows, Millar, 68, 185, 188
Butler, Howard Crosby, 28

Calkin, John B., 105
Cameron, George G., 83-84, 164
Carnarvon, Lord, 43
Carter, Howard, 43, 60
Ceram, C. W., 136, 170-74
Champollion, Jean François, 169
Chephren, 149
Chiera, Edward, 155
Colt, H. Dunscombe, 113
Conder, C. R., 28, 41, 49, 107
Contenau, G., 136
Cowley, A., 135
Cross, Frank M., 178, 191
Cyriac de Pizzicolli, 26
Cyril of Jerusalem, Bishop, 25
Cyrus, 120

Dagon, 77
Dalman, G., 106-7
Daniel, 177, 196
Darius I, 120, 143, 170
Darius II, 120
Darwin, 100
David, 107, 111, 135, 150, 159, 174
Debevoise, N. C., 83
De Buffon, Compte; see Leclerc
Dajani, Awni, 40
DeLaet, Sigfried J., 87
De Lagarde, Paul, 184
De la Peyrere, Isaac, 99
Del Medico, 54
DeMorgan, J., 133

De Saulcy, 54, 68
De Vaux, Roland, 125, 154, 185
DeVries, S. J., 121
Dhorme, Edouard, 76
Douglass, A. E., 70
Driver, G. R., 77, 175
Dubberstein, Waldo H., 21
Dumuzu, 134
Dungi, 130

Edwards, I. E. S., 81, 89
Eissfeldt, O. 194
Eli, 122
Eliezer, 156
Elijah, 90, 141
Elisha, 53, 165
Emerson, Ralph Waldo, 182
Ephron, 134
Epiphanes; see Antiochus IV
Erman, 150
Esarhaddon, 23, 27, 119, 148
Esau, 135, 161
Eshnunna, 133, 161
Ethbaal, 124
Eudoxia, Empress, 41
Eusebius of Caesarea, 25
Ezekiel, 139, 143, 161

Field, Henry, 34
Filson, Floyd V., 104, 190
Finegan, Jack, 90
Firkowitsch, 185, 193
Forrer, Emil O., 173
Franken, H. J., 51, 69, 126
Franken-Battershill, C. A., 69, 126
Fresnel, Flugence, 27
Friedrich, Johannes, 171
Fritsch, Charles T., 186, 188
Fuller, Reginald, 115

Gadd, C. J., 120
Gardiner, A. H., 148
Garstang, John, 39, 67, 126
Gaster, Theodor H., 77, 158-59, 179, 187, 189-90
Gelb, I. J., 77, 135, 137, 139, 168, 172-73
George and the dragon, Saint, 133
Gilgamesh, 132-33
Ginsberg, H. L., 77
Glueck, Nelson, 29, 51, 52, 54, 56, 103, 125
Gordon, C. H., 18, 77, 117, 138, 155, 156-57, 161
Gottwald, N. K., 158

Gray, John, 77
Greenburg, Moshe, 18
Gross, 106
Grotefend, G. F., 170

Hagar, 155
Haldar, A., 80
Hall, H. R., 38
Ham, 134
Hamburger, Herbert, 166
Hammurabi, 125, 129, 133, 161, 164
Harding, G. Lankester, 40, 56, 67, 75, 110, 113
Hathor, 151
Hattusilis, 136
Hawkes, Jacquetta, 23, 37, 99
"Hebrew," origin of name, 159
Helena, Saint, 25
Henry VIII, 99
Hercules, 133
Herod the Great, 53, 105
Herod Archelaus, 185
Hezekiah, King, 113, 114, 119, 121-22, 150, 165
Higgs, Eric, 101
Hincks, Edward, 170
Hippolytus, 188
Hiram of Tyre, 141
Hitti, P. K., 141
Hosea, 140
Hoshea, 119
Hrozny, Bedrich, 173
Huldah, 120
Huwawa, 133
Huya, 162
Hyrcanus I, John, 185

Ibrahim, Sheikh; see Burckhardt
Ikh-en-aton, 82; see also Akhenaton
Inanna, 134
Ipu-wer, 148
Irby, C. L., 28
Isaac, 90, 135, 155-56, 161-62
Isaiah, 142, 165, 177, 184
Ishmael, 155-56
Ishtar, 134, 148

Jaazaniah, Seal of, 108
Jacob, 17f, 135, 156-57, 162
Jacotin, Pierre, 27
Jehoahaz, 119
Jehoiachin, 119
Jehoram, 124
Jehoshaphat, 142
Jehu, son of Omri, 119, 121-22
Jeremiah, 15, 120, 141, 143, 175, 191
Jerome, 25, 106

Jesus, 16, 25, 29-30, 54, 89, 144, 158, 179, 189, 190
Jezebel, 124
Job, Sumerian, 128
Job, 143
John Baptist, 179, 189
Johnson, Aubrey R., 147
Jonathan, 160
Jones, William, 170
Joram, 122
Joseph, 126
Josephus, 68, 152, 188
Joshua, 80, 126-27, 142
Judas Aristobulus, 166
Judith, 135

Kahle, Paul, 184, 193-94
Kapelrud, A. S., 141
Kelim-ninu, 155
Kelso, J. L., 59, 105-6
Kennicott, B., 194
Kenyon, Kathleen, 32, 43, 58, 67, 69, 113, 126
Key, Andrew F., 159
Kirkbride, Diana, 55
Kitchener, H. H., 28, 41
Kittel, Rudolph, 194-95
Knudtzon, J. A., 79
Kraeling, Emil, 145-46
Kramer, Samuel N., 128-29, 131-33, 145

Laban, 17, 156, 157, 162
Ladagil-ilu, 148
Lamech, 74
Langdon, Stephen, 133
Lapp, Paul W., 59, 103
LaSor, Wm. S., 75
Layard, Austen Henry, 25, 27
Leah, 156-57
Leclerc, George Louis, 99
Legrain, G., 149
Leland, John, 99
Lerici, Carlo M., 71
Lightfoot, Bishop, 99
Lipit-Ishtar, 133, 161
Lloyd, Seton, 78
Luckenbill, D. D., 119

Macalister, R. A. S., 54, 164
Mace, A. C., 60
Manasseh, King, 114, 119
Mangles, James, 28
Marden, Luis, 70
Marek; see Ceram
Mariette, Auguste Edouard, 39
Mattiwaza, 123
Maundrell, Henry, 26
McCown, C. C., 107-8
Meek, T. J., 127, 159
Menahem, 119
Mendelsohn, I., 175-76

Mendenhall, Geo. E., 155
Mercer, S. A. B., 79
Meriggi, 173
Mer-ne-ptah, 126
Mesha, 124
Milik, J. T., 179, 191-92
Morgan, J. P., 23
Moses, 51, 80, 100, 127, 142, 152, 159, 178, 183
"Moses," origin of name, 159
Muhammed Ed Dib, 75
Muilenburg, James, 108
Murray, Margaret, 151-52

Nabonidus, 130
Naboth, 176
Naomi, 159
Napoleon, 25-26, 38, 169
Nashwi, 157
Nau, Michael, 26
Nebuchadnezzar
  Nebuchadrezzar, 114, 119-21, 160
Nefer-Rohu, 148
Nefr-tite,
  Nofer-ti-te, 83
Neufeld, E., 138
Niebuhr, H. Richard, 101
Nimrud, 122
Noah, 15, 74, 132
Noblecourt, Christiane De-roaches, 89
Nofer-ti-te; see Nefr-tite
Noth, Martin, 118, 155
Nuhuyu, 157

Olmstead, A, T., 23
Omri, 119, 124
Onan, 157
Oppert, Jules, 27, 170
Othniel, 122
Owen, G. Frederick, 113, 169

Patton, John H., 77, 144
Paul, 31, 104
Pedersen, Johannes, 118
Pekah, 119
Petrie, Sir W. Flinders, 19, 29, 31, 43, 81, 88, 113
Pfeiffer, R. H., 146
Philo, 188
Phythian-Adams, W. J., 107
Pietro della Valle, 26
Pilgrim of Bordeaux, 25
Place, Victor, 27
Pliny, 188
Pococke, Bishop, 26
Pope, M. H., 162
Price, Ira M., 171
Pritchard, James B., 105, 106, 108, 110-12
Ptolemy V. Epiphanes, 169

Quaresimus, 26

Raboisson, 107
Rachel, 17, 156-57
Ra-mose; see Ramses II
Ramses I, 126
Ramses II, 18, 126, 160
Rask, Rasmus Christian, 170
Rassam, Hormuzd, 27
Rauchwolff, Leonhard (Rauwolf), 26
Rawlinson, H. C., 27, 83, 170
Rebekah, 135
Reland, Adrian, 26
Rich, C. J., 27
Richardson, H. Neil, 110
Rim Sin, 129
Rist, Martin, 179
Roberts, Bleddyn J., 183-84, 193
Robinson, Edward, 28, 55, 103, 106-7, 109-10
Rockefeller, John D., Jr., 40
Rostovtzeff, M. I., 90
Rowley, H. H., 51
Ruth, 158-59, 162-63

Saad, Joseph, 40
Sachs, Curt, 150, 152
Safar, Fuad, 38
Samuel, 107, 109, 142, 160, 162-63, 174-76
Samuel, Archbishop, 73
Sarah, 134, 155
Sargon II, 23, 27, 119
Satan, 180
Saty al-hasri, 38
Saul, 107, 111, 122, 141, 150, 159
Sayce, Archibald Henry, 136
Schaeffer, Claude F. A., 76
Schechter, S., 179, 188
Schliemann, Heinrich, 29, 37
Schmidt, Felix (Fabri), 26
Scott, R. B. Y., 174, 177
Schumacher, G., 29
Seele, K. C., 82
Seetzen, Ulrich Jasper, 28
Sellers, Ovid R., 151-52
Sellin, Ernst, 67
Sennacherib, 23, 24, 27, 113-14, 119, 121, 150

Shalmaneser III, 27, 119, 121, 122
Shalmaneser V, 119
Shennima, 155-56
Shulgi, 130
Shuriha-ilu, 155-56
Sihon, King of the Amorites, 51
Simon, 166
Smith, Eli, 28
Smith, George, 17, 27, 60, 100
Smith, J. M. P., 127, 138, 184
Smith, Sidney, 37
Snefru, 141, 148
Solomon, 51-52, 122-23, 126, 135, 141, 158, 176
Speiser, E. A., 17, 137-39, 155, 161-63
Sprengling, Martin, 172
Starkey, James Leslie, 113
Steele, Francis R., 133
Steindorff, G., 82
Steuernagel, C., 127
Sukenik, E. L., 73, 75, 185
Sululi-Ishtar, 162
Suppiluliumas, 123
Swallow, Jason R., 19

Talbot, H. Fox, 170
Tammuz, 134
Tarmiya, 162
Taylor, J. E., 129-30
Testevuide, 27
Thiele, Edwin Richard, 121
Thorley, J. Palin, 59
Throckmorton, Peter, 69
Thut-Mose, 160
Thut-Mose III, 149
Thut-Mose IV, 149
Tiglath-pileser I, 170
Tiglath-pileser III, 23, 119
Titus, 106
Tobiah, 68
Tobias, 28
Tobler, Titus, 28
Torczyner, H., 113
Trever, John, 73, 75, 185
Tudhaliyas, 123
Tushingham, Douglass, 19, 56
Tutankhamen, 43, 89

Ungnad, 139
Uriah, 135
Ur-Nammu, 130
Ussher, Archbishop of Armagh, 44, 99
Utnapishtim, 132
Uzziah, King, 116

Van Kootwych, Johann (Cotovicus), 26
Vincent, A., 107
Virolleaud, Charles, 75, 76
Voltaire, 168

Wampler, J. C., 108
Watson, C. M., 27
Watzinger, Carl, 67
Weber, O., 79
Wellcome, Sir Henry, 113
Wellhausen, J., 151-52
Wen Amon, 144
Wheeler, Sir Mortimer, 43, 86
Whiston, William, 183
Williams, Walter G., 77, 141, 145-47, 164
Willis, E. H., 19
Wilson, J. A., 82
Winckler, Hugo, 136, 173
Winnett, Frederick Victor, 56, 127
Wiseman, Donald J., 121
Wood, Juliana, 106
Woolley, Sir Leonard, 18, 25, 34, 50, 133
Wright, George Ernest, 59, 104, 113, 115
Wright, William, 135
Wullu, 157

Xerxes, 170

Yadin, Yigael, 87
Yahweh, 134, 141
Young, Thomas, 169

Zacchaeus, 105
Zeitlin, S., 185, 191
Zelophehad, 159
Zilpah, 156
Ziusudra, 132
Zuallart, Johann, 26

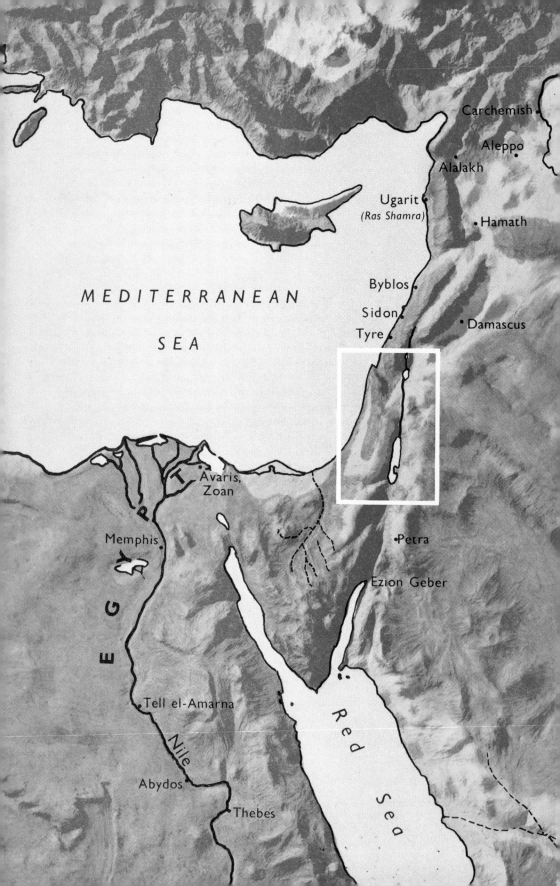

MEDITERRANEAN

SEA

Carchemish •

• Aleppo

Alalakh

Ugarit •
(Ras Shamra)

• Hamath

Byblos •

Sidon •

Tyre •

• Damascus

E G Y P T

Avaris,
Zoan

Memphis •

• Petra

Ezion Geber •

Tell el-Amarna •

Nile

Abydos •

Thebes •

Red Sea